No Rising

NO RISING TIDE

*Theology, Economics,
and the Future*

Joerg Rieger

FORTRESS PRESS
Minneapolis

For my parents and my late parents-in-law,
and their individual struggles against cancer,

and for the many others who struggle with what has
become yet another scourge of free-market capitalism.

NO RISING TIDE
Theology, Economics, and the Future

Copyright © 2009 Fortress Press, an imprint of Augsburg Fortress. All rights reserved. Except for brief quotations in critical articles or reviews, no part of this book may be reproduced in any manner without prior written permission from the publisher. Visit http://www. augsburgfortress.org/copyrights/ or write to Permissions, Augsburg Fortress, Box 1209, Minneapolis, MN 55440.

Cover image: *Fishbowl* (image number 2826153) copyright © hidesy / istockphoto.
Cover design: Paul Boehnke
Book design: Allan Johnson / PhoenixType, Inc., 235 N. Miles St., Appleton, Minnesota.

Library of Congress Cataloging-in-Publication Data

Rieger, Joerg.
   No rising tide : theology, economics, and the future / Joerg Rieger.
      p.   cm.
   ISBN 978-0-8006-6459-6 (alk. paper)
   1. Economics—Religious aspects—Christianity.   2. Free enterprise—
Religious aspects—Christianity.   I. Title.
   BR115.E3R54   2009
   261.8'5—dc22   2009032847

The paper used in this publication meets the minimum requirements of American National Standard for Information Sciences—Permanence of Paper for Printed Library Materials, ANSI Z329.48—1984.

Manufactured in the U.S.A.

13 12 11 10   2 3 4 5 6 7 8 9 10

Contents

Preface

Economic downturn is one of the stark realities that leaves hardly anyone unaffected today. The common response to this problem is, of course, that the economy goes in cycles and that we will be fine if only we have enough staying power. The tide will rise again for the economy, it is believed with religious fervor, and things will return back to normal.

Nevertheless, even if the tide rises again for the economy, many, if not most of us, will not be part of this rising tide. Many of us—the majority of the world's population—will be struggling with downturn for a long time to come. Not only are many of the jobs lost in this downturn projected to be permanent; pressure on most other jobs can be expected to grow.[1] Although the economy affects each of us differently, there are some common patterns. To which economic class we belong plays a role, for instance, but more and more of us are in the same boat, as the middle class is increasingly joining the working class. It is high time that even those who consider themselves middle class start thinking about these matters more seriously than ever before. The *logic of downturn*, developed in this book, will help us to make sense of what is going on, not simply in regard to economics but in regard to every aspect of our lives. At stake is not just money and finance. The way the economy shapes up affects us more deeply than we had ever realized, at all levels of our lives. Religion is one of the matters affected.

The purpose of this book, however, is not to savor doom and gloom. We will seek once again the path "from darkness to light," and religion will have a contribution to make.[2] Even though many contemporary economists and theologians have resigned to the belief that there is no alternative to the capitalist free-market economy, this is not the position taken in this book.

While there is no easy way out and while too many so-called alternatives turn out to be not much more than pie in the sky, we refuse to give in to what is behind the lack of belief in alternatives: the ongoing temptation of empire. The unique stance of this book can be found in the hopeful perspective that unfolds in stark contrast with an economy which displays the traits of empire and thrives on mounting class differentials. Although there have been numerous reflections on empire, the relation of empire and economics begs clarification from a religious perspective, and the notion of class has not been discussed in theological and religious discourse in the United States for a very long time.[3]

Religion and economics are often seen at the opposite ends of the spectrum. Those who feel this way tend to see religion as an affair that has mostly do to with disembodied ideas and with another world, while they see economics as a matter of realism, planted firmly in the concerns of this world. Living through a traumatic economic crash has shown us how untenable this all-too-common assumption is. Most of the established economists—commonly considered hard-nosed realists—lacked grounding in the realities of this world and did not see the economic crash coming, including Alan Greenspan, the former head of the Federal Reserve Board. They maintained their fervently held faith in a particular form of free-market economics. This faith was so strong that other voices that called for a reality check—including minority voices in the field of economics—were brushed aside. The fate of those people who ended up losing their homes, their jobs, their livelihoods, and their retirement funds in the economic crash cries out for such a reality check now. This has been long overdue, as people were falling through the cracks of the economy long before the floor fell out.

Part of the problem with the current economic crisis is that economics is based on an odd sort of faith, expressed tongue in cheek by the term "money-theism," which has been popularized by comedian Stephen Colbert. There are a few big faith claims, like the ideas that economic deregulation always promotes growth, that tax cuts for powerful corporations and the wealthy always spur the economy, and that wealth gathered at the top inevitably trickles down. This list of faith claims includes the well-worn belief that a rising tide will lift all boats, a belief that is maintained despite the fact that more and more people are drowning even in times when economic tides are rising. In the recent history of the United States, this should have become clear by the 1990s, when a growing economy left more and more people behind. Yet facts like these did little to deter the faith of the leading economists.

There are alternative voices in the economic community who are now talking about economics as a form of religion or even a form of theology[4]: economics as it is currently practiced, they note, is based on faith claims, and economists function like religious professionals when their main task is promoting the big ideas rather than crunching numbers. While this assessment is not necessarily made in order to rebuff the study of economics, it does not present a flattering understanding of religion. Religion is defined here, it seems, as that which people blindly accept, in terms of big ideas that do not need to be—and should not be—questioned. Religion, in this account, is the exact opposite of anything that can be supported by observation and evidence. Unfortunately, this is a misunderstanding with disastrous consequences, of which economic crashes are just the tip of the iceberg.[5]

Jesus did not demand blind faith. When John the Baptist began having doubts about whether Jesus would be the promised Messiah, Jesus did not encourage him to believe blindly and without question; rather, he provided some evidence when he told John's followers: "Go and tell John what you hear and see: the blind receive their sight, the lame walk, the lepers are cleansed, the deaf hear, the dead are raised, and the poor have good news brought to them" (Matt 11:4-5). Such efforts to tie faith to real life can be observed in other parts of the New Testament as well. Not even the Apostle Paul demands blind faith, although he is often misunderstood in this way. For Paul, the reality of faith is demonstrated in the fruits of the Spirit (Gal 5:22-26)—tangible and material examples of God at work in the world. The things that Paul lists, "love, joy, peace, patience, kindness, generosity, faithfulness, gentleness, and self-control" (Gal 5:22-23), are not religious fantasies but practical ways of living that are in stark contrast to the Roman Empire of his time—and to the free-market economy of ours. The following statement by Paul captures it best: "The only thing that counts is faith working through love" (Gal 5:6). This insight is deeply rooted in the Judeo-Christian traditions: God desires mercy—steadfast love—rather than the blind pursuit of a religion that promotes faith claims that must not be questioned (Hos 6:6; Matt 9:13, 12:7).

In other words, there are powerful reminders in the Judeo-Christian traditions that faith does not have to mean blind acceptance or a promise of pie in the sky that would not be subject to testing and questioning. Faith is tied to reality and the transformation of it. More specifically, Christian faith has to do with the transformation of the reality of the least of its followers, as Jesus' response to John the Baptist demonstrates (Matt 11:4-5). Without that particular transformation, faith does not make sense, and neither does economics. No doubt, things would be quite different if Christianity were to recapture such a sense of reality, and things would be just as different if economists would do the same.

Unfortunately, we are not there yet. In the current situation, too many people are still conditioned to accept things "on faith"—both in religion and in economics. What is most troublesome, especially in a country that is as religious as the United States, is that there appears to be a connection: people who accept religious principles on blind faith seem to be more likely to accept economic principles on blind faith, as well, no matter how detrimental to human well being they might be. Too many still forgo the sorts of questions that tie faith to reality. It is probable that more disasters will be the result—today the economy, tomorrow the church.

Nevertheless, there is real hope emerging in unexpected places. The struggle for alternatives had been going on long before the crisis, and it will continue afterwards. A crucial part of this struggle is constituted by those whom the system has taken for granted, overlooked, or even rejected. The Judeo-Christian traditions contain such stories in many prominent places, although mainline Christianity rarely picks up on them in ways that present a challenge to life as a whole. Jesus sums up the phenomenon to which I am referring, when he recites Psalms 118:22-23 to his opponents: "The stone that the builders rejected has become the cornerstone; this was the Lord's doing, and it is amazing in our eyes" (Mark 12:10-11). The rejection, itself, is no accident and does not come as a surprise; very early on in Jesus' ministry, it became clear that he would not conform to the rules of the dominant religious-political economy of his own day. That he healed a man with a withered hand on the Sabbath had consequences, and we learn that "the Pharisees went out and immediately conspired with the Herodians against him, how to destroy him" (Mark 3:6). Yet destruction and rejection are not the end of the story—as Jesus' own story continues through resistance and the production of an alternative way of life that is so surprising that not even his closest followers are able to understand it at times. It is this story that continues today, through cross and resurrection, and that may still have the potential to make a difference. But there is no need to take my word for it: "You will know them by their fruits" (Matt 7:16).

I would like to thank the following people for reading parts or the whole of the manuscript. They have made important contributions through their comments, but even greater contributions are made by the sort of work that each of them is doing in order to develop alternative ways of life: Rosemarie Henkel-Rieger, teacher and activist; Gene Lantz, radio host and lead organizer for North Texas Jobs with Justice; Néstor Míguez, professor of New Testament and systematic theology at Instituto Universitario (ISEDET) in Buenos Aires, Argentina; Jung Mo Sung, professor of religious studies and chair of the Graduate Program in Religious Studies at the Methodist University of São Paulo, São Bernardo do Campo, Brazil; David Brockman, research associate for the Progressive Christian Center in the South and adjunct professor at Brite Divinity School; and Kevin Minister, one of my Ph.D. students, who also prepared the index. I also thank the members of the

Progressive Reading Group, of North Texas Jobs with Justice and its Worker Rights Board, as well the striking Great Western Erectors Iron Workers with their organizers Martin Ramirez and Michael Martin. My daughters, Helen and Annika Rieger, and some of their friends constantly remind me of why the topics discussed in this book are important and that young minds are able to grasp the issues at stake. A Scholarly Outreach Grant, provided by Perkins School of Theology, has further supported the research of this book.

No Rising Tide: Religion, Economics, and Empire

1

In this book, we will take a fresh look at religion and economics and the relation between the two. Investigating this relation is especially instructive in light of economic crises, since economic crises are never merely about finance, capital, and labor; they impact all aspects of our lives, including matters of religion. Economic matters reach further than what we usually consider the discipline of economics. In what follows, we will explore this further reach of economics, just as we will explore how matters of religion are influential in shaping economic decisions. Bringing economics, religion, and theology (understood as self-critical reflection on religion) together in this way will not only lead to a deeper understanding of these crises but also to a clearer vision of what the alternatives might be.

No Rising Tide

"A rising tide lifts all boats," President John F. Kennedy used to say. This statement constitutes one of the strongest statements of faith in the free-market economy even today. It is one of the foundations of current mainline economics, which assumes that if those on top do better, everybody will be better off in due course. This statement-turned-doctrine, spread around the world by processes of globalization, is deeply rooted in the history of the United States, reaching back into the nineteenth century. More than one of the fathers of current mainline economics was convinced that the rising tide was the engine of all progress.

Nevertheless, the reality looks more and more different every day, not only during times of economic crisis but even during times of economic success. During the economic boom of the 1990s, an increasing number of people did not experience the lifting of the tide, not only globally but at home in the United States as well. Downturn had already become a permanent reality for many even before the economic fallout that began in 2008, which is the worst since the Great Depression of 1929. The first seven years of the new millennium showed no real increase for the working-age population, whose real income remained below its year 2000 level.[1] Downturn for working people — whose wages were systematically repressed and whose benefits were slashed — was one basis for economic successes at the top. The other basis was a bubble economy that was less and less in touch with actual economic performance, as in the stock market, or with real values, as in the housing market.[2]

The economic fallout of 2008 had global implications on a scale never before seen in history. "The crisis today is spreading even faster [than the Great Depression] and affects more countries at the same time," noted Pascal Lamy, the president of the World Trade Organization (WTO). Lamy warned that this could lead to political unrest on a large scale.[3] The situation was so severe that even Thomas Friedman, a longtime supporter of globalization, who continues to maintain great faith in the free market, concluded: "We are going to have to learn to live with a lot more uncertainty for a lot longer than our generation has ever experienced."[4]

Not all are affected equally, however. While the absence of rising tides is the reality for more and more of us — it has been estimated that the global economy lost as much as 40 percent of its value by 2009 — the tide keeps rising for some and remains stable for others. According to *Forbes* magazine's 2008 annual report on the four hundred wealthiest Americans, who each have assets in excess of $1.3 billion, the assembled net worth of the group rose by $30 billion to $1.57 trillion from the previous year, which is "only 2%," according to the report.[5] There were some changes at the top as some people's wealth was negatively affected by market performance; others, however, have seen tremendous gains. In addition to continued economic growth, economic policy — based on mainline economic theory — plays a role here as well, as the Bush administration's tax cuts benefited those four hundred wealthiest individuals the most. In 2006, the last year for which tax data are available, the wealthiest only paid 17.2 percent in taxes, down from 22.9 percent in 2001.[6] Author Tom Hertz identifies the following trend: "The middle class is experiencing more insecurity of income, while the top decile is experiencing less. From 1997–98 to 2003–04, the increase in downward short-term mobility was driven by the experiences of middle-class households (those earning between $34,510 and $89,300 in 2004 dollars). Households in the top quintile saw no increase in downward short-term mobility, and households in the top decile ($122,880 and up) saw a *reduction* in the frequency of large negative income shocks." The median household was no more upwardly mobile in 2003–2004, years when the gross domestic product (GDP) grew, than it was during the recession of 1990–1991.[7]

The result is that the gaps between the very wealthy and the rest of the population keep increasing, a situation that has all sorts of consequences that are often overlooked. What is overlooked most frequently is that these gaps are not primarily about income levels as such; looking at numbers often leads to this misperception. These gaps are ultimately about differentials of power and influence, because big money equals big power in the current economic system. Such power and influence determine who gets to shape the world, who gets recognized, and whose ideas count. But such power also determines matters of life and death. Most of us remember stories of Black Tuesday—the day the stock market crashed on October 29, 1929—about investors committing suicide. The downturn of 2008 and 2009 had its death toll as well, which even led to the creation of a new word—"econocide"[8]—although this time the deaths were kept more secret and made fewer headlines. The difference in that situation was that, while investors were once again committing suicide at alarming rates, common people increasingly did so as well. Sometimes they killed not only themselves but also their families. Calls to the National Suicide Prevention Lifeline were at a record high, up more than 25 percent in one year! A clinical psychologist in Beverly Hills, California, reported getting calls from businessmen with suicidal inclinations, a first in her eighteen-year career. These people, it appears, felt guilt and shame because they blamed themselves for not noticing sooner what was going to happen.[9]

In this context of a widening gap between rich and poor, abject poverty is and remains a challenge, and it kills more people. I have addressed it in many previous publications, and, as one of the genuine life-and-death issues in a globalizing world, we must never forget about it. But it is becoming clearer now that abject poverty is only one part of the problem, as many more lives are ruined by economic difficulties across the board. Life-and-death struggles are no longer just a matter for the poorest of the poor. What is going on in the economy affects more and more of us in negative ways—exactly at a time when economic issues reach ever further into our lives and affect us ever more deeply on every level of our being, from the emotional to the intellectual and the religious. Economist Steve Keen is right: "Economics is too important to leave to the economists."[10] The same could be said for matters of religion and theology, and this insight is writ large when the two fields overlap.

It is surprising that many people still do not seem to be aware of the seismic shifts that have been taking place. While nobody can overlook these mounting economic crises altogether, many maintain faith in the rising tide despite ever-more severe downturns. Keeping with the habitual time lag in the religious world and with a certain neglect of real-life issues, theologians and church people may well be the last ones to notice. Even more surprising, however, is the fact that for the longest time, many top economists and politicians did not seem to be much concerned about the long-term downward spiral that affects so many people either, and it remains unclear whether they have understood the severe nature of the problem yet. Oddly enough, there seems to be a time lag in the economic professions as well, combined with a peculiar neglect of real-life issues that at times rivals the religious world. An example are tax cuts to the wealthy—the most cherished economic and political tool of recent decades—which are still supported by many economists, despite the fact that there is little indication that they have benefited the economy and despite evidence that these policies have contributed to economic crises, since money saved at the top was often not invested, as expected, but hoarded.

Religion and Economics

In recent years, a great deal of research has been done around the globe showing the stunning connections and parallels between religion and economics. Pointing out these parallels, which have gone mostly unnoticed in mainline theology and economics,[11] does not imply a negative judgment on either discipline, as if the existence of religious underpinnings would make economics less serious or less scientific by default or as if economic interests would automatically disqualify religious thought. Pointing out these parallels merely places matters in a new and broader perspective and challenges us to investigate further what is still mostly hidden. In this new perspective, basic questions arise: On which authorities, powers, and energies do we rely? What is it that gives us ultimate hope, shapes our desires, and provides reasonable levels of stability?[12] Such questions are not always easy to address because the answers usually lie below the surface, in the realms of what might be called the "economic unconscious" and the "religious unconscious."[13] The next big challenge for theologians and economists will be to study these unconscious realms. In times when the global economy is moving from one slump to the next, having reached new low points, and when even the top economists do not really seem to know what to do except to plug the most glaring holes and to fill in the widest gaps, perhaps these matters will get more of a hearing, with a chance to bear fruit.

The basic question for an engagement of religion and economics today is whether we have perhaps relied on the wrong authorities and powers. This question should first be posed in terms of abstract theoretical matters but in terms of the practical consequences of contemporary economics—and particularly in terms of the constant and growing inequalities of rich and poor, which prevent more and more people from living decent lives. The economic fallout that began in 2008 serves as the starkest reminder yet that these inequalities can no longer be played down in the usual ways, either by insinuating that the gap between rich and poor might be the problem of only a few who occupy extreme positions on either end of the spectrum or by arguing that this gap is only a temporary one that will eventually close by itself. While the lower end of the spectrum has always been populated by large groups of people both globally and locally, this particular crisis hit home with a vengeance, as it pulled down even many of those who previously felt safe in the middle. Moreover, the sinking feeling that there may be no rising tide is no longer just related to growing economic hardships during times of recession. Economic inequalities, both global and at home, persist and grow not only during times of economic stagnation, but increasingly during times of economic growth as well. The so-called trickle-down theory, according to which wealth accumulated at the top inevitably trickles down, could not be corroborated even during the economic boom of the 1990s. When the global economy has produced growing wealth, this wealth has not even moved laterally, for the most part. If anything, economic production has aggregated into a flood of profit and wealth upward.[14]

Latin American economists and theologians were among the first to demonstrate the link between economics and religion: Franz Hinkelammert, an economist working in Costa Rica, and Hugo Assmann, a theologian working in Brazil, have published extensively on this matter. Jung Mo Sung, a Brazilian theologian, has developed some of these matters further in more recent publications.[15] European authors, both economists and theologians, have made their own contributions on this topic, most of them writing in German and some in English.[16] One of the pioneering texts in the United States was written by theologian M. Douglas Meeks.[17] Unfortunately, many of the critical studies are not available in English.[18]

But the case for the close relation of religion and economics has also been made by economists in the United States. John Kenneth Galbraith, for instance, has noted that neoliberal laissez-faire economics is built on theological grounds.[19] Robert Nelson, a professor of economics at the University of Maryland, has argued that economics now functions as religion. In two books, Nelson has shown the connection of religion and the free-market economy.[20] Reflecting on his experiences as an economist in the U.S. Department of the

Interior, Nelson points out that the main job of the chief economists was not to provide formal economic calculations, but to preserve key economic values and actively promote those values in politics through collaboration with politicians.[21]

Summarizing the assessment of an international group of religious scholars from different world religions, theologian Paul Knitter has concluded that contemporary economics can be perceived as a religion, since the dogma of the free market must be believed "with a trust that looks like blind faith." He finds the traits of a religion in the widespread impression that the authority of economics is unquestionable and often even infallible, and in the assumption that the current system is the only one that is viable. If the market is, thus, a religion, Knitter concludes, it needs to enter into a dialogue with other religions.[22] Such a dialogue would, no doubt, be worth considering. But, as with any dialogue, we will have to wonder whether it can be truly mutual if one side holds considerably more power than the other. More importantly, given that there are problems not only with current economic thought but also with religious thought, we need to go beyond a dialogue in order to develop a critique that cuts both ways.

While key economic positions are normally not presented in explicit theological terms—economists make few direct references to God, for instance, when they present their arguments—there are some efforts to do so. One of the most prominent supporters of a self-proclaimed "Christian theology of economics" in the United States is Michael Novak of the American Enterprise Institute. Though he disclaims a direct relation of theology and economics, he finds close connections between his conception of God and the direction that economics should take. According to Novak, Christian theology is relevant to economics because the incarnation of Jesus Christ challenges us to accept the world as it is and not to expect the reign of heaven on earth.[23] In other words, the economic status quo should not be challenged since this is the way God intends things to be. The logical conclusion is that God sanctions the current embodiment of the free-market economy.

Theological justifications of the economic status quo are usually not that blunt. It is more common that the connection between God and the free-market economy is simply presupposed without much reflection. The basic principles of economics rest on a deep-seated implicit theology, and, thus, they remain largely unchallenged. There is a chance that this implicit theology becomes more open during times of economic difficulties and growing economic hardship, but there is also a countervailing phenomenon since repression runs high in times of trouble. Consequently, this implicit theology is pushed further underground in some cases, and the beliefs on which it is based harden.

Economics appears to be closely related to such implicit theological perspectives, which are actively at work even in times of crisis. In the midst of economic fallout, the study of economic indicators often takes a back seat to reflections that are less solidly rooted in analyses of what is going on. No matter how bad the crisis, economists appear to hold on to an almost limitless faith in the reality of unstoppable progress that will follow seemingly inevitable depressions. When the floor fell out of the economy in 2008, for instance, this faith did not necessarily cancel out arguments for the need for economic stimulus and bailout, but it framed them. Even some of the most ardent defenders of stimulus and bailout never lost their faith in the free market, as we will see. Hope, even in the midst of the most severe economic crises, is thus built on the faith that things will eventually get better and that the reign of free-market economics will be reaffirmed. Due to the firm belief that things will get back on track in due time and that stimulus and bailout will not be needed indefinitely, even the economic assumptions of the Obama administration do not depart fundamentally from the past. As a result, economic hope resembles what might be called an otherworldly perspective, which is a perversion of the notion of transcendence.

This hope in the otherworldly reality of economic flourishing and success often covers up the role of severe failures that contribute to economic decline and hardship. For all the recent calls to limit their salaries, CEOs of large corporations, for instance, are still not substantially challenged, except in cases of crude moral failure or grotesque malfeasance. Even key figures in the world of free-market economics, such as Alan Greenspan, the well-known former chairman of the U.S. Federal Reserve Board, are held relatively blameless in the current economic crisis. While Greenspan has become the subject of some critique, it is rare that he is challenged in ways that would even remotely match the tremendous levels of praise that he has received in the past. In the 2004 elections, some sought to hold President Bush accountable for the economic crisis, but most people, including many of those most economically challenged, did not perceive the weak U.S. economy to be the fault of the government, its policies, or its leaders. In the 2008 elections, the state of the economy was more central, but, although President Bush's approval rating was extremely low, there was little clear assessment of the impact of his administration on the state of the economy. Neither his policies of economic deregulation, of noncompetitive government contracts in Iraq and New Orleans, of tax cuts to the wealthy, nor the tremendous economic costs of the Iraq war were much debated in public as causes of the full-blown economic crisis at the end of his second term, as faith in the self-healing powers of the economy prevailed in most quarters. Note that the economic costs of the Iraq war substantially exceed any other government expense: while the Obama administration has been criticized for planning to spend up to $1 trillion for economic recovery, the cost for the Iraq war will come to at least $3 trillion.[24]

The administration of President Obama does not seem to be interested in entering into debates that might challenge otherworldly economic hopes either; while it follows a slightly different approach in economic matters that will be discussed in more detail below, it does not seek to discredit the deeper assumptions on which the U.S. economy rests. This lack of debate of implicit theological principles and assumptions enhances and augments the problem of otherworldliness, which is a negative sort of transcendence that shapes up as a lack of connection to the real world. In this context, the insight of theologian M. Douglas Meeks that economics apparently cannot exist without some sort of divine or otherworldly sanction of its norms is corroborated.[25] For most economists and many theologians, the statement, "God bless America," with all the undertones of triumphalism that have been added in recent years, might easily be extended to mean, "God bless the American economy."

The intensity of the entanglement of religion and economics in the United States is perhaps harder to imagine for those living elsewhere. In Europe, for instance, great care is taken not to refer to matters of religion and transcendence in public in any way, let alone to God. Even most of the European churches are careful in this regard. When talking about economic matters, for instance, they rarely refer directly to images of God; they tend to refer instead to general moral premises and values, which they believe to be commonly acknowledged by everyone. One of the debates in European economics is whether the free market-economy is a merely formal mechanism of distribution, which can be dealt with through mathematical and statistical calculations, or whether the free-market economy is guided by other factors, such as, for instance, an implicit set of values that cannot be considered to be purely economic.[26] Nevertheless, even in Europe and other secularized places, economic theories appear to be based on certain embedded and unquestioned conceptions that push beyond mere sets of values and tend to assume a transcendent or quasi-divine reality, whatever it might be called.

The processes of economic privatization—an important aspect of free-market economics—may serve as an example. When the German Postal Service was privatized at the beginning of the 1990s, the shape of the new postal system did not emerge primarily from empirical observations and analyses of the local markets. Instead, management consultants from the U.S.-based corporation McKinsey and Company were flown in to promote universal ideas on matters of privatization. Their task was not to assess the German business situation, but to spark the imagination of their German counterparts through the promotion of concepts that were transcendent in the sense that they would apply independently of time and space. Universal economic values like deregulation and cost cutting were far more important in this process than economic analyses and studies; those values determined both the questions that were raised and the answers given.

More is at stake, however, than just the question of the role of values versus the role of empirical study and mathematical calculation in economics. There is a theological component at work even in Europe, as the following example will demonstrate: during an earlier period of decline in 2002, the German *Handelsblatt* reported that the incomes of the board members of the thirty largest companies rose, despite severely falling values of their stocks. The Daimler-Chrysler Corporation set the record at the time: the incomes of its thirteen board members rose by 131 percent, while the corporation lost 39 percent of its value in the stock market.[27] This phenomenon, which used to be challenged earlier in Europe than in the United States, cannot be explained if economics is ruled by purely mathematical and statistical calculations. Do the laws of the market, which are often referred to when the salaries of workers are cut, not apply to the upper levels of the economic world? Is there no competition at these levels from other competent business leaders who might do a similar or even better job for considerably less money? While standard economic calculations do not seem to apply at the highest levels, there is even more at stake than the question of specific sets of economic values. What is at stake here are not just values but what is of ultimate value or, to use Paul Tillich's descriptor of God, what is of ultimate concern. Here, we are entering the realm of the theological, going beyond the question of ethics or moral values. Questions of ultimate concern are theological questions.

It might be added that salaries of CEOs have decreased in recent years. In 2006, the average CEO made 364 times more than an average worker in the United States, down from over 500 times a few years earlier. However, there is another number that is perhaps more telling and much less known. The difference between the salary of an average worker and the top twenty private-equity and hedge-fund managers in the United States is in a different league altogether: on average, members of this latter group earned 22,255 times the pay of the average worker.[28] Such astronomical ceilings do their part to maintain high CEO salaries. Yet, at stake is not just the current plateau of salaries but the overall trends. During the previous decade, CEO salaries, when adjusted for inflation, have risen 45 percent, and worker pay only 7 percent; the minimum wage has gone down 7 percent in real terms in the same time frame.[29] It is hard to explain these differentials in terms of basic economic principles like the relation of supply and demand. Deeper values and concerns are at work here—indeed approaching ultimate concerns.

Economics with the Soul of a Church

In the United States, there is, however, a more existential level at which religion and economics are related. In the "nation with the soul of a church," as G. K. Chesterton described the United States in a different context, religion plays a special role. Unlike their European counterparts, large numbers of U.S. residents believe in God—as many as 92 percent, a recent survey by the Pew Forum on Religion and Public Life tells us. Of those 92 percent, 71 percent believe with absolute certainty.[30] Such deeply engrained religious attitudes cannot possibly be confined to matters of religion alone. Those who see religion as a private matter fail to understand how strong beliefs and convictions bleed over into other areas of life. Key components of life can never easily be compartmentalized, despite myriad efforts to do so, and, in the United States, religion is one such key component.

One of the core concerns of this book is the sense that people approach economics in much the same way as they approach religion. People who have been conditioned by their religious leaders to believe what they are told without the opportunity to question tend not to question what they are told by their economic leaders either. In other words, people who are used to accepting religion on the basis of a kind of blind faith tend to take economics on blind faith as well. Moreover, in our current situation, the relation of religion and economics is shaping up differently from the relation of religion and politics. While religious people are sometimes encouraged by their religious leaders to question political leaders, such questioning does not apply to economic leaders for the most part. One exception to this rule might be economic leaders who fail on moral grounds. At present, the principles of mainline economics are mostly taken for granted by religious communities, presupposed as part of the way things are, and virtually never discussed in critical fashion.[31] In other words, the ideal of the separation of church and state or church and politics has no parallel in the separation of church and economics. There is no debate about why church and economics or religion and economics might need to be separated.

Nevertheless, strong parallels between religion and economics exist, even if they are mostly hidden from view and located in the unconscious. Assmann and Hinkelammert have pointed out, for instance, that the rise in power of religious fundamentalism in the United States coincides with the rise in power of a sort of fundamentalism in economic matters.[32] But even outside the world of fundamentalism, it seems as if the deeply engrained religiosity in the United States takes shape in the spirit of economics as well. In the United States, there is generally a stronger faith in economic principles and in the way economics works than in Europe. This attitude has proven attractive to many others outside of the United States, as well, and one can only wonder what role this parallel between faith in religion and in economics plays in regions of the world that are often described as "developing" and where Christianity is currently growing. Does the perceived success of U.S. economics mirror the success of U.S. religion? Even the Europeans, despite their more secular disposition, have often admired such blessed assurance in some respects, if only in secret. It is not an accident that Europeans have been fond of hiring U.S. management consultants whose strength lies in holding strong convictions about universal economic principles and beliefs, rather than in the concrete and down-to-earth analysis of local economic phenomena. Today we know that the results of such faith-based economics have been a mixed blessing and have led to economic disasters, including the most severe global recession in history.[33]

There is another striking parallel between religion and economics. Just as there is generally very little public awareness of alternative approaches to the organized religion of particular faith traditions, there is very little public awareness of alternative approaches to the world of economics. In the popular mind, judging not only from widely accepted standard portrayals of the media but also from innumerable personal conversations, Christianity is a fairly uniform entity, and so is economics. As Beverly Harrison observed almost twenty years ago, "While some may mourn the loss of a consensual 'public philosophy' in this society, the truth is that there is hardly any public dissent—even in the academy—regarding the theoretical and practical paradigms that underlie policy prescriptions and diagnoses of American political and economic woes."[34] While there may be somewhat more dissent at the moment, a great deal of consensus on the basics remains. Christians, for instance, tend to assume that when they hear other Christians talk about God they basically mean the same thing. This is why it is so easy for politicians to talk about God and be supported by religious people for it. Likewise, when Americans talk about the free-market economy and about capitalism, they assume that this is one and the same thing all over what is sometimes called the "free world," including China. If they are made aware of differences—like, for instance, the much more generous vacation time of up to six weeks for workers each year in Europe, or a stronger social safety net that includes universal health care and even dental care—they are often confused and tend to conclude mistakenly that a situation that is so different from theirs cannot possibly be based on sound economics or, perhaps, that differences are due to other economic systems like socialism.

In this book, we will take a look at the overarching picture of economics that has been internalized by large numbers of people just as a certain picture of Christianity has been internalized. It is not that the myriad economic technicalities are unimportant, but, as Nelson reminds us, the task of the top economists is not to pursue small-scale technicalities and to crunch numbers, but to keep the big picture before us—a task that resembles the self-understanding of most theologians. Economists are the ones who need to make sure that the overarching picture is clear and has sunk in, and that we do not veer from the path on which the economy has embarked. Nelson goes even further when he compares the role of economists to that of priests.[35]

With this kind of priestly support, the big picture that continues to be presented even in times of economic downturn is one of nearly absolute faith in the so-called free market. As German sociologist Dirk Baecker has pointed out, society truly started to believe in free-market economics, or capitalism, when the socialist alternative disappeared, and the capitalist structure of society no longer needed to be supported by ideological arguments. People now relate to the free market as they used to relate to spirits and gods of old, Baecker claims. One has no choice but to conform to them since their temper and their decisions cannot be controlled. In this situation, no critique is permitted, and things must be accepted as they are.[36] Adam Smith's notion of the "invisible hand of the market" is also in the background here, although that notion may not necessarily be invoked openly. Since the market assumes such a central role, anything that might interfere with it needs to be kept at low intensity levels, especially government intervention, international restrictions on trade, and organizations of people like workers and all others who are not initiated into the system at the higher levels. Faith in the market currently commands high levels of conformity, including the need to please. This is demonstrated by the fact that even in times of economic boom there is a constant worry that the market can be "jinxed" by anything, if only by a critical remark or a pessimistic statement.

The various economic positions that converge on the topic of the free market are sometimes brought together under the notion of "neoclassical economics," or, especially in Latin America, under the notion of "neoliberalism," due to the preference for laissez-faire economics. While these theories have been around for a long time, the Chicago School of Economics has been among their most influential defenders for the past three decades, emphasizing both economic freedom and minimal government interference based on a strong faith in the powers of the free market.[37] The strength of this faith is demonstrated by the fact that it is maintained even in situations of obvious failure and downturn. The market takes on a central role here that assumes transcendent qualities, as it is the ultimate guide not only for economics but also for politics.[38] The Chicago School, most prominently represented by the late Milton Friedman, began its global ascent when Margaret Thatcher was elected prime minister in Great Britain in 1979 and when Ronald Reagan became the president of the United States in 1980. Both politicians were admirers of Friedman's work and were close personal friends with him. Reagan himself notes the initial success and the connections: "America astonished the world. Chicago school economics, supply-side economics, call it what you will—I noticed that it was even known as Reaganomics at one point until it started working—all of it is fast becoming orthodoxy. It's not just that Milton Friedman or Friedrich von Hayek or George Stigler have won Nobel Prizes; other younger names, unheard of a few years ago, are now also celebrated."[39] Since those days, economists who display strong faith in the market have become ever more influential in politics and public life, to the degree that it may not be an exaggeration to say that "the world has been remade in the economist's image."[40]

The idea of the free market is based on the simple idea of the interaction of buyers and sellers under the condition of scarce resources, which has assumed the status of a faith claim. The standard textbook definition is given by Paul Samuelson and William Nordhaus: "A Market is an arrangement by which buyers and sellers of a commodity interact to determine its price and quantity."[41] Faith in this market rests on the general assumption that it creates conditions of equilibrium, where supply and demand keep production and prices in balance, and that this arrangement invariably creates mutually beneficial results.[42] The market is thus the engine of happiness and balance, guaranteed by a *deus ex machina,* as it were: a god that functions automatically and can be trusted to arrive on the scene whenever help is needed.

One of the disagreements between mainline economists, debated with quasi religious fervor, is what part of this equation must be supported in times of crisis. During his tenure as president of the World Bank, Joseph Stiglitz, an opponent of neoclassical economics and the Chicago School, noted the agreement in a basic faith before pointing out the tension: After the end of the Cold War, "the ideological debates should be over; there should be agreement that while markets are at the center of the economy, governments must play an important role." The disagreement, according to Stiglitz, has to do with the role of government in creating a balance, but *"where that balance is may depend on the country, the capacity of its government, the institutional development of its markets."*[43] John Maynard Keynes, the father of the economic model from which neoclassical economics and the Chicago School sought to differentiate themselves, and whose theories are in vogue again to some degree with the Obama administration, argued that the economy would benefit the most when consumers (that is, buyers) had more money to spend. Consumers, especially when they are not wealthy, would spend these additional funds rather than save them, which would in turn stimulate the market. Neoclassical economics, represented for instance by supply-side economics, took the other position, arguing that the market would best be stimulated by tax cuts that favor producers and sellers. Supply-siders were often criticized, however, because they assumed that this could be done without cuts to government spending since increased economic output would "raise all boats." The neoclassical approach of Friendman and the Chicago School, dubbed monetarism, focused mostly on monetary supply—arguing that the main economic challenge for the government would be to keep the supply and demand for money in equilibrium. Nevertheless, all these schools, the Keynesians included, agree that the free market will ultimately produce the happiness of all. This is where faith ultimately rests.

Market Fundamentalism

In recent years, the faith of supply-siders and monetarists—summarized as the belief in a market with as little governmental regulation as possible—has had the upper hand in shaping economic policy. The success of these approaches—and with that success, the validity of their faith—is now in question. Economist Steve Keen describes this success in the following words: "The global economy of the early 21st century looks a lot more like the economic textbook ideal than did the world of the 1950s. Barriers to trade have been abolished or dramatically reduced, regulations controlling the flow of capital have been liberalized, currencies are now valued by the market rather than being set by governments; in so many spheres of economic interaction, the government's role has been substantially reduced."[44] This reflects the key concerns of the so-called Washington Consensus, whose days are not yet numbered: "liberalization, stabilization, and privatization" of the market.[45] While the Keynesian alternative to this approach has gained new currency through President Obama's stimulus packages, Obama has made it clear that things will go back to normal after the recession. Even the nationalization of banks and other corporations that was briefly discussed can be no more than temporary: privatization remains the ultimate goal. Meanwhile, the Cato Institute has put out one-page advertisements in the nation's major newspapers challenging Obama's temporary move and stating that in order "to improve the economy, policymakers should focus on reforms that remove impediments to work, saving, investment and production. Lower tax rates and a reduction in the burden of government are the best ways of using fiscal policy to boost growth." The statement was signed by approximately 250 U.S. economics professors.[46] What is overlooked by these economists, of course, is that the economy crashed precisely at a time when this approach was followed in economics in its purest form ever. And since no reasons are given for why we should still follow a failed approach, this statement appears to be based precisely on the sort of blind faith that seeks to avoid questions and challenges.

Some have called this position "market fundamentalism," a term that is more than a caricature because it connotes the parallels with a sort of rigid adherence to Christian faith that lacks consideration of changes in context or of the real needs and concerns of people. It should be noted also that, in this conception of the free market based on faith in the rules of supply and demand, workers play no role at all—an issue to which we will return in the next chapter. "Market fundamentalism," even in the judgment of investor and billionaire George Soros, "is today a greater threat to open society than any totalitarian ideology."[47] The problem, according to Soros, is that in this perspective markets are given too large a role: the market assumes a "magical quality," as if it really were able to produce consistently an equilibrium based on perfect competition.[48] Here we are back at the false transcendence of economics. What should give us pause is that despite a virtually ideal situation for the free market in the United States for the past twenty years, which was created and protected by those who fervently believe in it, things have hardly improved for large groups of people, and even fewer people are bound to profit from it in the future.

These various approaches all share a "hidden consensus"—we might call it an implicit faith—that Beverly Harrison identified almost twenty years ago.[49] There is a firm belief in the moral benevolence of the free-market system and private property, combined with a common acceptance among liberal, neoliberal, and neoclassical theorists that this is the only system that works. This system takes on quasi-divine and transcendent qualities when it begins to block any and all alternatives and challenges. Most adamantly rejected, of course, is any government intervention that is not unconditionally supportive of the market and that might question or challenge it. In this scenario, the only troubles with the market are seen as coming from efforts to regulate it, either by governments or by unions and other organized alternatives. Milton Friedman, in his Nobel Laureate speech of 1976, quotes British Prime Minister James Callaghan of the Labour Party: "We used to think that you could just spend your way out of a recession and increase employment by cutting taxes and boosting Government spending. I tell you, in all candour, that that option no longer exists, and that insofar as it ever did exist, it only worked by injecting bigger doses of inflation into the economy followed by higher levels of unemployment as the next step."[50] According to this position, the market is best left to its own devices. This is true even in cases where the market creates severe imbalances of its own, for instance, through monopolies. In the mind of another influential Chicago economist, Friedrich von Hayek, the creation of monopolies is less of a problem than antimonopoly intervention by the government.[51] Mainline economics is confident that the market will take care of the common good, and so the government's role is no longer the support of the common good itself, but to support the market which believes itself to be the provider of the common good. Whether this is expressed explicitly or not, economics is thus believed to be closer to ultimate reality than politics, with the result that the role of politics is reduced to the service of the market.

Just as any regulative involvement of the government in the economy is rejected, any lucrative involvement of the government in the economic realm is rejected as well and made subject to privatization. This does not mean, however, that the place for government in economics is minimal. While economic gain is privatized, losses are typically socialized, as the bailouts of large corporations show. Even before the bailouts of 2008 and 2009, the government supported corporations either actively, through financial and other subsidies, or passively, through the easing of tax burdens. Faith in the market holds that this will lead to the greater good for all. And while there has been a significant political change from the Bush to the Obama administrations, the economic bedrock remains virtually the same. The hidden consensus maintains a strong emphasis on the freedom of the market, tied to the implicit faith that the market will not only take care of itself but of everybody else as well. Within the confines of this market, the laws of supply and demand are believed to work generally towards an equilibrium; one particular way in which this is supposed to happen is through wealth "trickling down," so that—shifting to another metaphor—a "rising tide will lift all boats." Today, a stronger sort of blind faith than ever is necessary to hold on to this system, and this blind faith will need to grow stronger yet in the future, since it is based on little evidence.

This discussion cannot be exhausted, however, by focusing on economics in a narrow sense. The free market is increasingly taking over other areas of life and has become second nature to us. The market regulates other relationships, as well, and gradually assumes a position of omnipresence, expanding the reach of its transcendence. Even personal relationships are now commonly treated in good market fashion as commodities, for instance, as people tend to assess potential partners and spouses in terms of how their market value compares to their own. For the wealthier members of society, it is not uncommon to divorce their aging spouses and marry younger and more attractive "trophy wives," but this is not just a problem at the top. The all-pervasiveness of the market affects all of us. The real reason for high divorce rates may not be so much the much-maligned lack of traditional values, but the growing commodification of all aspects of life that reaches deeper and deeper and does not spare even our most intimate relationships.

In addition, the proponents of the free market have argued for its efficiency in regulating political matters as well. Free-market arrangements are now often seen as the most democratic way of relating. The idea of large numbers of sellers competing for even larger numbers of buyers has, indeed, some democratic qualities, as no single person is in control and everyone has some influence. This idea works best, of course, if all participants are seen as independent individuals, with none of them wielding substantially more control or power over the market than others. If the common tendency to concentrate power in fewer and fewer hands is not analyzed, democracy appears indeed to be the natural outcome when consumers are able to choose freely the products produced by individual sellers. In this scenario, the role of government is not merely to support the market but to eliminate, in the name of democracy, all critical forces that might threaten it. While the democratic qualities of the market do indeed need to be recognized, especially when compared to an older feudalist world where relationships and interactions were permanently fixed in hierarchical fashion, the neglected problem of the market is that it has produced another set of power imbalances that challenges not only economic distribution but democracy itself. What keeps us from noticing this is once again blind faith without concern for what happens in real life—especially in the lives of those who do not benefit from the economic system as it currently works.

Yet, this mystique of the market and its religious overtones begins to crack at the seams when it is taken into account that the worlds of small business and of big business are fundamentally distinct from each other. In the words of John Kenneth Galbraith: "The two parts of the economy—the world of the technically dynamic, massively capitalized and highly organized corporations on the one hand and of the hundreds of thousands of small and traditional proprietors on the other—are very different. It is not a difference of degree but a difference which invades every aspect of economic organization and behavior, including the motivation to effort itself."[52] Small businesses conform better to the commonly accepted view of the free market, and so it is this world that is usually presented to students of economics and to the public, while the world of big business remains under cover. As Galbraith has pointed out: "Economic education holds . . . that capitalism can best be understood by examining enterprises with little or no capital, guided by one or two people, without the complications of corporate structure and where there is no union. Part of its appeal is in the way it removes from the corporate executive all power, including the power to do anything wrong. It also has firm historical roots: economic life began with small firms, with small capital, each one under the guiding hand of a single master."[53]

Nevertheless, this is different from what happens in big business and the corporate world. This part of the economy shapes up differently, according to Galbraith: "It can hardly be doubted that General Motors will be better able to influence the world around it—the prices and wages at which it buys and the prices at which it sells—than a man in suits and cloaks."[54] What if the large corporation does not need to follow the classic ground rules of the free market slavishly, that is, the laws of supply and demand? This has consequences not only for economics but also for the shape of politics and many other aspects of life, including religion. After all, a not-insignificant amount of success in the religious world is based on the corporate model as well—manifest, for instance, in the way megachurches operate by following established business rules.

At a time when we are dealing with multinational corporations that are large and powerful enough to make their own rules and which, thus, have little trouble bending the rules of the market to their advantage, the free market is becoming a tenet of belief that has less and less connection to reality. This is where the real problem of religion in our time surfaces. The following statement is strongly worded but hard to refute: "The profits of alert multinationals have much less to do with their efficiency and sensitivity to customer preferences than with their astuteness in lobbying, bribery, and mutually profitable alliances with the politicians of many countries. Everywhere they appear to operate as a mongrel blend of politics and economics, negotiating tax concessions, subsidies, protections against unions, sheltered markets, and allied benefits from local, regional, and national governments."[55] The various free-trade agreements often contribute further to the support of the strongest participants in the market rather than to the weaker ones. It seems as if no real alternative exists any more.

While we will take a look at these issues in more detail later, let us note the fact that both this standard approach to economics and the standard approach to theology are based on the same thing: belief in a transcendent fix. In one case, it is the market that will mysteriously bring happiness and prosperity—no matter how badly it may perform this function at present—and, in the other case, it is a divine entity that will eventually bring happiness and salvation—no matter how bad things might be at the moment. The two positions come closest together in what has been called the "Gospel of Prosperity," which is based on both theological and economic perspectives. This economic theology promotes the idea that if your faith in God is strong enough, you will continue to move up the economic ladder of happiness and prosperity.

In both theology and economics, the problem is compounded by the fact that there are congregations which embody these beliefs collectively, made up of those who have benefited from these beliefs and those who hope to benefit in the very near future, and who, thus, create a protective bubble around these beliefs. Those for whom the standard account of theology and economics works flock together; those for whom it does not work have two options: become a member and have faith without any evidence or stay on the outside. Those on the outside have two choices as well: one is to rebel against the system and to resist and resent it; the other is to despair of God and the world and to perceive oneself as damned without hope (theology) or as hopeless loser (economics).

How can this faith possibly be challenged? One challenge will increasingly present itself based on the lack of a rising tide for more and more people: as the economy produces fewer and fewer benefits for everyone, the Gospel of Prosperity will lead to mounting disappointment—the sort of disappointment that can only be avoided if things go reasonably well for a substantial number of people. The other challenge necessitates looking outside the bubble of the blessed—paying attention to people's lives, especially to those who are not part of the establishment. Looking at what is happening in real life and on its underside can function as control both for standard theology and for standard economics—both of which are in danger of worshipping otherworldly deities that never really have to prove themselves, even in the deepest crises of life. Only when these perspectives are taken into account can we begin to understand which gods, if any, may be worth respecting.

Religion, Economics, and Empire

A crucial issue that needs to be considered at the intersection of religion and economics is power, and the most severe embodiment of power is in the form of empire. The economy is where tremendous power is lodged today. This power is not limited merely to monetary issues or to the distribution of wealth: the power of the economy is all-pervasive and affects all areas of life. Relationships of power negotiated by economic means can be found, for instance, at the macrolevels of the political; the power lodged in global corporations has tremendous impact on politics both nationally and internationally. Relationships of power negotiated by economic means also impact us at the microlevels of the personal and even in our most intimate relationships; shaping our desires and branding our tastes is one of the declared goals of the advertising industry.[56] Economic relationships also impact the way we think and what we believe. Even religion can no longer pretend to operate in a vacuum, undisturbed by other forces. Such an understanding of the power of economics relates to my definition of empire as "massive concentrations of power which permeate all aspects of life and which cannot be controlled by any one actor alone."[57] While imperialism is indeed about money and power on the macrolevel—this is what we usually understand when we talk about empire—it also shapes us all the way to the core of our being.

Unfortunately, the myth of individualism, to which both mainline economics and mainline theology subscribe in their own ways, makes it hard for us to see the imperial aspirations of the free market. Individualism is the founding myth of the mainline—whether in economics or in modern theology—and it covers up both questions of power and of empire. To be more specific, individualism is the myth of the privileged and the powerful, who tend to see themselves as independent and autonomous, and who need to convince themselves and others that their wealth and their success are self-made. This individualism has influenced many modern religious perspectives, especially where religion has been relegated to the private sphere, and has been sanctioned in recent times especially by the Gospel of Prosperity. Even when well-meaning religious leaders challenge individualistic attitudes, they still often presuppose that individualism is real. By admonishing people "not to be so individualistic," for instance, they overlook precisely that neither wealth nor power or privilege are ever based on individual accomplishment alone; wealth and power are always produced in close relation to others. More specifically, under the conditions of free-market economics, wealth and power are often produced on the backs of others in various ways. The myth of individualism therefore covers up the reality that those who made it all the way to the top are there not purely because of their own achievements but because they often had substantial help, and they know how to make use of others to their own advantage.[58] Likewise, the success of individual companies is never solely due to the exploits of individual managers, as we are often made to believe; no such success would be possible without the contribution of the workforce. Both economics and religion must, therefore, be understood in terms of relationships of power already in place. Only when this is seen can we hope to make a difference, which includes rearranging these pre-existing relationships where necessary. Myths like individualism are among the most important points of connection between religion and economics today. Individualism is one of the pillars on which both mainline theology and mainline economics rest.

The notion of self-interest is related to the myth of individualism, and here is another pillar of economic power. Mainline economic theory holds that all relationships, with the exception of family relationships, are governed by the self-interest of independent individuals. Milton Friedman himself can be seen making this point in an interview with Phil Donahue, which is now posted on the Web. Friedman begins his comeback to a challenge by Donahue with the statement that "the world runs on individuals pursuing their separate interest."[59] Such self-interest is often sanctioned religiously as an inevitable expression of fallen human nature or human sin. At the same time, this self-interest never becomes a real problem because it is redeemed by the activity of the market. The market magically transforms self-interest into the common good. Assmann and Hinkelammert find the "dogmatic core of a new orthodoxy" here, according to which self-interest is transformed from being the private vice of those who hold economic power into a public virtue. Mainline economists all agree on this blanket endorsement of self-interest, whether they are neoclassicists, Keynesians, or neoliberals.[60] Self-interest is never further investigated in this context, and the self-interest of the butcher, the brewer, or the baker to which Adam Smith refers (noting that we expect our dinner not from their benevolence but from their concern for their own interest)[61] appears to be no different from the self-interest of the colonizer, or the self-interest of the leadership of multinational corporations powerful enough to sway the course of whole nations. An odd reversal results from this assessment: those who pursue their own self-interest, even if they command large amounts of capital and wield quasi imperial power, are now seen as humble servants, while those who have no power in this system are seen as conceited, jealous, and perhaps even arrogant.[62] Assmann and Hinkelammert draw the conclusion that there has never been a religion that has been so deeply supportive of human self-interest and desire as the current religion of economics.[63] We will come back to this issue—suffice it to note here that the now-common understanding of self-interest in terms of radical individualism cannot even be found in the work of Adam Smith, himself, who, working in another time and another place, still understands self-interest in relation to the cohesiveness of a community.[64]

The connections of economics and empire, often sanctioned by religion, need to be kept in mind throughout the discussions in this book. In my recent book *Christ and Empire*, I have laid the foundation for this argument, noting that empire today shows itself most clearly in terms of economics. My notion of the "postcolonial empire" serves as a reminder that empire today is no longer based on the establishment of colonies and colonialism, best embodied in recent history by the British Empire. That the postcolonial empire is based on economic power was true even during the years of the administration of President George W. Bush, despite an aggressive foreign politics that did not shy away from war as an extension of the political. The Iraq war, for instance, did not result in the establishment of another colony but in production-sharing agreements that allowed U.S. companies to extend their power more firmly in new territories and to reap the profits of Iraqi oil. Empire rooted in economics will be even more important in the foreseeable future, and it will be an often invisible factor in the softer U.S. politics, both foreign and domestic, for which so many of the world's citizens hope. In this sense, we can agree with John Maynard Keynes's statement that "the ideas of economists and political philosophers, both when they are right and when they are wrong are more powerful than is commonly understood."[65] Economics is indeed too important to leave to the economists.

The flexibility of this postcolonial economic empire must not be underestimated, as it appears in many different shapes and forms. During recent years, a more pronounced authoritarianism has made a comeback as CEOs and other economic leaders once again claimed more unilateral top-down power just like the top politicians of the Bush administration. During the 1990s, by contrast, the notion of teamwork and the idea that "everyone can be a leader" were celebrated.[66] We should expect to see more of these approaches in the future as authoritarian models are once again losing some currency. At the same time, we must not forget that this softer approach still bears the traits of empire and has a long history, going back to early modernity and even to the sixteenth-century Spanish priest Bartolomé de Las Casas, who rejected the harsh models of imperial conquest only to embrace milder forms of colonialism.[67] These somewhat softer forms of empire, which are more typical for economic forms of power, are eerily reflected in the shrewd observation of colonizer Cecil Rhodes that British "imperialism was nothing more than philanthropy plus five percent."[68]

The postcolonial empire has become leaner yet meaner than any empire before. Economic models of lean production have blazed the trail, cutting out anything and anybody who is not absolutely necessary for getting the job done and ratcheting up the pressure for those who remain. No active domination or brute force is necessary, nor any official system of conquest and slavery. The postcolonial empire has finally caught up with an old insight of Adam Smith, the intellectual father of capitalism. Smith had little appreciation for the colonial enterprises of his own Britain in the eighteenth century. He realized that these efforts were too grandiose and too cumbersome, too expensive and too inefficient, with too little payoff.[69] Viceroys, governors, massive bureaucracy, extensive standing armies of clerks and soldiers are not necessary to make a profit in a free-market system. The important thing, of course, to keep in mind is that by giving up colonialism we have not given up the differentials of power on which the empire rests. If anything, these differentials of power have grown, but, since they have become less visible, both mainline religion and mainline economics often overlook their existence and, thus, tend to endorse them by default.

Empire is the mindset which sets the frame for much religious and economic thought. When thinking of a deity, the common response is to look up, either to the heavens or to high places of power and privilege. And even if the deity is envisioned as close and familiar, the hope is often that it will lift us up and introduce us to higher levels of power and privilege. Popular Christian images of what awaits the religious in heaven—like royal crowns and streets of gold—illustrate my point. When thinking of economic matters, the common response is to look up once again, this time not directly to the heavens but to the top floors of the corporate headquarters where the experts of high finance dwell, including the most prominent and successful investors like Warren Buffet, the most prominent and successful leaders of business like Bill Gates, or high-ranking officials like the head of the Federal Reserve Board, Ben Bernanke—although the latter has not yet achieved the oracle-like qualities of his predecessor, Alan Greenspan. We commonly hope and expect that economic matters will lift us up to higher levels of power and privilege, at least in the long run. The so-called victory of capitalism that was so enthusiastically celebrated in the 1990s raised many hopes in this regard. In addition, the future of those of us who are invested in 401(k) retirement plans depends on faith in this uplifting as well.[70]

Those expectations and hopes are now profoundly challenged by severe economic downturns which were thought to be confined to the past. Therein lies an opportunity for the critique of empire. If the economic bubbles are bursting all around us, can the religious ones be far behind? A deregulated economy has been allowed to produce an imperial bubble where the stock market, the housing market, and the lending sector built forms of power that were more and more disconnected from real values and real life. For over a decade, economic power based on the value of stock has risen often without direct connection to performance indicators—a situation I have interpreted elsewhere as one of the key elements of the postmodern situation.[71] Housing and mortgages have followed this trend as well, laying the foundation for severe economic crashes. Adjustable-rate mortgages, often used in subprime lending, were based on a belief in the "rising tide that lifts all boats" through housing values, salaries, and easy refinancing—beliefs that not only did not materialize for the majority of the population, but collapsed in drastic fashion. Organized religion may be lagging behind in terms of its own experience of a crash, but for too long it also has operated in a bubble. Its promises of power and success materialized in bubbles, such as in the relative safety of places like traditional middle-class Christian congregations during times of economic balance or boom. Outside of these special conditions, mainline religion is often of little help, as promises of power and success cannot be kept—a reality that is bound to sink in for more and more middle-class congregations as they struggle with economic downturn. Seen in this light, it is perhaps not surprising that in the United States neither religion nor economics have yet encountered the massive sort of critique that is typical in other parts of the world. This situation is likely to change, however, as both theologians and economists will encounter more and more doubts and questions as the rising tide fades.

It is the purpose of this book to formulate some of these questions and critiques ahead of the curve and, thus, to formulate some challenges to the powers that be. These questions need to be raised not simply because of recent dramatic failures, however, but because of the subject matter itself. The failures remind us that too often our common understandings of both religion and economics are out of touch with real life. This state of being out of touch and the tendency to create bubbles both in economics and religion are not harmless. They are signs of empire insofar as they are efforts to control all aspects of life and to create the impression that there is no alternative to the status quo. In addition, empire is the effort to orient all of life so that it conforms to the wishes and interests of those who occupy positions of power and privilege; the creation of bubbles where less and less attention needs to be paid to real-life experiences is the best example.

The good news, however, is that empires are never able to exert absolute control. As the ambiguities and ambivalences of empires are explored, resistance begins to build, and the alternatives become clearer. This is the reason for formulating questions and critiques: not to get bogged down in the past or in the present, but to develop clearer ideas of alternatives that have been available all along and that are available now, and to get an idea of what is to come. Most people are unaware that there are alternative visions and realities that exist both in religion and economics. They also forget that empire is not natural. A world where the power and wealth of some keeps expanding at the expense of others is not our only option, although this is what not only economists but also theologians often believe. In such a world, the trickling down of wealth would indeed be our only hope.

Under the auspices of the postcolonial empire, the standard accounts have been so dominant that alternatives have been repressed. Yet, alternative visions and realities have deep roots and a long history. It is no accident that the early Christians were considered to be atheists in the Roman Empire. The reason for this judgment had to do with the fact that they embodied a critique of dominant religion that looked up to the heavens and which expected to find gods of power and privilege that resembled those persons who held power and privilege in the Roman Empire. To be sure, the Romans had no problem with other religions and their gods in general. Their pantheon was full of gods, many of them imported from other parts of the world, including Egypt. The problem was that this Christian God would fail to match the expectations of the gods of empire and did not resemble those persons who held power and privilege—after all, the Christian God's son was considered to be a troublemaker; he suffered and was executed as a political rebel in the manner reserved for such people: death by crucifixion.

Dead Ends and Alternatives

At the end of this chapter, a few comments are in order about what this book is not trying to do. In this book, there will be no suggestion that religion will be able to solve the problems of economics from the outside. In a world where economics has become all-pervasive and one of the main engines of empire, religion needs to understand first of all that it has become part of the problem without being aware of it.[72]

Furthermore, in this book there will be no suggestion that the economy and economic reflection can be fixed by promoting moral values as distinct from economic values. Too often the debate of economics and religion is reduced to issues of morality—for instance, when greed is identified as the culprit in economics. As a result, individual CEOs and business leaders are condemned as greedy.[73] This approach is doubly problematic, as it neglects the real structures of the economy, and it sets up a false alternative. Even the most powerful CEOs need to act according to the dictates of the market, so the main problem is not a lack of personal moral values but the particular values produced by the market; that is, the ethics of the market. In this context, business ethics may well help in cases of blatant violations of the ethics of the market, which led to the collapse of corporate giants like Enron and WorldCom. In some cases, business ethics might even offer a critique when the free-market system goes out of balance; for instance, in the case of exorbitant salaries of CEOs. Business ethics is of little help, however, when it comes to the question of who benefits from the structures of the current economy and its embedded values, and who does not. Like the moral notion of greed, notions of jealousy and envy are not helpful either. All these notions cover up the systemic problems and lead to solutions that help maintain the status quo. One example, the common suggestion simply to let go of the values of the market, is particularly unrealistic because anyone who lets go in a competitive market will be gone. Tinkering with individual values without addressing the logic of the system as a whole will not help us here.

Merely repeating moral imperatives will not get us very far, and neither will the overuse of words like "ought" and "should." This is a common problem with religious thinkers, exemplified, for instance, by Chandra Muzaffar, who builds his response to economics on the obligation of religious people to put into practice their values, principles, and ideas. Emphasizing basic religious values, like interrelatedness, he argues that "this way of thinking means that the rich should help the poor and the strong should extend a hand to the weak, for the sake of the former."[74] Muzaffar's position is stronger than that of many other religionists because he recognizes the importance of self-interest of the rich (helping the poor is done for the sake of the rich)—a topic that is too often simply rejected out of hand as immoral. But Muzaffar's argument depends on the frequent repetition of the word "should." The following sentence further exemplifies the problem: "We should try to translate some of the values and principles in our universal moral ethic into institutions and policies."[75] The real question at this point is: Why is this not happening? For some reason, the moral imperative is never strong enough; people have all kinds of good intentions but are not able to carry them out. A systemic problem requires a systemic answer.

Finally, this book is not about integrating economically disadvantaged people back into society. This is the most common solution that is suggested when economic discrepancies are identified. Liberals and conservatives in both politics and religion agree on this point, although they disagree on the methods with which such reintegration can be achieved. Conservatives focus on individual ethics, encouraging economically disadvantaged people to get their act together, to get more education, to get a better job, and to conform to the expectations and demands of the system. Liberals, on the other hand, argue for more systemic approaches by which to reintegrate those who have fallen through the cracks of the system, including the provision of a robust social safety net.[76] To be sure, the social programs that grow out of these liberal efforts can be lifesavers for those at the very bottom who would not be able to survive without some measure of integration. The problem, however, is that in both conservative and liberal camps the deeper question is neglected: What accounts for the fact that there are economically disadvantaged people in the first place? This question can be neglected as long as the existence of disadvantaged people can be declared to be an anomaly. But such neglect is no longer an option when the ranks of the disadvantaged keep growing exponentially, even in the United States, and when more and more members of the middle class are joining these ranks. The existence of economically disadvantaged people is clearly not the exception but the rule. The challenge, therefore, is not first of all how to integrate all these people back into the system that has spit them out, but how to address the system that produces these problems in the first place. In order to address this challenge, we need to begin to pay attention to the real-life problems of those who are cut off by the system; these problems might be compared to the symptoms of a disease. The first step, however, must not be the effort to cure these symptoms. We need to let them guide us where no conservative or liberal has gone before: to the core cause of these problems.[77]

The only way to make progress on our topic, then, will be to bring religion and economics into conversation in such a way that the tensions and power differentials are worked out in light of the real-life problems of those who do not benefit from the system. The Christian concern for the least of these — for the ever-growing number of those who are reduced to the status of the "least" (no one occupies that status naturally or by sheer accident!) and whose lives are crushed by the current system — will help us dig deeper and hopefully unearth alternatives and a different reality altogether.

British Prime Minister Margaret Thatcher famously used to remind people that "there is no alternative" to capitalism. By this statement, she referenced the economic idea that unregulated free markets would be the solution for everything. That this position has been accepted with little challenge for the past thirty years is one of the most telling signs of pervasiveness of empire in our own time, and of the essentially religious nature of a free-market ideology that promotes blind faith. Yet, there are alternatives, as this book will argue. The intersection of religion and economics is not just part of the problem but also might become part of the solution, insofar as it can help us identify some of these alternatives.

There are big changes taking place in both theology and economics, which are unfortunately still too often overlooked. Sometimes this is no accident, as the status-quo representatives of these fields do not find it easy to deal with alternatives, and instead actively suppress them. Yet already in 1998, economist David Prychitko reported that the "status of economics as a *science* itself, and its potential as an a priori, value-free theory, is in dispute." In a volume edited by Prychitko, a group of economists reexamines the basic presuppositions of the field.[78] A whole new slate of questions will now have to be examined, beginning with questions of history, context, the existence of power differentials, the concentrations of power that distort the equilibrium of the market, and the belief in the effectiveness of its "invisible hand." Unfortunately, these issues rarely appear on the radar screens of mainline economists and theologians. None of this can be seen, however, without dealing with real pressures, of which the current economic crisis is only the tip of the iceberg. Perhaps Keen's insight not only for the field of economics, but also for the field of theology when he states that "for economics to change, it appears that things have to 'go wrong' on a global scale, in ways which the prevailing theory believed was impossible."[79] Things have now gone wrong on a global scale to an extent that none of the mainline experts were able to foresee.

In sum, I argue that whether we can find alternatives and reconfigure the interrelations of economics and religion depends in large part on a return to places similar to those where the initial insights of the pioneers of economic and religious alternatives were forged: places of great pressure. In this context, the contribution of theological and religious reflection to the further development of economics and the tremendous powers that it represents, is not primarily that of providing another set of ideas or a new state of mind, but of finding glimpses of an alternative reality. The best chances for this to happen are in places where the pressures of the economic and ecological status quo become unbearable, and are therefore being challenged. The different religions will be able to offer alternatives—not where they represent the smug symbols of regulated religiosity and moral values (the kinds of things that are easily commodified by the commercial spin doctors' efforts at re-enchantment), but where they draw on the irrepressible energies emerging out of the undercurrent of their own traditions and strengths as they have developed and continue to take shape in the midst of the pressures of life as a whole. In this book, we will explore the specific contributions of Christianity, but other religions have their own contributions to make as well.

   Economics, as it is practiced today, has a tendency to create its own reality that is often aloof to the struggles of real life. The same is true for theology. We need to make sure that economics and theology deal again with the "reality that hurts"[80] and out of this experience give fresh thought to the alternative realities that might save us all. The rest of this book is dedicated to the search for genuine alternatives in a world of growing pressure and suffering.

The Logic of Downturn: Class Matters in Religion and Economics

2

Downturn as the Rule

Even in the midst of an economic crisis, it is easily overlooked that crisis situations are no longer the exception, but the rule, as most people keep hoping for better times in the not-so-distant future. It is, after all, commonly assumed that the economy operates in cycles. Nevertheless, the truth is that, in the globalizing free-market economy, downturn is a constant fact of life for an increasing number of people, even during times of economic progress. This is true not only in the countries of the so-called third world, but for an increasing number of residents of the wealthier countries as well. Already in the 1990s, when the global victory of capitalism was declared, the global market no longer benefited the workforce of the so-called first world automatically, as it had done for some time. A warning about this problem was sounded over a decade ago by the authors of a book titled *The Judas Economy,* who confessed to be "great believers in the dynamism of the free market." The book concluded by pointing out that capital is divorcing itself more and more from the workforce everywhere. A telling example of this divorce was when, in the summer of 1996, the value of stocks retreated when the first real gains for wages in twenty years were announced.[1]

The disconnect between workers and the interests of the corporations is, of course, much older, and is in many ways part of the system itself. A court ruling of 1919 against the Ford Motor Company set an important legal precedent and continues to define the expectations of our current situation. According to this ruling, CEOs and their corporations are charged with maximizing the benefits of their stockholders rather than their workers—

a supremely significant regulation that, while not technically a law, is followed in praxis by all major corporations, but is not widely known by the public.[2] Even a business consultant, who in a recent conversation spoke of the beneficial nature of corporations that is promoted in much of the motivational literature, was not aware of this regulation. It might be argued, of course, that this line between workers and stockholders is increasingly blurred in today's economy, as workers may own some stock as well, but this argument fails to consider the matter of scale: the income of most workers who have some stock investments derives from their labor for the most part, and so they can hardly be considered to be the beneficiaries of an economy that maximizes the benefit of stockholders at the expense of workers.

Persistent economic hardships, which are not only visible in the widening gap between the richest and the poorest but also in increased pressures on large and growing sectors of the population, invite new questions. These questions will become more pronounced as more and more members of the middle class, even in the United States, move closer to the working class.[3] As more and more aspects of our lives are commodified and for sale, even those who used to enjoy certain free spaces in the middle between workers and the owners of large fortunes—the ones who consider themselves middle class—are being pushed into the ranks of working America. This includes members of the professional ranks like medical doctors, lawyers, ministers of religion, and university professors, who are feeling pressures they never knew existed, as their work is increasingly subject to economic calculations of profitability. This situation is bound to get worse in the long run due to ongoing shifts in power and wealth. The growing asymmetry between rich and poor is no longer just a matter of the absolute extremes—between multi-billionaires and people who are starving for lack of food—but manifest in the divide between those who labor for a living and those who control (although they may not necessarily own) the means of production and who command substantial amounts of capital. And, as we shall see, this growing economic asymmetry cannot be limited to financial matters alone, as it extends to every other aspect of life.

What is becoming ever clearer is that economic pressures are not limited to exceptional periods of decline. We are not just dealing with exceptional downturns, but with the continuing reality with which most people have to contend, even in the United States. This situation changes how we approach the question of religion and economics. Paraphrasing a famous statement by Walter Benjamin, who noted that "the tradition of the oppressed teaches us that the 'state of emergency' in which we live is not the exception but the rule,"[4] we might say that the experience of those who are not benefitting from the market teaches us that the current economic emergency is not the exception but the rule. This is why the view from the perspectives of working people—that is, from all those who have not much else to rely on for their income but their own labor—is so crucial. These perspectives help us better understand what is going on—here the rules of the system become clearer, and it is no accident that they are not given much consideration in the formulas of current mainline economics. Our approach is, therefore, in direct contradiction with mainline economics, where entrepreneurs are seen as the one who matter most and from whom the basic impulses flow; where entrepreneurs are seen as the "revolutionaries of economics," as Joseph Schumpeter put it.[5] Mainline theology is no different in this regard from mainline economics, as it also tends to look to the top religious leaders for inspiration and guidance, rather than to the common people. What is too often overlooked, however, is not limited to the fact that even the most ingenious entrepreneurs are ultimately dependent on their workforce.[6] Those in the workforce might also provide alternative views that cannot be seen from the perspective of the entrepreneurs, but which might prove more truly revolutionary to economics than anything proposed at the top. We will need to take these alternative perspectives into account as we take another look at religion and economics.

At present, when economics is charged with taking the shape of a religion and when theology shows increasing interest in studying economics while being (mostly unconsciously) shaped by its logic, fresh reflections on the intersections of these disciplines are imperative not only in order to understand the interplay of religion and economics but also in order to develop better alternatives. The reality of severe economic downturn adds urgency to these reflections, but also brings fresh perspectives. The silver lining in an otherwise rather depressing situation is that, in times of economic downturn, conventional economic and religious forms of logic otherwise taken for granted tend to be more visible and open to question. The logic of downturn helps test the perennial optimism which rules when things go well, and brings to light hidden presuppositions. As a result, the otherwise hidden connections between economic, religious, and other powers become visible. In this situation, I identify a logic of downturn, which broadens the horizons and opens our view for alternative resources.[7] Being increasingly pushed to the margins, more and more of us are endowed with an unexpected potential to see more clearly. This clairvoyance not only lets us analyze more competently what is going on; it also enables us to envision better what our options are and what the alternatives might be. There is an "epistemological surplus" here that relates to what I have called a "theological surplus" in an earlier project and, hopefully, to a "surplus" in economic imagination as well.[8] As I will argue more explicitly in the chapters to come, this logic of downturn is also one of the key elements of Christianity, as it is closely related to the logic of the incarnation of the divine in Jesus Christ: God does not become human just anywhere, but in a family of construction workers and day laborers,[9] located on the underside of a small part of the powerful economy of the Roman Empire. This perspective has the potential to shed some new light both on the study of economics and on the future of the study of theology.

One of the key challenges of becoming aware of the reality of downturn is that it pushes us to pay attention to concrete situations of conflict and suffering. This is more crucial than one might think at first, because this is exactly what is lacking in the economic and theological status quo, which is either blissfully unaware of conflict and suffering or is anxious to cover it up. We are dealing with an old problem here, which goes back hundreds, if not thousands, of years. Even the prophet Jeremiah must have been aware of it when he transmitted the divine judgment: "They have treated the wound of my people carelessly, saying, 'Peace, peace,' when there is no peace" (Jer 6:14). We will not be able to understand the economy and its impact on all of our lives unless we consider it in light of the conflicts and tensions that it produces, and from the perspective of those who have to endure the brunt of these matters. Neither will we be able to transform what is going on without these perspectives.

Class Matters in Economics and Religion

In our current situation, it is convenient to perpetuate misunderstandings of both religion and of class. Mainline economics firmly believes in a deregulated market, and the free-market economy appears to function best when both religion and class are at work below the surface and out of sight, sheltered from investigation. The 2008 election season in the United States was a pristine example of this. Among the efforts made to erase what little is left of the notion of class in this country was the promotion of the views of "Joe the Plumber," one of the heroes of the McCain campaign who appeared to be quite worried about rising taxes for the upper class. Believing in the American dream, Joe the Plumber appeared to see himself as a potential member of the ownership class—that is, the people who own or at least control a significant share of the means of production and who command capital. This erasure of class happens on various levels, and racial issues play an important role: working-class whites are actively lured into identifying with ruling-class whites rather than with working-class Blacks, Latinos, Latinas, or Asians; sometimes this lure includes the granting of small benefits and favors.[10] These efforts explain in part the old American phenomenon of a lack of class consciousness, especially among the white working class. No wonder that Joe the Plumber and all other white plumbers might tend to feel more connected with a white billionaire like Bill Gates than with their Latino colleague José *el plomero*. Doing away with notions of class by whatever means possible makes the system run more smoothly. If all participants in the free market can be lured into considering themselves to be winners, they will not raise questions; even the ones who have lost so far can see themselves as potential winners in the future.

A similar dynamic is at work when it comes to religion: if the concept of religion can be confined to a narrow frame that extends no further than the personal, the moral, or, perhaps, the cultural, questions can be avoided about the role that religion plays in public matters, whether in the economy or in political struggles for power. However, it is becoming ever more difficult to maintain such a low profile, as religion has become a power to be reckoned with in U.S. politics in recent history. Moreover, religion is also increasingly becoming a power to be reckoned with in economics, as well, although this is not yet as explicit as in politics; things have generally been moving more slowly on this front and, perhaps, more undercover, but with no less consequence. Religion is an integral part of the discourse on class and economics, as will become clearer in this chapter.

There can be little doubt that the topic of class is among the most taboo subjects in the United States. The old advice not to talk about politics, religion, sex, or money in polite company preserves these taboos. Since class is not supposed to exist in any substantial way in this country, the advice of what not to talk about is often given without explicit reference to the taboo of money. That class is not supposed to exist does not mean, however, that class is not on people's minds. The German adage that "money is not what one talks about; money is what one has" (*über Geld spricht man nicht, Geld hat man*) gives expression to this: the moneyed classes are aware of their privileges to such a degree that the matter is better left undiscussed. Media presentations on the "lifestyles of the rich and famous"[11] might seem an exception to this rule, but what is discussed there is the stuff that those people own—their yachts, their houses, their cars, and so on—rather than the deeper meaning of this stuff, which translates into power and influence, and how it is generated. In general, the upper classes seem to be more aware of their class interests than the lower classes—as shown, for instance, by the number of lobbyists in Washington, D.C., or by the existence of exclusive neighborhoods, clubs, and even churches and religious organizations. At a time when the labor unions have been losing members and lobbying power, the number of lobbyists for monied interests has been on the rise.

While class, thus, remains real but mostly undiscussed, there is a certain stigma that adheres to being lower class. When we launched a program for "disadvantaged youth" at Perkins School of Theology a few years ago, the youth resented this classification for good reason. Talking about the "lower classes" is part of the same set of problems, as the blame tends to fall back on those who are "lower" or "disadvantaged" with a vengeance—more so than ever in recent decades.[12] The way forward at the time for what became the Perkins Youth School of Theology was to talk about "youth under pressure," a term that arose out of my theological reflections on matters of liberation theology. The term could be appreciated by the young people, since it put the blame not on them but on outside pressures. The problem was no longer with them but with the system. Of course, this is where the real challenge of class discourse starts: How do we understand these pressures that keep people down, and how do they influence our lives? This is where our learning process is just beginning, not just for our young people and not just in the realm of economics, but also in theology and religious studies.

The problem is that, even where the topic of class comes up, it is mostly discussed in ways that diffuse the challenges. Class is discussed, for instance, in terms of diversity of tastes and cultural preference, like the distinction between "lowbrow" and "highbrow" culture. Class is also discussed in terms of social status, depending primarily on income levels. The typical function of this discourse is the drawing of the poverty line, implying that there is no need to be concerned too much about anyone above this line. This is true not only for popular discourse but for mainline religious and economic discourses as well. Consistently missing from these discourses, however, are reflections on class in terms of relationships of power. Yet it is precisely in this context that the matter becomes interesting for our subject, since one of our basic definitions of economics has to do with relationships of power, and it is the matter of power that also helps us better understand religion.

Before continuing, let me note the tremendous challenge that these reflections on class pose to the current system. It is probably no accident that Martin Luther King was assassinated exactly at the point in his career when he began to pay serious attention to matters of class, and class remains a dangerous subject in the United States today. Moving from the observation of class differentials to the support of oppressed classes—as King did, when near the time of his death, he supported sanitation workers in Memphis— touches raw nerves, especially when it comes from religious people who are considered more or less allies in the world of economics.

What do we mean when we talk about class? The notion of class is not only left underanalyzed but is fundamentally misunderstood when it is defined primarily in terms of income levels, social stratification, or social status. The deeper levels of the notion of class have to do with questions of power, and with the particular sets of relationships that produce class differentials in the first place. In other words, income levels and social stratification must be seen as the result of class differentials, not as their cause. Note that income levels are dependent on many other factors, and are not always directly correlated with the underlying questions of power which are key to the notion of class. It is quite possible, for instance, to imagine service providers to the extremely wealthy—whether chauffeurs, chefs, or chaplains—who may get paid very well but who have little power when it comes to determining the work that they do. This issue is significant because the work that we do for a living shapes us to a large degree, and who holds the power over this work determines who ultimately benefits from it.

The implications of this observation are surprising at first sight: if class is defined not primarily in terms of income levels but in terms of the power and authority that people have in and over their work, most Americans are not middle class but working class: 62 percent of Americans belong to the working class in this scenario; 32 percent are middle class; and only 2 percent belong to the ruling class—that is, to the class that controls the means of production and commands capital.[13] White-collar workers in cubicles, for instance, bear an uncanny resemblance to blue-collar assembly workers in terms of the power and authority they have over their own work. Even academics who work outside the traditional tenure system know what it means to have limited power and authority over their own work—something that is also increasingly true for those of us who work within the tenure system but whose performance is increasingly measured in terms of the parameters of corporate America (like the maximization of profits, efficiency, and so on). Even an examination of labor in the churches, especially those churches that have direct influence on the salary of their pastors, might lead to surprising insights about limited power and authority at work; the related lack of power would go a long way toward understanding the often-lamented phenomenon that pastors do not preach from their pulpits the more challenging theologies they have encountered in their seminary education.[14] In other words, religion is impacted by the dynamics of class just as much as the rest of society, if not more. Add to that the observation that class is fundamentally about the distribution of power—and images of the divine often tend to reflect the power structures of society—and it becomes clearer how deeply interrelated economics and religion really are.

An understanding of class framed not primarily in terms of income but in terms of power picks up a classic understanding of class as related to the ownership of the means of production, and broadens it: those who have little or no ownership or control of the means of production have few other options than to sell their labor to those who own or control the means of production. And thus, those who are forced to sell their labor belong to the working class, which has little power over its work. Those who own or control significant shares of the means of production, on the other hand, mostly derive their wealth from the surplus that is produced by those who work; they belong to the ruling class because they are entitled by law to determine the work of others. The fundamental character of this distinction is also reflected in the commonly accepted economic logic that the interests of the stockholders trump the interests of the workers. Obviously, these things are becoming ever more complex in our current situation, and there are some grey zones, the most important one of having to do with the middle class.

Based on what has been said so far, it should not come as a surprise that being in the middle is not as comfortable as it sounds, as it means being in a place of tension. While members of the middle class may own no means of production (or at best only a small part, as small business owners, owners of a few rental properties, or some stocks), they may still have some element of control over the work process, perhaps as managers, supervisors, or independent professionals. This position, however, frequently places them in the midst of the tensions between the working class and the ruling class—that is, between the class that has little control over its work and little access to capital, and the class that determines much of the work process and commands capital. In this perspective, the problems of the middle become clearer, as they manifest themselves, for instance, in the tensions to which supervisors and foremen find themselves subject in their daily work. The law reflects this tension as well, as supervisors and foremen are prohibited from being part of the collective-bargaining processes of the workers, yet they are not the ones who determine salaries. Independent professionals may have more freedom, but even these professions are experiencing more and more pressure to conform to the expectations of the market, without direct recourse to the stronger organizations that safeguard the interests of workers. And even though members of the middle class are likely to be stockholders, this does not change their situation substantially, since their ownership of stock is fairly modest, and their power and influence as stockholders is of little consequence for the overall direction of the corporations. Unfortunately, the middle class is put in the straits of these tensions without most of the benefits of power and financial status and without the broader political influence that the ruling class accrues. As a result even this short examination of one of the grey zones of class—in the contemporary academy an emphasis on grey zones is often combined with an aversion to binary oppositions—points us back to the fundamental distinction between working and ruling classes as a distinction that continues to be relevant.[15]

The fundamental distinction between working class and ruling class, both broadly conceived, takes on particular interest when we note that the relations of power at work organize not only production but, at the most fundamental level, all other relationships as well. Since so many hours are spent at work, since so much of people's sense of self is generated in work relationships, and since some of the most existential questions of everyday life are negotiated at and through work, the relations of power at work are significant building blocks of human life and affect all other areas—including culture, the realms of the emotional and the personal, and even religion, where power relations of the workplace find expression in self-selecting religious communities. In this context, a broad social-scientific study of the influence of class on the shape of religion would be of great service.[16] It seems that even the Gospel of Prosperity changes its form, depending on the class context: while in a lower-class context the promise of prosperity needs to be repeated over and over again with great intensity, in upper-class contexts there can be polite understatement of these matters to such an extent that the topic of prosperity never needs to be addressed at all (although it remains at the heart of things, since it is taken for granted by the members of the community). This all-pervasiveness of class, based in power relations at work, is one of the key insights of the so-called New Working Class Studies, which investigate how class function not only in the workplace but also at home and in communities.[17] This is where fresh investigations of class and religion will have to begin.[18]

Those who have traditionally considered themselves middle class will have to pay particular attention to these matters. In a pioneering work that is almost as painful to read as it must have been to investigate, Barbara Ehrenreich has captured the despair of formerly successful members of the middle class who have been laid off and who spend long months, if not years, searching for jobs. What if these people who are experiencing the logic of downturn in their own bodies were no longer the exception but the rule? The longer their job search continues, the less likely they will be able to find their way back into the system that has cast them out. To add insult to injury, they are often blamed for their own misery. Ehrenreich reports on a seminar for job seekers in which she participated. In this seminar, the leader strictly prohibited the blaming of others, including the blaming of tough economic times. Discussing the situation of Kevin, a thirty-six-year-old operations manager who contemplates starting his own business in response to expected layoffs, the leader of the seminar poses the question, "The person who is stopping Kevin is who?" to which the other participants who have also lost their jobs respond in unison, "Kevin!"[19] The victim is the one who is stuck with the blame. Many others who are still holding on to their jobs in a situation that has increasingly grown worse live in permanent insecurity, often haunted by a form of depression that has been called "survivor syndrome."[20] In this context, churches and religious communities have sought to help by offering their own job-search seminars and by offering spiritual support to unemployed members. Yet religion is used here mostly in order to help participants adapt to the situation rather than in order to challenge it.[21] Having experienced some of these efforts firsthand, Ehrenreich wonders in her book: "Maybe one of the functions of the evangelical revival sweeping America is to reconcile people to an increasingly unreliable work world: you take what you can get, and praise the Lord for sending it along."[22]

The problem cuts deeper yet, calling for a reexamination of the pre-suppositions of the middle class in both economics and theology. Even the pride of the professions—which is lacking to a large degree in other areas of work, including the business world, that are not built on credentials and diplomas—is increasingly challenged.[23] Medical doctors, for instance, have begun to organize themselves in trade unions because the ethos of the free market encroaches more and more into their work, and introduces the principles of lean and mean production into the relationship with their patients. In the context of the free market, even the value of professional credentials and diplomas is subject to erosion. The world of the academy offers many more examples of this problem, as leaner and meaner forms of production are reshaping time-honored traditions even in the world of the so-called ivory towers. Beverly Harrison describes the particular problem that arises from the lack of class consciousness for the middle class: "The failure to see and name pervasive class dynamics in this society is robbing middle-strata people—especially men—of the critical insight needed to become aware of their subjugation or to act creatively and effectually against human oppression."[24] Failure to understand the pressures impending upon the middle class, as they derive from free-market economics, is a substantial impediment to our work in both economics and theology. I have observed this dynamic in the classroom for over twenty years, particularly as white male seminary students of the middle class tend to feel, consciously or unconsciously, that they have no other choice than to root for the system. In the mainline churches, the situation is often similar or worse, since there is even more pressure to conform to middle-class perspectives, due to a more pronounced lack of diversity and to the fact that some of the top donors also sit in the pews. Without a clearer awareness of what is going on, things can only get worse.

While lack of class consciousness is an old American problem that affects even the working class itself, there are also explicit efforts to cover up class differentials. Through 401(k) retirement plans, for instance, the masses have been integrated into the ownership of capital to a certain degree and, thus, they share in the interests of the ruling class to some degree as well. As the owners of stocks and bonds, holders of 401(k) plans appear to have become full members of the class that owns the means of production and that commands capital. This can lead to tensions among workers, who now have an interest in the profit that is made from the work of other workers.[25] What is covered up here is the fact that these holdings of stock are miniscule compared to those of the bigger shareholders, and that very little real power is connected to them.[26] Such mystifications of class interests are not innocent, as they lead people to overlook their real interests—which are not just their own private interests as individuals but also the interests of their families, their friends, and their communities. In addition, they prevent a more accurate understanding of power.

In the spirit of the logic of downturn, we might say as a rule of thumb that people ought to be able to know that they are not members of the ruling class if they are not benefitting from the system in any substantial way. But much of this has hit home only in more recent times. For a while, it looked indeed as if the free-market system was benefitting a broad range of people, not only at the top but also in the middle. 401(k) plans were part of this excitement, as people were led to believe that the problem of pensions could be solved through modest contributions that would grow in sync with the stock market. That this shifted the risk from employers to employees who were responsible for their own plans seemed to be a small price to pay for the opportunity to become truly wealthy. This bubble, too, has now burst in a way that even the most clear-sighted critics could not have imagined even a few years ago. William Wolman and Anne Colamosca pointed out as early as 2002 that a stock market that was designed to benefit the financial interests of the wealthy would not be able to carry the weight of producing benefits for the nation as a whole. While Wolman and Colamosca never quite state it this way, it becomes clear that class distinctions are necessary for understanding even the financial future of the middle class, and for understanding that it is simply impossible for the market to make everyone wealthy.[27]

In the United States and other industrialized countries, even some workers could consider themselves to be pretty well off, especially if they had union-backed jobs in prominent industries. A sense that they belonged somewhere in the middle class gave many workers false confidence in the system; sometimes this sense was strengthened by joining middle-class churches and other religious communities. This sense has still not quite worn off, but troubling economic developments have taken their toll. Workers in the auto industry, for instance, who enjoyed decent jobs and benefits only a few years ago now face an uncertain future as even the big three U.S. carmakers are struggling for survival, at least as far as their business in the United States is concerned. The economic fallout that started hit home in 2008—marking the worst downturn since the Great Depression—has heralded a new era. To be sure, the loss of funds that is tied to these events is not the key determinant of class, but the existential nature of these losses for many people reveals their positions of power in the system. Contrary to conventional economic wisdom, the real risk of downturn and the failure of whole industries is borne by the workers, whose existence is destroyed when jobs are eliminated in whole regions and whose housing values implode as a consequence. CEOs and other high-level business leaders, in the meantime, often tend to be able to hang on to their golden parachutes or to move on to the next assignment.

Religion, as we have observed, is tied up with these dynamics of class. While religion has oriented itself for the most part toward the upper classes, there are alternative forms of religion that are related to the lower classes as well. This has been the case throughout history and in all religions: for this reason, a simple switch between religions without attention to the dynamics of class—like the somewhat fashionable switch from Western to Eastern spiritualities, both Christian and non-Christian—will not present us with a solution. In this book, we will explore the question of what positive differences Christianity, as a particular form of religion, will be able to make in this context.

Growing Inequality: Some Numbers

The whole extent of what is going on cannot be depicted in numbers. Yet some numbers might help us to see more clearly. The following numbers do not simply make us recognize the tremendous economic stratification, which is real, even more importantly, they push us to think about the underlying relationships of power and what all of this means.

The absolute poverty rates in the United States have long been worrisome, as the United States is located at the bottom end of industrialized countries in this regard. According to a United Nations Human Development Report, the poverty level in the United States was 15.2 percent in 2007, which puts us on rank 17 of all industrialized countries.[28] But poverty in itself does not say anything about relationships of power. The distribution of income is more telling in this regard, as it depicts the relationship of the poorest to the rest of society. In this perspective, the United States ranks last out of all Western industrialized countries and many other less wealthy nations, just slightly ahead of Hong Kong and Singapore. Here are some numbers: in the year 2000, the share of the national income received by the poorest 10 percent in the United States was at 1.9 percent; the poorest 20 percent at 5.4 percent; the richest 20 percent at 45.8 percent; and the richest 10 percent at 29.9 percent. The ratio of the income share of the richest 10 percent to that of the poorest 10 percent was 15.9, which is a Gini coefficient of 40.8. (The Gini coefficient is the standard measure of economic inequality, according to which 0 signifies perfect equality and 100 absolute inequality.[29]) Amy Glasmeier also reports the changes over time in the distribution of income in the United States: in 1977, the lowest 40 percent of families received 17 percent of earned income (income earned over a calendar year) while the upper 20 percent received 44 percent. In 2002, the lowest 40 percent received 12.5 percent of income while the top 20 percent received 50 percent, with the Gini index at 46.4.[30] All this needs to be seen in the context of the fact that in 2005 the United States occupied the second-highest place in terms of Gross Domestic Product (GDP) per capita, bested only by Luxembourg.[31]

The U.S. Census Bureau sheds further light on the historical development of this level of inequality. Beginning in the 1980s, the Gini coefficient increased dramatically, leveling off a bit in the period from 1993–1998.[32] However, there is a major oversight in these numbers—which points in turn to a major oversight in the understanding of relationships of power—since in earlier data the numbers for the wealthiest Americans were left out of the calculations: the data show a major gap between 1993 and 1994, when the growth in the Gini coefficient for the income of families jumped from roughly 13 percent to 20 percent (at the same time, the growth in the Gini coefficient for the income of men went from roughly 16 percent to 26 percent). The U.S. Census Bureau gives the following explanation:

> In 1993, the Census Bureau began using a new method of collecting income data, allowing respondents to report greater income values in the Current Population Survey. A change that may affect only a small number of cases (particularly those at the upper end of the income distribution) can have a considerable effect on inequality measures, like the Gini coefficient and shares of aggregate income, while making little or no change to median income. This had a profound effect on the upper end of the income distribution by recording income levels that had been previously underreported. The impact of this change on measured income inequality was quite large, and we are unable to determine precisely the proportion of the increase in income inequality between 1992 and 1993 that is attributable to this change.[33]

While adjustments have been made, and the greater transparency at the top has added some clarity to the relationship between classes, we still do not really know the numbers at the very top; the precise value of any income above $1 million is not allowed to enter the statistics. One must seriously wonder how the numbers would change if higher incomes were taken into consideration and what this would tell us about relationships of power.[34] The following numbers (not supplied in the Census Bureau report) speak volumes about the development of the relationship of the wealthiest and the poorest: between 1979 and 2000, the top 1 percent gained 201 percent in after-tax household income, while the top 20 percent gained 68 percent. The bottom 20 percent gained 9 percent, and the next-highest 20 percent gained 13 percent.[35]

All these numbers, however, still leave out other even more important details. The greatest discrepancies—not just in terms of money but in terms of the underlying relationships—can be seen when the assets owned by individuals are taken into account. The top 5 percent of the population owns 67.5 percent of the nation's wealth, and the top 20 percent owns 91.3 percent of the nation's wealth.[36] Upon closer look, the often-quoted discrepancy between CEO pay and worker pay, which began its steep ascendance in the 1960s, pales in comparison. A United Nations Human Development Report of the year 1996 notes: "The assets of the world's 358 billionaires exceed the combined annual incomes of countries with 45% of the world's people."[37] What this means is that the world's wealthiest 358 individuals own as much as nearly 3,000,000,000 people earn in a year. The United Nations Human Development Report of 1999 adds the following statistic: "The world's 200 richest people more than doubled their net worth in the four years to 1998, to more than $1 trillion. The assets of the top three billionaires are more than the combined GNP of all least developed countries and their 600 million people."[38] Behind these numbers is a process of monopolization that adds important insights for the question of relationships between the wealthy and the poor, with all the implications for the middle that we discussed earlier: "The recent wave of mergers and acquisitions is concentrating industrial power in megacorporations—at the risk of eroding competition. By 1998 the top 10 companies in pesticides controlled 85% of a $31 billion global market—and the top 10 in telecommunications, 86% of a $262 billion market."[39] The United Nations Human Development Report of 2000 continues the story: "Meanwhile, the superrich get richer. The combined wealth of the top 200 billionaires hit $1,135 billion in 1999, up from $1,042 billion in 1998. Compare that with the combined incomes of $146 billion for the 582 million people in all the least developed countries."[40]

Understood in terms of relationships of power, this is more than anyone can really fathom or bear, and so it is perhaps no surprise that the word "billionaire" does not occur any more in the Human Development Reports after 2000, and the data are more and more defused. The only time that the rich at the very top are named again is in the report of 2005. One must, of course, wonder whose interest is really served by toning down this analysis. Is it to avoid upsetting the "rest of us," or is it because something needs to be hidden because it is just becoming too blatant? On the whole, the reports use more and more generic talk about the "richest countries," or the "richest 20 percent," which levels the greatest discrepancies and the asymmetrical relationships expressed by them. While the United Nations Human Development Report of 2005 brings back another reference to the wealthy, by talking about income rather than assets, the numbers seem less dramatic: "The world's richest 500 individuals have a combined income greater than that of the poorest 416 million. Beyond these extremes, the 2.5 billion people living on less than $2 a day—40% of the world's population—account for 5% of global income. The richest 10%, almost all of whom live in high-income countries, account for 54%."[41] Of course, the relationship expressed here is still stunning: the wealthiest 500 individuals earn as much as the poorest 416,000,000 people.

All these numbers point to stunning discrepancies—not just in terms of money but in terms of power and influence—that mark the world in the twenty-first century. On the whole, these discrepancies are growing, through times of economic boom and bust, and they are much greater than any discrepancies in the history of the world. Never before have so few individuals owned so much. Some have compared this situation to feudalism, another period in history when discrepancies between the rulers and their subjects were pronounced. But feudal rulers were not individuals in the contemporary sense: they were not at liberty to spend all their wealth on themselves. They had some obligation toward the common good and the welfare of their subjects, an obligation which is increasingly eroded in the current system. The particular development of this matter in the United States needs to be kept in mind: in 1982, there were only 13 billionaires in the United States; in 1996, there were 179; and in 2005 there were 374.[42] In the current situation, individuals are drifting in and out of this bracket, but the number as a whole keeps rising. These numbers are often seen as showing the advanced state of the U.S. economy, as there are fewer billionaires elsewhere, even in all the countries of Europe together. This judgment, of course, only makes sense if the question of relationship is neglected, as this massive gain at the top is achieved by massive losses in many other places. This is what the numbers show, despite ongoing claims that religiously repeat the mantra that a rising tide will lift all boats.

What has kept the system afloat in the past was the American Dream. Large numbers of people still hold on to this hope that anyone can make it to the top, a message that is also propagated in many religious communities across the theological spectrum. Yet the numbers tell a different story. Workers in the United States are less upwardly mobile than in many other countries, and small business failures are common not just in times of downturn. Economist Tom Hertz finds in his research that "by international standards, the United States has an unusually low level of intergenerational [economic] mobility: our parents' income is highly predictive of our incomes as adults. Intergenerational mobility in the United States is lower than in France, Germany, Sweden, Canada, Finland, Norway and Denmark. Among high-income countries for which comparable estimates are available, only the United Kingdom had a lower rate of mobility than the United States."[43] That is not the news that most people expect to hear. Hertz also points out that "children from low-income families have only a 1 percent chance of reaching the top 5 percent of the income distribution, versus children of the rich who have about a 22 percent chance." Race is a compounding factor: "African American children who are born in the bottom quartile are nearly twice as likely to remain there as adults than are white children whose parents had identical incomes, and are four times less likely to attain the top quartile."[44]

In this context, greater wealth for individual families has most commonly been achieved not because salaries have grown but because women have joined the workforce in large numbers. In this context, it is important to keep in mind that the United States, unlike most countries in the world, never signed the United Nations conventions on freedom of association and collective bargaining.[45] At the writing of this book, the United States is one of the very few industrialized countries where large groups of workers do not have the right to organize. Since the United Nations Declaration of Human Rights endorses collective bargaining as a human right, the United States must be considered to be in violation of international human rights law. The religious aspect is of interest here, too, as many religions and a good number of Christian churches explicitly support the right of collective bargaining, a fact which is not widely known and which is rarely promoted by the churches themselves.[46]

Surveys have shown that between 25 and 60 million workers would like to organize in unions, but only 500,000 actually are able to do so each year.[47] The Employee Free Choice Act before Congress in 2009 may change this situation by allowing workers to choose between different methods of organizing unions, but it is amazing to think that the country that prides itself on its civil liberties has laws that restrict the free organization of free citizens so severely that only between 1 in 50 and 1 in 120 workers can realize the choice to be unionized. Under the current law, the employers determine the process of how unions can be organized: they determine the time frame, and they have the right to campaign against unions during work hours, while pro-union forces are only allowed to campaign after hours. None of this is by accident, as the current state of things is actively promoted by interest groups: in the United States, freedom of association and collective bargaining is actively blocked by the dominant economic interests. In early 2009, a major informal effort against the Employee Free Choice Act which included top CEOs—some hailing from companies that had received government bailout money—was reported. Bernie Marcus, the cofounder of Home Depot, who was one of the leaders of the meeting, stated that this legislation would mean "the demise of a civilization." Shareholders, he suggested, should sue CEOs who did not oppose the Employee Free Choice Act.[48] If this is not sheer cynicism, it must have to do with a firm belief in the free-market economy and its beneficial nature for all. This belief is so strong that it is allowed to trump both democracy and human rights.[49] The result is a form of class warfare that is commonly waged from the top: in the taped phone calls that are part of the *Huffington Post* report, there are frequent mentions of "the business community," which functions as a class that makes sure that its interests are maintained by ensuring that the workers will be prevented from forming their own communities.

There is a gender component that adds to matters of inequality. A study by Heather Boushey makes the following observation about the recession that started in 2008:

> Since . . . December 2007, employers have shed 2.6 million employees—a decline of 1.9 percent—with most of that occurring in the last four months of 2008. Not all groups, however, have been affected equally: Over the first year of this recession, job losses and unemployment have spiked higher for male workers than their female counterparts. This recession began with the bursting of the housing bubble, which has led to sharp job losses in male-dominated industries, especially construction, through 2008. As a result, the share of men in the United States with a job is at its lowest point ever, 69.7 percent. Over the past year, however, women's jobs have been sustained by hiring in the government and health care sectors. As a result, since the recession officially began adult women's unemployment has risen by 1.6 percentage points, to 5.9 percent in December 2008, from 4.3 percent a year earlier, while adult men's unemployment has risen by 2.8 percentage points, to 7.2 percent from 4.4 percent over the same period.

What may look like a reversal of gender oppression becomes clearer when it is considered that "among full-time, full-year workers, women earn only 78 cents for every dollar a man earns."[50] Since women provide cheaper labor, cuts are made to more expensive male labor. This trend can be seen even in the world of construction, a traditional stronghold of male labor: "Even within construction men have lost a disproportionate share of the construction jobs. Men make up 87 percent of the construction workers, but they have lost 95 percent of the jobs over the course of the recession."[51] There is a deeper structural problem: ever since the early 1980s, men's unemployment has risen over women's unemployment during recessions. The increasing feminization of certain professions points to a similar problem, as it is a move that usually comes with a cut in prestige and salary. Not even the church is missing here, as the feminization of ministry progresses and women fill in especially the lower ranks of the profession. Other factors like race and age also need to be considered in this context.

Amy Glasmeier sums it up, pointing out the factors of gender, race, and age: "American society is based on paradoxes. Its citizens are at once among the richest and the most economically insecure in the developed world. While income inequality was once on the decline, over the last twenty years the distribution of wealth and prosperity in the nation has become more unequal. Individuals and families at greatest risk for poverty are men with less than a college education, people of color (especially blacks and Hispanics), working families and families headed by women, and a significant number of the nation's elderly."[52] The rising tide is not materializing for these people and neither is it for many others. In 2003, a person of color still had a one in four chance of being poor, while for whites the ratio was one in ten. Households headed by females had a one in three chance of existing below the poverty line; black female-headed households had a slightly higher chance of 38.9 percent. All children had a 17.6 percent chance of living in poverty, and black children a chance of 33.6 percent.[53]

What matters are not so much the absolute numbers but the underlying asymmetries of power. As the rising tide fails to materialize for many, the other side also needs to be mentioned. The richest 1 percent of Americans were able to increase their after-tax income by 200 percent between 1979 and 2000, at a time when the real median family income went down—from $60,670 in adjusted 1959 dollars to $43,318.[54] The consequences of these discrepancies are hard to explain outside of the United States: in the country that has the most billionaires, there is no substantial social safety net, and while the country has the best doctors and hospitals in the world, there is no health care for 18 percent of the U.S. population under the age of 65.[55] These discrepancies do not occur by accident, and they are related both to economics and to religion, as I will show.

In this context, it may be surprising that a challenge comes from the business community itself. Already in 2006 the following assessment was made by a top investor, as reported in *Fortune* magazine: "'About half of American industry has grossly unfair compensation systems where the top executives are paid too much,' says Charlie Munger, Warren Buffett's partner at Berkshire Hathaway. Florida governor Jeb Bush—a pro-market conservative—is even more blunt. Out-of-control compensation, he believes, is 'a threat to capitalism.' Says Bush: 'Large rewards for great results can still be attacked, but they're very defensible. But if the rewards for CEOs and their teams become extraordinarily high with no link to performance—and shareholders are left holding the bag—then it undermines people's confidence in capitalism itself.'" While these statements may be unexpected, the real question is, what is the underlying problem? Are CEO salaries merely inexplicable accounting mistakes? The position of top investor Warren Buffett, currently the richest man in the world, throws some light on this: "the only cure for better corporate governance is if the small number of very large institutional investors start acting like true owners and pressure managers and boards to do the same."[56] Note that this challenge to CEO salaries comes from those large investors who wield tremendous power based on ownership—made visible by the fact that their incomes are many times higher than those of the CEOs. Other investors are now following suit. Tom Gardner, cofounder of *The Motley Fool,* puts it this way: "For years now, heartless people have been running many of our world's banks and investment houses, and our laws have been insufficient to restrain them. Boards of directors, CEOs, and their leadership teams created incentive systems that rewarded self-interest, impatience, and bottomless greed. That's a deadly three-punch combo that can flatten employees, customers, and shareholders alike." The conclusion is that until the excesses of CEOs are reined in, there will be no more investor confidence. Not long ago, the following comment would have been unthinkable coming from the finance sector: "Until there are new regulations in finance, there will be no rebound in investor or consumer confidence."[57] Yet the substantial gap between CEO and worker compensation that is challenged here covers up another gap that is even more substantial: the gap between the major shareholders and workers. In order to understand what is really going on, we need to keep observing these matters from the underside, which, in this case, includes both workers and smaller shareholders.

Viewing these matters through the lens of relationship rather than through the lens of absolute wealth should make us realize that the problem is not primarily economic wealth but power. As economist Michael Zweig has pointed out: "Economic problems arise not because some people are rich but because private profit and the power of capital are the highest priorities in the economic system."[58] Those who hold the most power—whether CEOs or large investors—make sure that no one is in a position to challenge them. CEOs seek to prevent the workers from organizing themselves because their own profits might be reduced. The top investors seek to prevent CEOs from writing ever-larger checks to themselves because otherwise their profits are cut. The struggles at the top are not primarily about money, however: both top CEOs and top investors have more money than they could ever spend. These struggles are about power and more power, and profits are crucial because they back up the power of those who get to pocket them. In this situation, the old topic of the ownership of the means of production still plays a role, although the situation has become more complex. Those who ultimately control the means of production—that is, those who hold substantial amounts of shares in a company—are the ones who have the ultimate say, as Buffett's comments remind us. Those who do not control the means of production, even those who own small amounts of shares, need to work for those in control in one form or another and are, thus, dependent on them. The real problem with this sort of control over the means of production—which must not be confused with the ownership of private property in general, as will be pointed out in chapter 5—is that it skews relationships among people and creates sometimes severe asymmetries of power, a fact that is generally more visible from the perspective of the workers, who have to endure the pressures of this arrangement. While small-business owners often find themselves in the middle and, thus, may have some sense of these problems—they own some means of production but still often need to work in order to make ends meet—the owners of large amounts of shares in big corporations have a harder time understanding what is going on. As a result, any efforts to level the playing field will seem foreign and unfair to them. For this reason, the view from below turns out to be significant for anyone who wants to develop an understanding of the whole, both in economics and in theology.

Religion, Economics, and Class

What is becoming clearer now is that economic downturn for the majority of people, even during times of economic growth, is not simply an accident—or a succession of mere accidents—but is tied to a system that distributes power in unequal fashion. There is an emerging logic here, what I call the "logic of downturn," which has tremendous potential because it provides a real alternative to the dominant logic of economic growth that is supposed to lift all boats. This logic of downturn not only provides new insights in economics; it also helps us better understand the phenomenon of religion. Like the notion of class, the notion of religion is frequently and conveniently misunderstood. The notion of religion is not only left underanalyzed but fundamentally misunderstood when it is defined in terms of personal or communal belief systems or practices that are independent from politics and economics.[59] To put it as succinctly as possible: the problem is that attention to religion, when paid primarily to belief systems, cultural-linguistic phenomena, or religious practices, not only neglects but tends to cover up the many aspects of life that have to do with questions of differentials of power, especially with the deeper questions of economics and class. And even when questions of power, economics, and class are addressed, they are often considered as optional strata of investigations—as the niche projects of certain scholars based on their personal interests and tastes—rather than as essential topics which need to be investigated whenever religion is investigated.

There is a long history to this compartmentalization of religion, economics, and other aspects of life, but the pressures of downturn make us take another look at how everything belongs together. Just as we are beginning to understand that definitions of economics and class are deficient if they do not take into account the asymmetry of power in everyday life and at the workplace and the resulting pressures, we also need to consider that definitions of religion that neglect these issues are deficient as well. The experience of downturn makes us painfully aware that our lives cannot be compartmentalized, since all aspects of our lives are affected by it. In reference to our discussion of class, we might say that sticking with reflections on belief systems in terms of religion is just as inadequate as sticking with reflections on income levels in terms of class. Just like income levels are the result, rather than the cause, of relationships of power as they shape up in class divisions and the division of labor, belief systems are the result, rather than the origin, of the practices of religion and the relationships of power that are worked out in this context.

Despite the fact that maintaining a definition of religion is an existential issue for religious studies and theology, once we begin to pay attention to the flows of power in everyday life, religion can no longer be seen as an independent phenomenon that can be defined in abstraction from other parts of reality. Whether religious studies and theology have been aware of it or not, religion has always been a part of life as a whole. What is still often overlooked is that it is this relation of religion to life—rather than a sense for academic adventure or sheer curiosity—that compels us to engage in interdisciplinary studies like the current one. In this context, the question of how religion relates to class introduces another level of investigation and a more embodied form of the study of the role of power. The particular questions to be considered in terms of religion and class are these: How does power as it is embodied and shaped in relationships at the workplace contribute not only to economic and political phenomena (the more typical focus of the study of class) but also to the shape of religion and belief systems? And what alternatives can we possibly envision? Such questions will push us beyond current modes of investigation in religion that function in terms of what might be caricatured as idealism—that is, modes of investigation that operate mostly in the realm of ideas without deeper reflections on how these ideas are produced.[60]

In a next step, a similar question will need to be raised of the economic sciences, which—and this may come as a surprise to those who can see the idealism of theology and religious studies but not the other idealisms that shape our current situation—have often operated on the level of abstract and disembodied ideas as well. After all, it takes a substantial amount of faith and a strong commitment to the world of ideas to believe that the market will take care of all our problems, especially if the track record of the market is shaky at best. The following statement by two self-proclaimed Christian economists is not atypical of economics in general: "Markets generate economic incentives and rewards that are important for personal freedom and material well-being. Both tend to erode economic gaps over time. Under the best competitive circumstances, unwarranted prejudice gives way to market rewards that enhance productivity."[61] The logic of downturn, combined with a deeper awareness of class structures, forces us to reassess such idealistic assessments.

In this context, practical engagement with real-life issues as they shape up in situations of great economic pressure is a first step toward developing deeper reflections on both economics and religion. In Dallas, for instance, this was one of the reasons for the founding of a Workers' Rights Board through North Texas Jobs with Justice.[62] The work of such boards, whose members are recognized community leaders who have credibility with the public, is to support particularly those workers who have little other organized support. The work of a workers' rights board is based on hearings in which the members of the board—mostly middle-class people with high visibility in the community, such as lawyers, government officials, pastors, teachers, professors, and others—begin to listen to the stories of workers. These stories often broaden the horizons of the board members, who for the most part have few first-hand encounters with the rising pressures that bear down on average workers. In recent meetings of the Dallas-based Workers' Rights Board, for instance, construction workers from Texas and Arizona reported that they are not given water to drink in the brutal heat of the summers of the Southwest; that they have to perform dangerous jobs without safety equipment provided by the companies; and that their personal or family needs get little or no consideration. In response to these abuses, the Workers' Rights Board seeks to communicate with employers and raise their awareness of what is going on through meetings and letters. If issues cannot be settled in this way, the abuses are made public so as to raise broader awareness. In this context, workers' rights boards also become epistemological tools, broadening the horizons of board members, employers, and the broader public by dealing directly with what might be considered yet another and more severe logic of downturn. A theology that takes seriously these issues and questions can lead to new insights on the nature of religion, and it might develop new insights that are relevant for the study of economics as well.

Paying attention to class in the study of religion and economics forces us to revisit one of the foundational myths of U.S. history: the notion of individualism. This notion is still widely accepted and defended by religious people and economists alike. Even those who oppose it and argue for communitarian models of life instead, however, lend support to the notion of individualism because they assume that it exists. Both individualists and communitarians assume that individualism is real—the difference is that one group celebrates it while the other laments it. Various interpretations of religion are tied up with either of these perspectives, and some of the biggest conflicts in recent theology have been bound up with these two camps. Unfortunately, these fights lead nowhere. The logic of downturn further underscores our earlier argument that individualism is a mirage. Taking into account the experience of downturn in light of the notion of class, we are beginning to understand that individualism is the myth that helps to buttress the power of the ruling class, as it allows this class to see itself in separation from the working class.

Even common understandings of class in terms of income levels or so-cial stratification perpetuate this myth of individualism, as discussion of class in terms of these phenomena does not require a reflection on how the vari-ous classes are related. In fact, the opposite is usually the case: the various levels or strata are usually discussed in isolation from each other, as if there were no connections between them.[63] An understanding of class in terms of power and the larger economic context, however, demonstrates that indi-vidualism is a myth—the favorite myth of those on the top, who have made it, and the scourge of a myth that haunts those at the bottom. The myth of individualism allows those on top to proclaim that their success is self-made, just as it allows them to maintain that the misfortune of those on the bot-tom is self-caused, a myth that is often internalized by those on the bottom. The American Dream—that anyone can make it to the top based on indi-vidual achievements—further feeds the myth of individualism, and consis-tently works against those at the bottom and in favor of those on the top. It discredits the aging busboy and endorses the youthful billionaire—leaving the former with nothing but an idealistic dream and the sort of religion that resembles Karl Marx's notion of religion as "the opium of the people," no matter how complex that notion may be.

In this context, something else comes to the fore that is even more dif-ficult to bring up in polite company than politics, religion, sex, or money: the notion of class struggle. Talk about class struggle usually results in the ac-cusation that those who dare even to mention the term are the ones instigat-ing the struggle. But the reality is different: the current situation—in which the rich not only get richer but also more powerful, and everyone else, the middle class included, gets poorer and is increasingly stripped of power—points to a systemic problem. Clearly, the reality of downturn does not affect everyone in the same way. The ultra-rich keep increasing their wealth and power at the expense of everyone else—even if only relatively so—by par-ticipating in a sort of class struggle that is mostly invisible. In the construc-tion industry, for instance, workers have been told that their salaries had to be reduced due to the recession, so that the company could deliver more competitive bids in a depressed market; in reality, the bids were often deliv-ered virtually unchanged.

The struggle that is waged by the defenders of the free-market econ-omy against worker solidarity is perhaps the most telling example of what is going on. While the declining state of the unions is often attributed to a loss of interest among workers, the reality is that there have been increas-ing numbers of systematic attacks against workers organizing themselves that have mostly gone unnoticed.[64] Economist Robert Brenner notes that the trump card of the U.S. economy is "a labour force that has, so far, proved not only incomparably more exploitable than, say, those of Western Europe or Japan, but increasingly over time." Brenner further notes that "since the end of the New Economy bubble-driven boom, between 2000 and the present [2006], corporations and government have unleashed one of the fiercest assaults on workers in U.S. history."[65] These assaults, referencing the legacy of the Bush administration, include cuts of increases in pay and wage, major intensification of workload, reneging on pension plans, reductions in health care, and increasing resistance to the organization of labor.

This sort of class struggle is justified by the philosophies of trickle down economics, and by quasi-religious beliefs that the market will benefit everybody in the long run and that a rising tide will lift all boats. Workers are being told, for instance, that in order to save their companies they need to make compromises, accept cuts in pay and benefits, and cease forming unions. In this context, workers and unions are often blamed for making unreasonable demands that jeopardize their companies, despite evidence to the contrary.[66] And here religion plays an essential role: the success of the class struggle that is waged against those who are less privileged and less powerful depends on keeping the beliefs in the beneficial character of the market alive. No matter that these beliefs fly in the face of reality, as the lack of a rising tide becomes the fate of more and more and nothing of substance ever trickles down.

In this context, there are different options for the work of theology and religious studies. One option would be simply to ignore the clash between the classes, which is the default mode now and which explains the high level of discomfort when the notion of class struggle is even mentioned. Another option would be to declare this clash as real, but part of another discipline or another world that is irrelevant in the spheres of religion. Yet another option would be to use religion to heal whatever clash might exist and to put to rest the remaining tensions—a common response, especially from mainline religious communities which quickly resort to notions of peace and harmony when confronted with tensions of any kind. None of these approaches, however, really captures the problem because none is in a position to address the underlying power differentials. As a result, theology and religious studies miss an opportunity to engage some of the key issues of life that shape religion, as well as the question of what difference religion might make in this context, which is a question that Marx missed in his own way.

The insights of liberation theologies, broadly conceived, are especially relevant at this point. A non-theologian, economist Michael Zweig, makes a significant observation about the difference of this approach to theology: "Liberation theology can be distinguished from liberal theology in that the former recognizes class conflict . . . and positions itself consciously as an ally of one class against the other; whereas liberal theology, which also seeks to ameliorate the conditions of capitalism and sees the need for structural changes, denies the class-conflictual nature of society and proposes instead a plan for social harmony among all the classes."[67] While this assessment may sound harsh and tendentious, similar conflicts and tensions are at the basis of the Judeo-Christian traditions from Moses to Jesus and Paul, and things tend to become clearer when conflict is recognized rather than repressed. In addition, taking sides does not imply a lack of care about the other side: when Jesus took the side of the common people against the side of the privileged of his own day, he cared about the salvation of both sides, knowing that true harmony can only be achieved if the tensions are addressed and overcome rather than repressed. His impassioned speeches against the Pharisees in Matthew 23 provide only one example for this: accusing them of having neglected "the weightier matters of the law: justice and mercy and faith" (Matt 23:23) implies not so much an ultimate rejection but an invitation to conversation and a new beginning.

Unfortunately, in both theology and economics, conflict is too often repressed and pushed out of sight, so that it becomes even more harmful. It is frequently overlooked, for instance, that prominent economic moves that are recommended based on seemingly scientific economic arguments, like tax cuts for the wealthy, also create conflicts. Unlike supply-side economists in the 1980s, who assumed that tax cuts to the wealthy could be had without reduction in government spending, economists now know that these tax cuts have to be bought with cost reductions elsewhere. Those who support tax cuts to the wealthy usually endorse reductions to welfare for those at the lower end of the spectrum; even subsidies for school breakfasts for disadvantaged children have been cut in the past in order to finance lower taxes for the wealthy. Endorsing a move like this is either cynical or shows the extraordinary faith that is put in such tax cuts; in some cases there might be a bit of both. As president of Americans for Tax Reform, Grover Norquist famously stated: "My goal is to cut government in half in twenty-five years, to get it down to the size where we can drown it in the bathtub."[68] Statements like this make it look like no one gets hurt when government is reduced. Nevertheless, what is really announced here is a deepening conflict and struggle between the classes: the cuts to welfare that result from such programs, for instance, are stunning and clearly intentional, as Norquist's statement shows, and many other public services that support people in need are also put in jeopardy.

The logic of downturn helps identify a distortion of perspective that occurs both in economics and in religion. It is commonly presupposed that those on top represent the common interest—what is good for all—while those on the bottom represent various special interests. Public opinion in the aftermath of the devastation of New Orleans by Hurricane Katrina is a case in point. When the evacuees of New Orleans were given some funds to purchase the bare necessities of life, the common public sentiment was that they would surely squander this money without sense and reason. There was, however, no comparable outcry when large and lucrative contracts were awarded—often without competitive bids—to large corporations for the purpose of rebuilding the city. Just as there was a general distrust of those at the bottom, there was a general trust that those at the top who represent the world of business would do the right thing. The truth is that tremendous sums of money were squandered by those at the top, not only due to a lack of competition when no-bid contracts were awarded, but also because many companies did not perform well without oversight, with some taking the money and running.

Dealing with the issue of class, we need to ask ourselves what would change in economics and religion if common interest were not to be found at the top but at the bottom. In the case of hurricane-damaged New Orleans, would not those who have lost everything have a greater interest in rebuilding not only their own properties but also their communities as quickly and efficiently as possible, since they know that they are not able to survive long without them? Those whose lives get crushed by catastrophes, including catastrophic downturns of the economy, are the ones who cannot afford to waste time, money, or energy when seeking for solutions; and they are the ones who might help us to develop new insights into the things that contributed to these destructions. Already the Apostle Paul, turning a classical imperial notion of society as a hierarchically ordered body on its head, understood that "if one member suffers, all suffer together with it" (1 Cor 12:26a). While the imperial model of the body implied that top-down power and subordination were natural, that they should be accepted without question, and that the emperor knew what was best for everyone, Paul identified the location of common interest at the bottom, with those who suffer. The trade-union movement expresses a similar wisdom in this way: "An injury to one is an injury to all." Common interest is found at the bottom, because pressure applied to the weakest tends to spread to everyone sooner or later. Conversely, gains made in this context also spread: the unions have found that when wages are raised for some workers and when their working conditions improve over time, the wages and working conditions of all workers tend to improve. In Paul's language: "If one member is honored, all rejoice together with it" (1 Cor 12:26b). The Christian thing to do, in this context, is to take a stand with those who suffer and to work for change, which will ultimately benefit all of society.

One of the most important advantages of identifying common interest at the bottom is that new and constructive ways of interacting can be identified from here. Negotiations of employers and workers organized in unions, for instance, introduce a bottom-up form of negotiation that allows for a negotiation of the real issues, related to where the pain is. Rather than negotiating things through a seemingly omnipotent outside party like the Department of Labor, which may be out of touch and would have to interfere from the top down in order to be effective, strong unions could provide the input that is really needed from the bottom up—especially if it is seen that workers tend to have an interest in the well-being of their company which is often stronger and in many cases more existential than that of the owners themselves.

The same dynamic applies in religious discourse. If the matters of Christianity, for instance, are negotiated in relation with those who seek to live their faith in everyday life, the real issues of life can no longer be repressed, as they often are in the work of religious professionals and academics; the often-questioned relevance of Christianity would not be a problem either. And rather than negotiating the matters of faith from the top town, the people themselves could provide the input that is really needed. Both economics and theology would greatly benefit from such reversals.

One more issue must be raised in this context. The factor of human sin, generally affirmed by Christianity as a serious theological issue, is often used as an argument in favor of the free-market economy. A widely held position is summarized by one Christian author in this way: "Capitalism . . . begins with human beings as they are, coordinating the self-interested actions of self-interested people so as to produce an unintended beneficial outcome, and enabling the actions of ignorant people to be informed by more knowledge than such people could ever individually acquire." By the same token, socialism is rejected by this author because "it postulates virtually omniscient, omnibenevolent beings."[69] This position, despite having been argued countless times, actually has it backwards: while capitalism does indeed note the selfish nature of human beings to a certain degree, it appears to be hopelessly naïve and groundlessly optimistic about what happens when selfish human beings interact in the free market and about the market's power to turn evil into good, especially in situations of grave asymmetries of power that transcend small-scale individual selfishness. An observation of market systems that does not romanticize the relations between buyers and sellers, but instead takes into account the logic of downturn—which points us to the often-serious distortions in power, for instance, in the relation of employers and employees or in a world of monopolies—cannot easily affirm such optimism.

The logic of downturn pushes beyond this trivialization of sin and relates to those Christian theological perspectives that recognize that sin never affects just individuals but also systems and relationships.[70] In this context, it appears that socialism takes sin more seriously by inviting a more sustained look at how free markets have actually shaped up in real life and by noting the accumulation of the means of production in the hands of a few, with the result that human selfishness becomes compounded; it might be argued that anti-monopoly regulations seek to address a similar problem of compounded human selfishness. The misunderstanding of socialism in the above remarks is of course a common one and has to do with a portrayal of the core concern of socialism as government centralism, which would result in a naïve reliance on the benevolence of government. The real concern of socialism, however, has to do not with totalitarian attitudes but with a concern for democracy—especially with what might be called *economic democracy*. Ethicist Beverly Harrison is one of the few working from within a Christian perspective who have understood this. For neoclassical economists, she points out, socialism means "centralized economic planning." Historically, however, "a socialist approach to political economy *meant* economic democracy. It implied either shared resources or worker control of production and participation in determining the use of created wealth. All types of socialists addressed the specific alienations effected by separation of work and ownership."[71]

How such a democracy can be achieved will have to be debated, but economic democracy is necessary precisely because the logic of downturn leads to a deepening awareness of what Christians would call sin. This deepening awareness of sin does not allow for the sort of optimism about human nature that is content with leaving leadership in the hands of a few who, in the case of economic leadership, are not even democratically elected. Christian ethicist Reinhold Niebuhr's famous phrase might be interpreted in this broader context of economic democracy: "Man's capacity for justice makes democracy possible; but man's inclination to injustice makes democracy necessary."[72] This more realistic assessment of human nature maintains a healthy sense of sin and evil and begs the question of why notions of political and economic democracy ever got separated.

The Logic of Downturn and the Future of Religion

Once we begin to address these deeper tensions in economics and religion, the interesting question is whether religion might contribute to negotiating these relationships of power in constructive ways. Understanding how religion helps negotiate economics, class structures, and the clash between the classes introduces a new level of insight into the study of theology. Such an investigation of religion and class opens the door to deeper analyses of the complexity of power: How does religion help negotiate other power struggles related to economics, politics, culture, race, gender, sex, and so on?

One of the questions that can be pursued on the basis of these observations is how religion assumes different functions in different class contexts, rather than being limited to the role of the "opiate of the people." This was, of course, one of Karl Marx's most famous statements about religion, which must be seen in its own historical context. Many of the particular forms of mainline religion which he was able to observe in his time functioned precisely in this way. Religion in Marx's time helped reduce the pain of the working class by being the "sigh of the oppressed creature and the heart of a heartless world," but it did not contribute to resolving the burning issues of the day.[73] As we investigate this issue further in our own time, it might help to see that religion is not opium for everyone: religion is not opium for the ruling class, for instance, when it reinforces its power and helps extend its reach through quasi-religious ideas about the free market that govern the logic of economics. The interests of the ruling class are also supported by certain religious ideas embedded in the minds of the working class, such as the Gospel of Prosperity. By the same token, we need to take a closer look at what difference religion makes for those who experience the logic of downturn in their own bodies, especially the members of the working class and the middle class, who are increasingly experiencing similar pressures as they build their own logic and an alternative sort of power from the bottom up. This has nothing to do with reductionism—that is, the reduction of religious ideas to economic matters. Just the opposite: the term *religion* is liberated from reductionistic notions that place religion in a limited sphere. Placed in a broader context, religious positions can be observed in terms of the difference they actually make, one way or another.

This alternative use of religion does not have to be understood in narrow and exclusive terms. What difference does religion make to the poorest of the poor, for instance? What difference might it make to those white-collar workers who are often made to bear the brunt of economic downturn when they are let go by their employers and who have so internalized the myth of individualism that they blame themselves and thus withdraw from their peers?[74] The dilemma of white-collar workers is neatly summarized by Thomas Frank: they have no say but they are held responsible for what happens.[75]

The relation of religion and class takes a special shape in the United States: whereas, particularly in Europe, workers have long since left the churches, which for centuries supported the ruling classes and their economic and political interests, in the United States many workers have remained in the churches. Yet these churches are not necessarily serving their interests, and they are often not doing much to help them develop alternatives and constructive solutions. In Texas, for instance, a large number of trade-union members are also members of churches, yet these churches give virtually no support to their causes. If these churches address economic or political issues, they often side with the employers. In churches that are attended both by employers and workers, the employers are usually the ones who make their interests heard; it has frequently not even occurred to the workers that they could do the same. While we will discuss the theological reasons for this situation in the next chapter in more detail (if God is seen as being at the top, those who occupy the top positions appear to be closer to God), it appears as if this behavior is closely related to financial contributions made to the church. Yet, although employers are certainly in a position to make bigger individual contributions to the church than workers, the collective contributions of workers are most likely not insignificant either, and, for this reason alone, things might change if worker solidarity were to develop in church. Fortunately, this is more than a dream, as there is a strong but little-known history of church and labor in the United States,[76] and current religion and labor coalitions are witnessing to solidarity being built from below, which makes a difference.[77]

As solidarity emerges from below, the role of the middle class can be seen in a new light as well. This class, which is literally in the middle between the two conflicting groups, is often so strongly tied to the system that it is unable to make any contributions of its own. It is this class that is often most closely related to the religion of the market, as it is more dependent on religious hope than the ruling classes, due to its weaker economic status. But there are also some options here. One option took shape in Argentina early in the new millennium, when the middle class took to the streets in protest of the collapse of the country's economy—unearthing the common interest of working and middle classes, as both benefit from the system only in a limited fashion. The middle class in the United States will ultimately have to face these issues, as well, as its economic status is declining amid the housing crisis and the crisis of the stock market, and it is beginning to develop an inkling that its economic fortune can no longer be expected to rise even at the rate of average economic growth. In this context, Barbara Ehrenreich makes an interesting suggestion for unemployed middle-class people: "No group is better situated, or perhaps better motivated, to lead the defense of the middle class than the unemployed—assuming they could recognize their common interests and begin to act as a political force."[78] One can only imagine what contribution the mainline churches could make to such a development. Yet, in order to conceive of this, new kinds of theological reflections that deal with the common pain and that do not shy away from the logic of downturn are necessary.

In the following chapters, the notions of the divine, of hope, and of desire will be examined in light of this logic of downturn. Examining the ground of our hope and the role of desire in the interplay of theology and economics can lead to the development of constructive alternatives. What if we have put our hope in the wrong things? What if many of the gods in which 92 percent of Americans believe are false gods? What if our desires are tied up with things that are harmful? Constructive alternatives of hope and desire help re-shape the current situation that causes undue pressures and the distortion of life—and even death—for large numbers of people. Is there hope at a time when, for much of humanity, things do not even minimally go as anticipated by mainline economic and theological models, and when economic models fail to take into account the existence of those on whose labor they are built? What images are able to generate such hope for all of humanity? How can desire be reshaped in ways that are life-giving for all of humanity?

God and the Free-Market Economy | 3

What Gives Us Hope

As the rising tide anticipated by free-market economics fails to materialize long term for more and more of us—in spite of the claims that the economy goes in cycles and that there will be ups and downs—the question is: What gives us hope, and what keeps us going when things do not go as anticipated? This question, part of the logic of downturn, ties together not only those who are down on their luck in the economy at one point or another, but most people who work for a living, not only blue collar but more and more white collar as well, including large numbers of small-business people. It is the appropriate question to ask at the beginning of an exploration dealing with our images of God.

What gives us hope is an important part of what keeps us going, particularly in the face of adversity. Hope is tied to images of what is ultimate and on which we can depend. In this hope, we find another area of overlap of theological and economic images. The question of what gives us hope is at the heart of all other questions; it tells us more than many other questions which are commonly raised in either theology or economics. Asking this question in situations where things do not go as anticipated helps filter out a certain self-congratulatory undercurrent that tends to infiltrate even descriptive statements and seemingly objective claims. Considering questions of hope and motivation in light of these crises pushes beyond superficial descriptions of economic and theological processes and urges us toward investigations of deeper levels of reality. The intersections of theology and economics at the core of this project are not artificial. While they are in place all the time, these intersections are intensified in times of pressure when things do not go as anticipated.

In Christian theology, the question of what gives us hope is tied to specific images of God. These images are not always fully explicit—and often the most influential images are the ones that are least visible. Nevertheless, Christians are able to name some of the key images of the divine to which they subscribe. In economic theory, on the other hand, it is less obvious where hope is grounded. Yet economics is not without sources of hope either, as we shall see. In this chapter, I will elaborate how economic hope takes shapes similar to Christian hope in the United States. The parallels and intersections of theology with other areas of public life, including economics, are perhaps more visible in the United States than in other economically privileged countries. Here, religious discourse continues to play an important role in almost all areas of life. It is common, for instance, for the presidents of the nation to make public references to God. Devotions and public prayers in the White House have remained a fixture under all recent presidents. And while prayer and devotion have come under scrutiny in certain areas—most visibly perhaps in restrictions on prayers in public schools—in the business world prayer and devotion seem to have a stronger foothold than in many other areas of public life. Countless organizations of businesspeople are dedicated to religious purposes, seeking to link together God and success in business.[1]

Even most of the Christian churches tend to go along with this trend to link God and economic success. Although not all preach the so-called Gospel of Prosperity, which proclaims that God and the Christian faith guarantee economic success, very few churches see the need to question the intricate relation of faith and economics. While the principle of the separation of church and state is commonly noted—even though it is not necessarily realized—there is little concern for similar distinctions when it comes to the church and economics. And while there has traditionally been some concern for the lack of distinction of faith and politics in U.S. Christianity, for the most part the distinction of faith and economics is not widely recognized as a problem. We will need to investigate the deeper connections which prevent a clear separation of the underlying phenomena of religion, politics, and economics.

A devastating economic crisis like the one that was in full swing at the writing of this book is not just a crisis of the financial sector: it has to do with a long-term crisis of hope. Much of the fallout of this crisis will not be known for years to come, as people are only gradually beginning to realize that they placed their hope in the sorts of things that cannot ultimately endure. At the same time, hope was a powerful engine that helped to drive the economic successes of the 1990s, some of it lasting into the early years of the twenty-first century. Much of the economic boom that followed the brief economic dip caused by the events of September 11, 2001, has been built on the hopes of middle-class and working-class families. When the Bush administration's tax cuts to the wealthy failed to stimulate the economy, low interest rates opened the floodgates of borrowing for those less well off. Combined with an increase in subprime mortgages and lax lending practices which included adjustable-rate mortgages, these lower interest rates (together with bubbling property values) lured people into maxing out their credit. The stock market played a role in raising hopes as well, as it went from one boom to the next, with only a few busts in between. In these and other ways, hope was generated that the American Dream might be just around the corner. Yet this hope is increasingly failing for more and more people, as both the housing and stock-market bubbles are deflating and as the economy, as a whole, has experienced the most severe crash since the Great Depression.

Despite the fact that this hope in the market was tied to some actual economic developments, it had the features of an unhealthy utopianism. Nevertheless, the effects of this unhealthy utopian hope for the American Dream were real enough, as it made cash flow for a while and supported what is often decried as "consumerism" (a term that has its own problems, as we will see in the next chapter). For a while, the effects of this utopian hope allowed even those who were not so well off financially to live like those who were better off, as they were able to borrow more and more money. Adjustable-rate mortgages were particularly insidious in this regard, as they started with lower rates that were initially affordable. But when rates increased substantially after a few years, the hope that was put in rising housing values and personal economic improvement had often failed to materialize, and so many of the homes bought with these mortgages had to be foreclosed. Home-equity loans added another burden. At the basis of it all was an unhealthy utopian hope for the future, the sort of hope that could not be sustained because it was not rooted in what was actually going on in the real world—upon which economics and theology purport to reflect. This sort of unhealthy utopian hope is most pernicious when consumption and the growth of capital are disconnected from labor and production.

Using slightly different terminology, one might say that this latest economic boom was built on faith in a transcendent reality that was not able to deliver. This sort of faith is closely connected to unhealthy utopian hope because it directs attention away from real-life issues—in economics it directs attention away from what happens in production and labor, the basis of the economy; in religion, it directs attention away from the struggles and tensions of life, so that the divine itself becomes a bubble. Yet the more this unhealthy faith is challenged by real events, the greater the defensiveness of those who consider themselves true believers. As a result, those who question this faith are seen as the worst enemies of all, because they touch on the shaky foundations of the system. They are, therefore, seen as the ones who will surely not enter the promised land or partake of heavenly bliss, whatever that may look like.

The good news is, however, that this unhealthy hope is not the only option; hope and faith can be based on more solid grounds. And it is these grounds that we will have to explore in the remainder of the book, after we gain more clarity about unhealthy hope and the sort of faith that keeps leading us into one economic crisis after another. This sort of faith remains a major obstacle to any real future alternative.

Invisible Hands

When it comes to the relation of religion and economics, the most prominent images of God in the United States can be found in the so-called Gospel of Prosperity, which has been on the rise during the last two or three decades. The statement, "God blesses prosperity, and God wants to make his followers successful and wealthy," is the message preached by the prophets of prosperity. The divine blessings expected are often spelled out concretely: larger cars, larger houses, boats, and bigger paychecks and bank accounts are only the highlights of a much longer list. Even if the requests are not so big and less centered on luxury items, the hope of the adherents of the Gospel of Prosperity is always for more success and prosperity in life, which are seen as signs of God's blessings for faithful individuals. Prosperity for the community, if it is an issue at all, will come through the blessing of individual community members who make their way up in the system. The bestseller *The Prayer of Jabez,* authored by Bruce Wilkinson, incorporates the various elements of this theology. It is based on an obscure Old Testament passage in 1 Chron 4:10: "Jabez called on the God of Israel saying, 'Oh that you would bless me and enlarge my border, and that Your hand might be with me, and that you would keep me from hurt and harm!' And God granted what he asked." Wilkinson encourages Christians to invoke this prayer for themselves on a daily basis: "I challenge you to make the Jabez prayer for blessing part of the daily fabric of your life. To do that, I encourage you to follow unwaveringly the plan outlined here for the next thirty days. By the end of that time, you'll be noticing significant changes in your life, and the prayer will be on its way to becoming a treasured, lifelong habit." The key, according to Wilkinson, is not just to know about this prayer but to believe it: "It's only what you believe will happen *and therefore do next,* that will release God's power for you."[2] This sort of success is not seen as limited to people's religious lives, and so the website of Wilkinson has a link titled, "Enlarge the boundaries of your business," right under the quotation of the prayer from the Bible.[3] This message is expounded in various forms by almost all television preachers. It is also one of the staples of many megachurches and many churches in the Pentecostal tradition.

The Gospel of Prosperity has often raised eyebrows not only with critics of religion but also with adherents of mainline Christianity. "How can good Methodists, Episcopalians, Presbyterians, and Lutherans believe that sort of thing?" was the incredulous question raised by journalist Jeff Chu in a phone interview. One of the authors of a report on the Gospel of Prosperity in *Time* magazine in September of 2006, Chu sought to draw a clear line between mainline Christianity and the Gospel of Prosperity.[4] My response to Chu did not make it into the article, probably because it did not fit this basic effort to draw the line. While mainline Christianity may not preach the Gospel of Prosperity as blatantly as other traditions, I told Chu, we share similar theological presuppositions. Both mainline Christianity and the Gospel of Prosperity tend to take for granted, for instance, that God is to be found at the top, with the wealthy, the successful, and the powerful. This is what most Christians assume implicitly, and this is what many seem to hear when they follow along in the liturgy and chant: "Holy, holy, holy Lord, God of power and might." My theological statement, however, was not enough for Chu, and so I had to come up with further evidence. Even a cursory glance at the leadership of the church supports my point: the laypersons who serve on the most influential boards and committees of a church are commonly the ones who enjoy relative levels of power and wealth in the community. This is not just for the more obvious pragmatic reasons, like, for instance, the expectation that members of a board of trustees will donate more money to an institution that they help govern; there is an underlying theological rationale that is of more interest here. If God is envisioned as being on top, those who are closer to the top are more like God than others. And since the question of what "being on top" means is never explicitly discussed, "being on top" is defined by default—yet very effectively—by the top echelons of society.

This logic is also reflected in the so-called outreach programs of many mainline churches: when churches reach out to others through social programs, the implicit hope and expectation is often that these others will be provided with the opportunity to become more like their benefactors, who consider themselves to be closer to God not just because they are members of the church but also because they are somewhat closer to the top of society (no matter how far from the upper classes they might be). The invitation to others in need is often to better themselves, to be "uplifted" in various ways, and to share to some degree in the success of their benefactors. Similar processes are also at work inside the church itself: for instance, when certain members are afforded the opportunity to "work their way up" into the ranks of leadership. To be sure, the problem here does not primarily have to do with the personalities of people who seek to help and to do the right thing, but with an implicit theological logic that operates mostly below the surface, according to which God and success in life are closely related.

There is a close connection between these explicit and implicit hopes and what happens when economists, explicitly or implicitly, rely on Adam Smith's notion of the "invisible hand of the market," a quasi-theological concept which symbolizes the force that guarantees economic prosperity and success. According to Smith, a merchant who only intends his own advantage is "led by an invisible hand to promote an end which was no part of his intention." Moreover, "by pursuing his own interest he frequently promotes that of the society more effectually than when he really intends to promote it."[5] It is the invisible hand of the market, which, in miraculous fashion, turns self-interest of individuals into the common interest of the community. At first sight, this reference to a transcendent factor like the invisible hand of the market might look like a theological leftover of outdated worldviews inherited by Smith, which is no longer relevant today. This is, however, not the case, as this factor remains the foundation of contemporary free-market economics; certain quasi-theological assumptions are part of what is going on in economics even today. Whether there is a stated belief in transcendence or not does not matter. What matters is that the free-market economy continues to count on the existence of certain beneficial powers inherent in the market that promote economic prosperity and success. This can be seen, for instance, in the belief in the self-regulating powers of the free market and the resulting rejection of any kind of corrective intervention, whether by government or by other organizations like those of labor. This belief in the self-regulating powers of the free market rests squarely on the assumption of a transcendent factor. Faith in a regulating invisible hand, as it were, makes efforts to stage corrective interventions in the market appear like unfaithfulness or even blasphemy. It is the principle of the invisible hand of the market, which guarantees that human self interest—considered to be one of the strongest sources of energy of the free market—is transformed into common interest, thus benefitting the community as a whole. This does not necessarily have to be called a transcendent factor or an invisible hand—what matters is the common and unfaltering conviction that this is the way the world works. What is most telling is that no alternative vision is allowed—this one point is not negotiable—and anyone who dares to question this assumption risks being discredited by the guild, which amounts to a form of excommunication.

This logic of the invisible hand, first captured in its official form by Smith but maintained in less explicit forms even today, has far-reaching implications and pushes beyond the theological logic represented by mainline Christianity. Since we must have complete faith in the market to create the common good out of self-interested acts, it is important that people act exclusively according to their self-interest. Any other way of acting would be detrimental, and those who refuse to follow their self-interest in order to pursue the common good are seen as doing more harm than good: "I have never known much good done by those who affected to trade for the public good," states Smith. Fortunately, he continues, "it is an affectation . . . not very common among merchants, and very few words need be employed in dissuading them from it."[6] In his *Theory of Moral Sentiments,* Smith goes even further, noting that it is the the natural selfishness, rapacity, and convenience of the wealthy that puts the invisible hand to work and, thus, results in the common good: "The rich only select from the heap (of the harvest) what is most precious and agreeable. They consume little more than the poor; and in spite of their natural selfishness and rapacity, though they mean only their own conveniency, though the sole end which they propose from the labours of all the thousands whom they employ be the gratification of their own vain and insatiable desires, they divide with the poor the produce of all their improvements. They are led by an invisible hand to make nearly the same distribution of the necessaries of life which would have been made had the earth been divided into equal portions among all its inhabitants."[7] Smith continues: "When providence divided the earth among a few lordly masters, it neither forgot nor abandoned those who seemed to have been left out in the partition. . . . In what constitutes the real happiness of human life, they are in no respect inferior to those who would seem so much above them."[8] While there have always been some who were inclined to validate Smith's argument that the wealthy invariably contribute to the benefit of the poor, the conclusion of the paragraph gives us a hint at how little sense this must have made even in Smith's own day, at least to the common people: "The beggar, who suns himself by the side of the highway, possesses that security which kings are fighting for."[9] To be sure, there are simply not that many sunny days on which a beggar could sun himself in England, and what happens when it rains? At this point, the logic of downturn has caught up with us, and it should be clear how little awareness Smith had of what was really going on at the bottom of his own society. While the differences between the rich and the poor may not have been as great in Smith's day as now, and while it was not possible to hoard extraordinarily large sums of money in stock or other virtual forms of wealth then, Smith could have taken a clue from the plight of those who obviously did not benefit from his system—like beggars, child laborers, and the majority of factory workers. What sneaks in through the back door, of course, is not just

the belief in the free market but also the God-givenness of private property,
an issue to which we will come back in a subsequent chapter.

In any case, Smith trusts that it is the way of providence to care even for
those who are endowed with less and who do not belong to the small group
which was chosen to own the earth. As one of Smith's interpreters observes,
Smith's rather negative view of humanity is balanced by his optimistic view
of the world, since nature makes sure that justice is established.[10] Here, we
begin to understand that the theory of the free market only works because it
touches some sort of transcendent reality. Of course, this transcendent entity
does not necessarily have to be called "God"; one might also call it the "nature of the world"[11] or the "order of things," or one might call it that "which
keeps the world together at its core."[12] In this context, human intervention
can only be harmful, especially if it dares to second-guess providence, that
is, the invisible hand of the market. Worse yet is organized human intervention. For Smith, the biggest threat was interference by the state, and, for contemporary proponents of the free market, organized labor has become an
additional threat that they feel needs to be eliminated at all cost. The union-
busting efforts and the general discouragement of the organization of labor
which have increased exponentially in recent decades can now be understood
better in a theological context. We are, here, dealing with nothing less than
a holy war, based on ultimate principles. This is surprising at first sight, because the philosophical argument of Smith seems quite dated in terms of
the history of philosophy; nevertheless, it parallels developments in religious
studies where, despite significant progress in theology, some of Smith's arguments and the quest to define what is "natural" and true without variation still have some currency as well. The interesting question is, of course,
whether this transcendent reality is reliable, or whether it is more like the
unhealthy utopian hope in the growth of the market which has let us down.

On this backdrop, the freedom of the market takes on the form of a
new creed,[13] although it is for the most part not recognized and addressed as
such. It is simply seen as an objective description of the nature of the world
and of human nature, always and everywhere. Nevertheless, we are dealing with a form of theology here which is so strong that it ultimately transcends the realm of the purely economic and shapes all other areas of life.
No wonder that the principles of the free market have more and more become the principles of life as a whole.[14] The economic order of the free market is, thus, turned into the blueprint for the order of society. Based on this
blueprint, even government is supposed to receive its marching orders from
the logic of the market, as its main task is to create the framework within
which the market can continue to operate freely even under the most ad-
verse conditions. To paraphrase a well-known bumper sticker: "The freedom
of the market is not free." Enemies are all those who seek to interrupt this

freedom—whether they are social reformers, organized citizens or workers, foreign nations that seek to impose restrictions on trade relations with our industries, or terrorists. Government is supposed to protect the market against all these challenges. No wonder that this position has been called "market fundamentalism" (see above, chapter 1).[15] This conflation of economics and theology is what economist Duncan Foley has called "Adam's fallacy." Foley identifies two related fallacies of economics in the tradition of Adam Smith. One is a logical one: neither Smith nor anyone else has been able to demonstrate exactly how private selfishness turns into public altruism, and so this claim is ultimately faith-based. The other one is psychological, and "requires a strategy of wholesale denial of the real consequences of capitalist development."[16]

The basic problem of modern economics in terms of religion can now be seen in a new perspective. The problem is not secularization—as is often assumed—but a kind of hidden religiosity that promotes the worship of the gods of the free market. Brazilian theologian Jung Mo Sung identifies the core of this religiosity in the promise to achieve the impossible, namely an equilibrium in which all needs and desires are completely satisfied.[17] Hugo Assmann and Franz Hinkelammert agree: such trust in the function of the market as coordinating private initiative and self-interest for the common good can only be considered faith in a providential deity.[18] The work of this deity is presupposed to such a degree and with such confidence, it seems, that it never even needs to be named. This argument does not imply, however, that mainline economic theory must be seen as monolithic. Within the mainline, there are different schools of economics at work, just like there are different schools of mainline theology. Yet there are also commonalities and family resemblances. In this case, it is the belief in the invisible hand of the free market that is held both by Keynesians and their rivals, the followers of the Chicago School of Economics, as well as many other economists. This belief in the invisible hand of the free market might be considered as the element that makes mainline economics mainline, just like a common belief in "God at the top" is what makes mainline theology mainline—no matter whether it shapes up in liberal or conservative forms. And since in both economics and theology few people are aware of the alternatives, the dominant mode is tremendously influential despite some internal diversity.

From the perspective of downturn, however, there is another aspect that has not yet been considered and that points in the direction of a real alternative. The market is not just based on the exploits of capital, but also on the productive capacity of labor. What is neglected in the dominant vision of the market and its invisible hand is that its lifeblood—capital—is produced through labor: by siphoning off the economic surplus produced by labor, as it were. Unless labor is recognized and honored for its contribution to the economy, wealth will continue to flow up to such a degree that "trickling down" is hardly an option. We will come back to this topic in the final chapter.

Transcendence of the Market

Despite experiences of severe downturn, hope in the invisible hand of the market does not yet seem to have suffered great losses. This is perhaps understandable because it is the necessary hope of anyone who has a mortgage or who keeps investing in a 401(k) retirement plan, and whose personal future depends on these things. In order to believe in the continued success of the market in a situation where downturn is becoming the rule rather than the exception, one has to have an ever-stronger faith in transcendent realities. At the same time, however, faith in the transcendence of the market will become more and more difficult to maintain when faced with the ongoing lack of a rising tide. At first sight, this might be akin to the hope against hope of which the Apostle Paul talks in his letter to the Christians in Rome (Rom 4:18). But the two contexts are on opposite ends of the spectrum. Paul's hope against hope sought to point out a viable alternative in a situation where the dominant hope of the Roman Empire did not allow for alternatives; the hope in the free market, on the other hand, is the dominant hope on which the system rests, and it is this hope that does not allow for alternatives. In our own search for alternatives, it is precisely this dominant hope that will have to be tested.

Not a theologian, but a literary scholar made the following statement in the midst of the recession, during the early days of the Obama presidency:

> The high doctrine of Economic Correctness of the Reagan-Bush-Clinton-Bush years is as bankrupt as Soviet Communism. It is all but officially dead. Why then are the president's economic advisers paid to prop it up and apply a sickly rouge and embalm it and set it in motion with galvanic shocks to simulate life? All the money proposed to be donated to bankers and brokerage houses to keep their enterprise private is a proof of religious belief. The hundreds of billions to indemnify a class of private owners represent a sacrifice to our own God that failed—an idol we cannot surrender the habit of adoring. And the plucking of state subsidy out of taxpayer pockets to ensure that nothing is state-owned: a form of savage prayer or burnt offering.[19]

This is strong language, but the question that is raised is hard to dismiss. If the free market, increasingly deregulated and left to its own devices, has experienced substantial rates of failure, why maintain such fervent faith in it, and why try to shore it up once again?

When talking about the transcendence or even the divinity of the market, there are, of course, some fundamental distinctions that must be made.

There is a difference, for example, between envisioning the order of the free market as one that was "made" or as one that is "spontaneous." This is the way in which Friedrich von Hayek was presented the issue.[20] According to this distinction, those who assume that the order of the market was made assume a transcendent maker; this is probably a smaller group, although it should not be underestimated. Those who assume that there is a spontaneous order, on the other hand, can afford to leave the question about a transcendent being open; there is probably a larger group of economists in this camp. Nevertheless, the similarities may be greater than the differences, as both perspectives trust in the benevolence of the market and maintain the optimistic hope that it will keep developing in the right direction, despite occasional downturns. As economist Sheila Dow points out, such presuppositions "can only be regarded as an article of faith," even when (or perhaps especially when) evolutionary schemes are embraced and the "crutch of a mechanistic system to represent order" is given up.[21]

The problem with this sort of transcendence, however, is not unlike the problem with a particular sort of transcendence that is promoted by certain Christian groups, namely "otherwordliness." This does not mean that this sort of transcendence is focused on life after death, but it means that we are dealing with a sort of transcendence that does not pay attention to what is really going on here and now. As a result, whatever is considered to be transcendent is declared absolute and must be accepted without question. To be sure, this is not the sort of transcendence that Christians believe is manifest in the incarnation of the divine in Jesus Christ: here, *transcendence* has to do not with otherwordliness but with transcending a particular form of immanence that is determined by the status quo (e.g., the Roman Empire, establishment religion) in order to embrace a different form of immanence (in a stable, on the margins, with the "least of these").[22] In this sense, the incarnation of Jesus Christ is closely related to the logic of downturn. The transcendence of otherworldiness, on the other hand, is based on another logic. It often finds its place with those who do not have to worry about taking care of the everyday realities of the body because they have some means, and it is those groups that make sure it gets proclaimed to others. Economist Warren J. Samuels points out the problem with this sort of otherworldliness in economic thought and the tensions that it creates: "The supreme irony resident within economics is that we tend to adopt an official positivist methodology which presumes that the economy is independent and transcendental to man . . . while at the same time we seek policy implications and recommendations . . . which presume that the economy is not independent and transcendental." Unfortunately, these tensions are often overlooked, and Samuels's conclusion that "it would be better if this particular process were out in the open" is relevant both to theology and economics.[23]

If things are not "out in the open," however, and if the core of economics is not seen as transcendent, its pronouncements gain power exponentially. In the words of another economist, "the belief that economic theory *is* sound, and that it alone considers 'the big picture', is the major reason why economics has gained such an ascendancy over public policy."[24] Unlike in the 1980s, during the rule of British Prime Minister Margaret Thatcher and U.S. President Ronald Reagan, we do not even need to be told anymore that there is no alternative to capitalism. We simply believe it, unaware of the transcendent status that this particular form of economics has assumed. As a result, we do not raise questions—even if our livelihoods, our jobs, and our personal economic futures are at stake.

If the economy of the free market, thus, assumes a transcendent status, the only thing that remains to be debated is how best to serve it. One of the biggest battles between Republicans and Democrats, which has raged for decades, is precisely the debate on this issue. Republicans, despite divisions and demoralization after the 2008 elections, and despite the fact that their preferred economic policies have not worked, are rallying around the key issue that they continue to hold in common: massive tax cuts to the wealthy and to those who control production. The Democrats, on the other hand, prefer other forms of economic stimulus, which have traditionally been more in sync with the needs of the common people, by seeking to infuse economic support from below—assuming that this support eventually will make its way up. The Obama administration has developed yet another variation on this theme by infusing money into the big financial institutions and other large-scale enterprises in order to create economic stability and ultimately growth. In all cases, the question is the same, however: How do our actions best serve and service the free market?

Holding on to the transcendence of the market, which is supposed to fix things if correctly serviced, President Barack Obama is pushing back behind the sort of mainline economics favored since President Reagan came to office, which favors incentives to big business and the wealthy, in the belief that tax cuts and other means of support to those who control production will stimulate the market. There are several alternative options, one of them being the large-scale bailout of troubled corporations that began in the final months of the Bush administration. Another alternative, which is also endorsed by Obama to a somewhat lesser degree, was presented initially by John Maynard Keynes and pursued between the time of World War II and the Reagan presidency; today, it is supported by economists like Nobel Prize winner Paul Krugman.[25] This alternative seeks to create economic stimulus by supporting lower-income groups which can be expected to spend any additional income, since they cannot afford to hoard it like the affluent. Yet this return to Keynes is expected to be only a temporary fix.

Krugman, for instance, is adamant that this is an appropriate response to an emergency, which will pass; reforms, he notes in passing, can be discussed at a later time.[26] To be sure, none of this has anything to do with socialism, as some of the detractors fear. The objective in either case—whether in Reaganomics, in Keynesianism, or in the bailout of large corporations—is to shore up the free market and to ensure the free flow of capital. In the current situation, Keynesianism and bailouts appear to be necessary in order to prevent the economy from cycling out of bounds and hitting rock bottom, as the last vestiges of Reaganomics implemented by the Bush administration in the form of tax cuts to the wealthy and further deregulation of the market have failed.[27] Nevertheless, in neither case is the system required to change fundamentally. Neither do these approaches necessarily require any major corrective actions to the market itself; what little corrective action there is, is aligned with the best interests of the free market, for instance, the cutting of unnecessary excess in CEO salaries.

Even a Keynesian approach, which empowers people at the bottom to a certain degree and, thus, addresses some concerns of the logic of downturn, ultimately affirms the transcendence of the market and does not directly challenge the sorts of imbalances of power that are inherent in the so-called free market. The transcendence of the market is affirmed, therefore, across the board since nothing is allowed to touch on its fundamentals, which are safely stashed away in otherwordly realms. Perhaps the best test of the pervasiveness and depth of faith in the otherwordly transcendence of the free market is whether we can even imagine an alternative. At present, most people in the United States appear to find it easier to imagine the end of the world than the end of capitalism.

Contemporary Consequences

Thomas Friedman, celebrating economic globalization in his popular book, *The Lexus and the Olive Tree,* is a somewhat more enlightened voice in the sea of true believers in the free market. Friedman does not believe in leaving the market completely to its own devices. He points out the fallacy of the Republican Congress in 1994, which did not believe in government support even if it would have made the market more successful and safer: "I heard men and women who insisted that the market alone should rule, and who thought it was enough to be right about the economic imperatives of free trade and globalization, and the rest would take care of itself."[28] Friedman argues that it is not sufficient for the United States as a "benign superpower" to exert itself in support of the free global markets, noting that "the hidden hand of the market will never work without a hidden fist. Markets function and flourish only when property rights are secure and can be enforced."[29]

Friedman, while believing in the invisible hand of the market, makes up for a certain lack of faith by adding a little pressure: "With all due respect to Silicon Valley, ideas and technology don't just win and spread on their own."[30] And with this assumption—an assumption that we have seen more clearly at work during the years of the administration of President George W. Bush than ever before in recent memory—Friedman adds another aspect, namely that "neither the hidden fist nor the hidden hand will work . . . without also the open hand." What he envisions by that is "an America ready to use its wealth to pay a little more than others to stabilize the system and lend a more generous helping hand to others to stabilize the system."[31]

The images of God implied here deserve attention, as the invisible hand of the market appears to be in need of a little help. Thomas Friedman's explicit theological reflections on God at the end of his book go in a similar direction when he notes that it is *our* task to make God present in this world. In this book, the deep faith in the invisible hand of the market that will make everything right entirely without our help no longer comes through, although Friedman desperately seeks to keep the faith.[32] Friedman's position is probably more typical of free-market economists than a position that relies on faith alone. John Perkins's confessions about his work as an "economic hit man," for which he was authorized to use any means to get developing nations to accept huge loans that they could not repay in order to gain influence over their economies, shows the range of efforts to spread the reach of the market. Milton Friedman's endorsement of the "shock doctrine," according to which people need to experience trauma and terror in order to be converted to the free-market doctrine, which was first applied in the support of the military takeover in Chile in 1973, goes in a similar direction.[33]

Thomas Frank, in a book provocatively titled *One Market Under God*, has chronicled the fundamental shifts in economic policy which took place in the 1990s. These shifts are still with us, although in somewhat more hidden form. Politically, this takes us back to the administration of President Bill Clinton and to a time when Americans would not have used words like *empire* to describe what was going on. The optimistic attitude at the time did lend itself to the assumption that economic power was liberating rather than oppressive. The free market was seen as the ultimate source of democracy and welfare.[34] What changed from the 1990s onwards, Frank argues, is that there is now "the general belief among opinion-makers that there is something natural, something divine, something inherently democratic about markets," and this idea trumps all other ideas to such a degree that it was seen as worthy to be extended over the whole world.[35] The mood at that time was, no doubt, that of the "victory of capitalism" in the wake of the collapse of a particular form of state socialism in the Soviet Union and many of its allies. Frank identifies in the 1990s "an intellectual consensus every bit as ironclad as that of the 1950s," despite postmodern affirmations of difference and ethnic diversity that accompanied it. As a result, "in a manner largely unprecedented in the twentieth century, leaders of American opinion were in basic agreement on the role of business in American life."[36] In recent decades the transcendence of the market has indeed found deep and varied support.

This consensus about the role of the market and of business in American life seems to have outlasted even the fairly substantial political shifts of recent history. With President Obama's appointments of Timothy Geithner as Treasury Secretary and Lawrence Summers as the director of the National Economic Council, two protégés of Robert Rubin (first director of the National Economic Council and then Treasury Secretary under the Clinton administration), are carrying on the banner of the free market.[37] Rubin took a prominent role in deregulating the market in regard to derivatives—tools of financial speculation whose values derive from the values of more common financial tools, like stocks, bonds, and the value of commodities. Key for maintaining hedge funds, derivatives are even further removed from the processes of production than are stocks and bonds.[38] Together with Alan Greenspan, who was chairman of the Federal Reserve Board at the time, and with Summers, Rubin opposed the regulation of derivatives, which was suggested by the Commodity Futures Trading Commission (CFTC) in 1997. Rubin's recommendation was that Congress should take the power of regulating derivatives out of the hands of the CFTC altogether.[39] Lawyers for the Treasury Department went even further, arguing that merely discussing new regulations would pose a threat to the derivatives market.[40] This argument exposes the faith-based mechanism undergirding the whole situation without acknowledgment: we cannot even afford to critique the market without turning it against us. The slightest insinuation of lack of faith in the free market would be a mistake—a mistake that would almost be as bad as the lack of faith that manifests itself in calling for economic regulations.

Regulations, of course, have been discussed again in the wake of the economic crash of 2008 and 2009, including firmer regulation for derivatives. But Geithner presented the case as if we were dealing mostly with a new problem that did not exist before, without acknowledging the systemic problem: "I believe that our regulatory system failed to adapt to the emergence of new risks," he commented in a written response.[41] It is not surprising that there was broad agreement among representatives from both major political parties that Geithner was the right candidate for the job, although he had to face some embarrassing questions about personal tax evasions at his hearings before the Senate. Republican Senator Charles Grassley noted that Geithner, who worked closely with the Bush administration on financial bailouts as head of the New York Federal Reserve Bank, was "possibly the only man for the job of healing the recession before us and a very fractured economy."[42]

Grassley's response is telling, not only because it shows rare bipartisan support, but because the emphasis clearly is on healing the economy rather than restructuring or changing it. It should also be noted that the economy responded positively to Geithner; with the growing hope that Geithner would be confirmed, the stock market went up on the morning of January 21, 2009. Whatever subsidies were being provided for economic recovery, the goal was to get the markets working again and, thus, to restore faith.[43]

Despite the fact that this sort of extreme deregulation was at the core of the worst economic crisis since the Great Depression—what collapsed in the housing bubble were precisely the derivatives linked to mortgage-backed securities—deregulation of the market appears to remain an ongoing commitment. Any and all regulations that are discussed in this situation, including the nationalization of banks and other failing ventures, are only seen as temporary measures that will be reversed when things are back on track. The faith in the market to solve most of our problems remains virtually unbroken. Few people represent this faith as clearly as Alan Greenspan himself, who from 1987 to 2006 chaired the Federal Reserve Board, linking the legacies of four presidents (Reagan, Bush senior, Clinton, and Bush junior). Enlightened self-interest of individuals was his credo, based on "a resolute faith that those participating in financial markets would act responsibly," betting "the health of the nation's economy to that faith," as one journalist put it.[44] It is interesting that Greenspan was considered to have oracle-like qualities which, according to some observers, made him almost god-like. It is, therefore, not surprising that he was virtually never questioned when he gave presentations to Congress and other lawmakers. Some of the decisions of Greenspan, based on his firm faith in the transactions of the market, are now under scrutiny. But that faith itself, although it belongs in the realm of unhealthy hopes and unfounded otherworldliness, is not being abandoned just yet.

In the midst of the recession, President Obama challenged Wall Street. Distributing $20 billion dollars in corporate bonuses in a faltering economy was "shameful," he stated. Bonuses were distributed even by corporations that had received bailout money from the government. Nevertheless, even this challenge does not yet amount to a challenge to the system, as Obama made it clear that "there will be time for them to make profit and there will be time for them to get bonuses."[45] While Obama is responding to public outrage over these matters, picking up a theme of his election campaign, he is leaving the door open for the future. We may have to tighten our belts for some time, the message seems to be, but the system itself is not in danger. Not even such moderate appeals, however, resonate with the financial world. "It is a complicated thing," the Wall Street response was summarized, "to apportion compensation in a bear market. First of all, profits do not stop; they often ebb. Second of all, losses move unequally, so the law of the jungle should still apply: you eat what you can kill." But can the financial windfall of government bailouts be considered profit? And whose losses are being discussed here? In the same report, a Wall Street lawyer is quoted as saying: "I think bonuses should be looked at on a case by case basis, or you turn into a socialist."[46] Socialism was generally the specter raised in response to Obama's comments, although socialism has nothing to do with any of this.

The political differentiations of the mainline—Democrat or Republican—matter little in this context. No alternatives seem to exist when it comes to the faith in the free market. Even the bailouts that were certainly not supposed to be necessary according to mainline economic theory, and which smack of the sort of government interference in economics that was frowned upon for three decades, were designed to prop up a market that failed precisely by following its deepest creeds; these bailouts were not designed to challenge the market and its creeds. While in Germany bailouts to banks were offered under the condition that CEO salaries would be restricted, initially no such conditions were leveraged in the United States. And while in Germany there was a discussion as to whether banks should be run and controlled by the government, this topic was broached only much later in the United States. Even the German discussion, however, was interspersed with professions of faith by detractors who stated that government would never be able to run banks as successfully as the private sector. Yet the irony of this faith in the private sector should not be hard to identify in a situation where the private sector had just run the banks into the ground. In the United States, there was also some talk about the nationalization of banks, supported from various sides.[47] But any such nationalization was only supposed to be temporary. After the government brought things back to "normal," the private sector would take over again. At that point, even the faith of the worst doubters would supposedly be restored.

For good reasons, David Sanger in the *New York Times* called nationalization "the most politically delicate question about the financial bailout."[48] Democrat Nancy Pelosi, the Speaker of the House had this to say: "If we are strengthening [the banks], then the American people would get some of the upside of that strengthening. Some people call that nationalization." Nevertheless, she also noted: "I'm not talking about total ownership," adding: "Would we have ever thought we would see the day when we'd be using that terminology? 'Nationalization of the banks?'"[49] Hybrid models of ownership have been suggested as an alternative. At present, the government is the biggest shareholder of Bank of America and Citigroup, owning 6 percent and 7.8 percent of these companies' stocks respectively. Geithner and Summers, the economic leaders of the Obama administration, went on record against nationalization during the Asian financial crisis in the 1990s, stating that "governments make lousy bank managers."[50] One of the problems with the government running the banks, Geithner and Summers argued, is that there will be increased pressure on the government to stop foreclosure or lend money to projects in need; apparently their assumption is that such a sense for the common good could not possibly be expected from private owners. Another model that was discussed briefly was to create a "bad bank," which would be owned by the government, and whose role would be to assume troubled investments. Sanger sums up what should be obvious: "But in that case, taxpayers might well be the losers: They would have all of the bank's worst assets and none of their performing loans."[51] Mainline economic efforts to socialize losses and to privatize gains continue full force in this model. The interesting thing to note about Sanger's statement is the use of the conditional "might": anyone concluding that taxpayers might not be the losers in this system must maintain strong hope and faith in the free-market system. But is it not exactly this hope and faith, which keep telling us that in the long run everybody will win, that has failed us?

Note also that temporary nationalization is not a form of, but the exact opposite of permanent nationalization: the role of the government in temporary nationalization would be to bail out the banks; to assume the responsibility for bad loans and other financial failures. When the banks are back up to speed, they will be in private hands again. This attitude indicates one of the key problems with faith in this case: it is not guided by evidence but by claims in a transcendent reality that is not required to prove itself, even in the face of evidence that it has failed us and that it will fail us again with great probability. It seems to be this faith, though, that is assumed to be necessary if we want to prosper. Moreover, this faith is not just required of business leaders, but of everyone. Those who are not part of the establishment, but who hope to gain from its exploits, are required to believe more firmly than anyone else.[52] Once again: those of us who know that our retirement accounts, our life savings, and, therefore, our future depend on the market feel we have no other choice. Just like the hope of an afterlife after death is often seen to depend on belief in certain religious doctrines, the hope of life after employment—whether permanently in retirement or temporarily through unemployment—seems to depend on belief in certain economic doctrines. Here is where this matter of faith hits home. In this situation, the logic of downturn not only makes us raise deep questions, but requires us to identify and develop alternatives.

"Idealism"

One more aspect of the relation of religion and economics needs to be explored at this point. When religious people talk about money, we usually talk about how faith should influence the use of money. Consequently, there are numerous resources on religion and economics that seek to develop the theological lessons for economics. The usual question asked is: What are the implications of faith for economics? The question that is rarely asked is how faith, itself, is influenced by the flow of money. What does money do to how we view the transcendent? What does money do to our images of God, even the ones that we consider to be classical and therefore "safe" because they originated before the advent of capitalism?[53] This question is crucial once we have understood that money is not just purchasing power but also social power[54]—a power that shapes everything. In other words, rather than simply reflecting reality and conforming to it, money increasingly creates its own reality. One example how this happens in the realm of the economy itself is the creation of a bubble, where the values of stocks, for instance, are less and less tied to actual performance.[55] Walter Benjamin has observed one aspect of this larger question, wondering how many connections money had to establish with myth before it was able to attract so many mythical elements from Christianity so that, in the end, it was able to construct its own myth.[56] We are not able to conduct such a study here, but it seems that capitalism has been quite successful in this matter. The other aspect of the question not addressed by Benjamin is how the capitalist myth is feeding back into Christianity so as to reshape its core images.

Religious communities usually do not give much thought to money as an actor. Theology is even worse when it comes to thinking about the agency of money; the question simply never shows up. Money is thought of as something to be acted upon, but not the other way around. Could a statement along these lines not also be made about economic theory—namely, that even in economic theory money is thought of as something to be acted upon and to be used, but not necessarily as an actor itself? My question here is whether money somehow influences how we think about God, and how we think about what is transcendent and of ultimate value. In order to address this question, we need to take a closer look at religious communities.

Religious communities often tend to assume that they have the answers to the questions of life—economics included—without wondering how they themselves might be part of the problems that underlie these questions. Nevertheless, the assumption that faith is independent from the world in such a way that its answers come straight out of nowhere is hard to maintain, especially when it comes to matters of money and economics. Even our most cherished beliefs are somehow shaped by what is happening around us, especially when what is happening goes so deep and is so all-pervasive as the broader understanding of economics that we are developing here. The image of Christ as Lord, for instance, is commonly shaped by the images of those who are in power at any given time. This does not mean that there are no alternative ways to understand this image—the powers that be are never able to take over completely, as I have shown elsewhere—but theologians need to learn to take into account the gravitational pull of the factors that most determine our lives in order to maintain these alternatives.[57] The problem is that these influences mostly work below the surface and, thus, are hardly noticed.

If religious people want to talk about how faith can impact their use of money, they first need to understand how the use of money impacts their faith. "The bottom line tends to drive us," was a comment that someone made at a United Methodist clergy meeting years ago. Many of us who were present nodded; no one objected. Somehow, most insiders intuitively know the truth of that statement. Most leaders of churches and other organizations understand that the flow of money impacts our operations. The practical consequences are fairly obvious. Deep down, we know that pastors are not free agents, especially in a situation where their local churches pay their salaries and where these churches need to raise certain amounts of money in order to keep their doors open. These insights are currently becoming clearer to those of us who work in academia as well. While our salaries may not be as directly dependent on the good will of donors as are those of pastors, private universities, in particular, still need to raise substantial amounts of money in order to keep their doors open and to thrive.

These practical consequences of the flow of money are not, however, the biggest problem. The bigger, and perhaps more interesting, problem has to do with the things that happen below the surface, in the theological unconscious, of which we are not aware and which we cannot see. What if money were to shape not only our actions and programmatic initiatives, but also our faith and our most cherished images of the divine, without anyone noticing? This is a difficult and painful question to address, especially for religious people who would prefer to see their faith as pristine and pure, but we need to deal with it. Failure to understand the divine jeopardizes everything: Why should Christians bother with church, for instance, if it fails to relate to the Christian God? In other words, a phenomenon like the Gospel of Prosperity, for example, is not only problematic because of its practical consequences for the lives of religious communities. It is problematic because it tends to construct an image of a god that radically differs from the image of the Christian God.

If we perceive the flow of money as a top-down phenomenon, trickling down from those who have most to those who have little, is it surprising that our most common images of God are top-down images? Or, if we understand the flow of money in terms of the image of the rising tide that lifts all boats, is it surprising that we perceive people at the economic top to be closer to God and that, when we care about less fortunate others, our idea is to "lift them up" so that they will move closer to the top? Along the same lines, the ancient confession that "Jesus is Lord" is now commonly interpreted as if Jesus were a successful business leader or a CEO. One book boldly proclaims this parallel in its title, but large numbers of Christians simply presuppose the linkage between Jesus and the powerful by default because they are not aware of any alternatives.[58] None of this matches, however, how the four Gospels of the New Testament envision Jesus. In one of his temptations, Jesus explicitly rejects a top-down approach to the world (Matt 4:8-10). In addition, Jesus constantly gets in trouble with those who consider themselves to be the "leaders." His work might be better understood in terms of what is now commonly called "servant leadership," due to his insistence on the greatest being the servants (Matt 23:11), but this term is now also used by the Wal-Mart Stores, Inc.[59] The real test for notions of servant leadership, whether in the church or in the world of business, is whether they maintain an awareness of Jesus' critique of power: his idea of servant leaders is not only about leading "from below" but also about challenging leadership "from above." In Jesus' theology, not only will the last be the first, the first also will be the last (Matt 20:16). Unless these issues are addressed, the flow of money will continue to determine our images of the divine by default.

Another example of how money shapes our images of God has to do with how Christians envision the work of God in the world. Once again, top-down images come to mind. The classical theist notion of omnipotence, which has no real match in the Bible if perceived as an absolute top-down category, has been revitalized by the top-down flow of money in the free-market economy. In addition, God's work is often envisioned in terms of a "fix-it" approach, not unlike the current actions of the government intended to bring the free market up to speed again. Such a fix-it approach does not challenge or transform the status quo—it simply restores it. The top-down activity of the divine is expressed perhaps most dramatically in bombing campaigns during war times: not only is the activity of throwing bombs out of airplanes that are worth many millions of dollars envisioned as clean and effective (we are supposed to believe in "surgical strikes," which do no harm to noncombatants), it can also be seen as approaching the classical idea of omnipotence, as few casualties among the aggressor's own forces are to be expected; the one who is envisioned as omnipotent in this way acts but is not acted upon. In addition, the airplanes that carry the bombs are so valuable economically that they are piloted by high-ranking officers, who are closer to the top than any other active combatants. These images of God at work from the top down are in stark contrast with images of the Judeo-Christian God, who elects a people enslaved by an ancient empire in Egypt; who accompanies them when they are later exiled by the Babylonian Empire; and who becomes human in Jesus Christ, whose life's work is in constant tension with the Roman Empire and its vassals, and with the religious establishment that lends supports to these powers.[60] Clearly, when the heirs of these ancient traditions confess the power of God today, there are very different ways of doing so.

In our investigation of what money does to the concept of God, we need to take into account that our images of God are not always fully explicit; the most influential images often tend to be the ones that are least visible. The problem that occurs when we fail to look for the deeper roots of these images is what I am calling *idealism* here. Idealism, in this context, has to do with a failure to examine the links of our mental images to material reality; and, thus, our tendency to take these images at face value, as if they had fallen straight from the sky. Idealism runs its course when it never occurs to us that even our most deeply held and cherished beliefs might be shaped by the flow of power, which in our world is synonymous with the flow of money. That material realities shape ideas is not the problem here; this happens all the time. The problem is that if these mechanisms are not recognized and taken into account, the status quo is affirmed by default and no room can be given to alternatives. Assmann and Hinkelammert are right in noting that behind the abstract notion of "the market" hides real society with all its complexity, and, we might add, the same is true for abstract notions of "the divine."[61]

We can now pick up the parallel between religion and economics once again, for there appears to be a parallel between this sort of theological idealism which is not aware of the deeper roots of its faith, and what might be called economic idealism, a notion that seems to be a contradiction in terms at first sight. A slightly different way of framing the issue might be to talk about a parallel between unhistorical theology and unhistorical economics. Like ideal or unhistorical images of God, ideal or unhistorical images of the market are problematic because they fail to attend to the real disparities in the flow of money in the current economy—which are, ultimately, disparities in the flow of power. Nevertheless, this economic idealism usually presents itself as "realistic" and even as "scientific"; a similar fallacy exists in theology, where the academic value of an approach to theology is often mistakenly thought to increase the more considerations of the actual context decrease.

Various alternative economic approaches have pointed out that such abstract reflections are illusory and that, as a result, the notion of the free market that is based on them is problematic. Economic institutionalism, a school of economics based on the work of Thorstein Veblen, notes, for instance, that the market is never a purely formal entity but rather is always already shaped by interests. In this perspective, power structures—related to the evolving distribution of wealth, property rights, and technology—are what ultimately shape the distribution of resources.[62] According to economic institutionalism, economic theory is neither universal nor can it be studied in an ahistorical fashion. In a changing world, there is nothing that can be presupposed as absolutely given or natural—not the free market, and not even property rights (an issue to which we will return in the final chapter). In addition, institutionalism understands that the most important relationships in society are relationships of power, and power in this perspective has to do with the myths which enable one group to dominate another.[63] One of these myths is the idea of individualism, which we have already discussed. Racism is another one of these powerful myths that are constructed to maintain the status quo. The result is a vicious circle: while the myth keeps people down, their low standard of living is used as further evidence in support of the myth itself.[64]

Another such myth is the idea of the invisible hand of the market that creates equilibrium, with the result that differentials of power are overlooked. Assuming an invisible hand of the market that is unaffected by anything and cannot be swayed is like assuming an idea of God that is unaffected by anything, which happens to be another feature of classical theism. Yet just like our images of God are shaped by interests and differentials of power, so are our images of the invisible hand of the market shaped by interests and differentials of power. Building hope on either the market or God as abstractions without examining the deeper roots, results in building hope on the mostly invisible powers that shape these terms. This has disastrous consequences for both economics and theology. No wonder that neither an abstract notion of the market nor an abstract notion of God is of much help in a situation of persistent downturn. After all, it is the logic of downturn that reminds us that neither one of these images has really delivered what was promised: unlimited success, a rising tide, or at least some form of trickle down.

In this context, we need to explore alternatives. Since the sort of idealism described here is ahistorical, historical thinking provides an important first step. The old insight applies here: when a conceptual problem cannot be solved on its own terms, it helps to historicize it. As early as the late-nineteenth century, for instance, the limits of the free-market economy were understood by some German economists of the Historical school of economics when they began to analyze the bigger picture. When viewed in light of the historical context, it became clear that free trade was advantageous for the British because their industries were more developed than others and because their interests were protected by the British fleet. For the Germans, on the other hand, free trade was disadvantageous because their industries were less developed than the British ones.[65] Yet reflection on the historical context, as such, is not enough. The historical context needs to be analyzed in terms of power, best seen from the underside. In our example, the Germans were able to see what the British could not see precisely because they viewed history from the underside. Even if the British had looked at things from a perspective that considered the historical context, they would most likely still have ended up with a firm conviction in the benefits of the free market. Only a historical analysis from the underside reveals the sorts of tensions that are lost to the mostly top-down idealist point of view. This is not unlike the development of the Judeo-Christian traditions: while the Egyptian pharaoh at the time of Moses must have been convinced that the divine was on his side, the slaves perceived the divine differently. The God who spoke to Moses is tied to a particular history that is often overlooked in favor of his cryptic claim, "I am who I am" (Exod 3:14); this history is that of "the God of Abraham, the God of Isaac, and the God of Jacob" (Exod 3:15), whose history is one of perseverance in the face of hardship and of resistance to the powers that be. Here, another kind of hope emerges that is diametrically opposed to the unhealthy utopian hope we encountered earlier. This hope might be termed "dangerous hope," because it is historical hope and because it presents a real alternative to the status quo. Those who are afraid of this dangerous historical hope tend to eclipse history in favor of universal statements. No wonder that when standard history is recorded, it usually glances over these dangerous perspectives from below.

The powerful myths of individualism and racism can be deconstructed along the same lines as the myths of an abstract divinity or of an abstract market are deconstructed. Viewed from the logic of downturn, there are no self-made individuals, and there can be no easy equilibrium between individuals because of grave differentials of wealth and power. Furthermore, none of these differentials are natural, in the sense that they have always existed,[66] or universal, in the sense that they will always exist. Big landownership, for instance, is not a natural form of existence; rather, it developed because some individuals were able to expropriate what used to belong to others and to take advantage of them. This is an issue whose early history can be already be observed by the times of the Old Testament and against which the prophets in the eighth century BCE and many others protested.[67] Racism, too, can be deconstructed when viewed historically. Racial differences between humans have no biological basis; nor are they natural, in the sense that races would have always existed in the way they are viewed today; nor are they universal, in the sense that they will always exist. Racism is a perspective that developed historically at various times when it was convenient to classify human beings according to race. The pernicious racism of European and North American chattel slavery, for instance, is a powerful product of history and has little precedent in earlier views of race; its efforts at biological explanation of racial differences have no scientific merit.

We can now see the deeper problem with the sort of idealism and ahistoricism that we have described: these positions are useful because they cover up real differentials of wealth and power and justify them implicitly. In the words of economist Michael Zweig: "The ahistoricism and individualism of mainstream economics . . . has a class stand."[68] Individualism is, thus, not just a myth; it is the myth of the ruling class, as it covers up the relations of power that benefit some and not others, and is thus quite effective and powerful. The same is true for the powerful myth of racism: it is a myth that plays into the hands of the ruling class, as it covers up the relations between people who otherwise have a lot in common—like white and black field hands, white and black workers, and so on. The lack of historical perspective points in the same direction: it supports the powers that be. Yet even if history is done in universal fashion, the problem is not resolved. Universalism has its own history, which is related to the rise of the modern ruling class; its purpose is yet another cover-up of who benefits from the status quo and who does not. From a historical perspective that embraces alternative perspectives and perspectives from below, it becomes clear that the universal perspective does not exist; to wit, not even the individualism of the status quo—one of the pillars of free-market economics—can be seen as a universal phenomenon: Adam Smith assumed a different sort of individualism than we take for granted today, since his thoughts on self-interest still presupposed the cohesiveness of a social community.[69]

In the end, the invisible hand of the market becomes a hand that is quite visible; idealism is a mask that cannot be sustained long-term. In the words of Beverly Harrison: "United States economic history must be read not only as a story of the acceleration of concentrations of wealth and power but as a story of the increasing mobilization of the state in the service of existing economic power."[70] At the time when this comment was made, Harrison was not yet aware of the historic bailouts of 2008 and later, but the particular ways in which the government acted in this context might illustrate her point. Even the Bush administration, which seemingly rejected government interference in the market, decided to step in as a *deus ex machina* and provided a sizeable $700 billion bailout, which was designed particularly for the financial institutions. The auto industry, on the other hand, which employs many thousands of people, had a much harder time being considered by this "visible hand of the market."

Some theologians and economists have begun to push beyond these idealisms and abstractions. Since we will give more consideration to theologians in the next two chapters, let me give some examples of economists here, all of whom are fairly mainline. Even the standard textbook of economics by Paul Samuelson and William Nordhaus notes a bias in the history of economics: "The rising business classes needed a spokesperson for their interests. Smith provided them with the laissez-faire ideology that served their purposes, offering intellectual support for free enterprise with minimal government interference."[71] This observation points to one of the key insights missing in what I have called *idealism*: the reflection on power. Only when the underlying power structures are made visible can they be examined and can alternatives be devised. Yet insights such as the one put forth by Samuelson and Nordhaus need to be explored further from the perspective of those who are exposed to the pressures of the system. One example might be the perspectives of women.

Economist Frances Woolley notes two problems of bias in economics when it comes to matters of gender: "The first, the use of mistaken stylized facts, is easier to combat than the second, the invisibility of women. Invisibility is more pervasive, more persistent, and harder to fight."[72] The factual information on this topic, arguing that women earn less than men for the same jobs, is not controversial and is published in mainstream economic journals.[73] The deeper challenge to neoclassical economics, according to Woolley, is that there seems to be no rational foundation to this inequality; that people, therefore, do not act rationally, and that the outcome of the market can, therefore, be other than equilibrium.[74] At this point, the problem of bias in economics should be clearer, without having even touched yet on the problem of the invisibility of women.

Perhaps the most important service of feminist perspectives in economics is to point out a "masculinist bias" in neoclassical economics, which sees itself as neutral. This bias is not hard to spot and helps to create awareness of the problem of bias in other areas as well. On these grounds, feminist economists question such neoclassical ideas as the "separative self," the ubiquity of self-interest, and the primacy of competition over cooperation.[75] Proposing alternatives, they define economics "in terms of real-world issues of concern to women, men, and children, rather than as merely the examination of choice under the conditions of scarcity."[76] Once the idealist assumptions of economic theory are called into question, a tremendous opportunity for fresh research opens up in all areas.

In this context, we need to talk about ecological factors as well. The neglect of what the economy does to the environment is another instance of idealism and ahistoricism in economics. Yet only a clearer view of ecology from the logic of downturn will help us here, as ecology can easily lead to another idealism, wherein the systemic issues that threaten the environment are covered up in favor of romantic visions of "harmony with nature."[77] The Worldwatch Institute Report of 2009, with the ominous subtitle, "*Into a Warming World,*" would be a good place to start this discussion, into which we cannot enter here.[78]

What Is Ultimate? Who Is God?

While fundamental images of the divine and of ultimate reality are at work both in theology and in economics, the basic problem at the intersection of theology and economics is not that both espouse hopes and faith and that both presuppose images of God and of ultimate reality. The basic problem—even more pressing than usual in the midst of economic crises—has to do with the question of how those hopes and faith-claims mesh with the reality of what is going on and whether they truly support life. Whatever is declared to be ultimate and divine makes a tremendous difference, and so the god of the market has substantial influence, no matter whether this god "really exists" or not. In the Judeo-Christian traditions, this matter can be discussed in terms of idolatry. While false gods are "not real," their worship cannot be simply shrugged off as inconsequential. Idolatry creates problems because it has powerful effects on human life and negatively influences the well-being of people.

In economics, the question of what is ultimate is only gradually rising to the level of awareness and will need to be developed much further. A good start might be the insight of Samuelson and Nordhaus, who report on Adam Smith's confidence in the invisible hand, which creates balanced markets, but then also note the "realistic limitations of this doctrine." "We know," Samuelson and Nordhaus write, "that the market sometimes lets us down, that there are 'market failures,' and that markets do not always lead to the most efficient outcome." The major failure that concerns them, however, is merely "imperfect competition."[79] Without this problem, it seems, the market would be fine. The first question that we need to ask here, by contrast, is, what is creating imbalances in the market? Is the problem labor unions, for instance, or is it monopolies? Another question would be whether the problem of market failures is more fundamental, having to do with unequal distribution of ownership and control of the means of production, and, thus, with another divinely sanctioned system. It is quite telling that Samuelson and Nordhaus's list of market failures—although they consider "unacceptable inequalities of income and wealth," among other things—addresses neither labor unions nor ownership or control of the means of production. We will come back to this latter issue in the final chapter.[80]

John Kenneth Galbraith adds another important insight to this debate about what is ultimate when he reminds us that the question of capital and power was neglected in economics for a long time because it was assumed that no one had a great deal of power. No ultimate power was assumed, as economic textbooks envisioned a world of small companies. In this context, it appeared that prices, wages, and profits were all set by the market. Only Karl Marx differed from this assessment, Galbraith notes, when he pointed out the power of those who command capital and that their collective interest would influence prices, wages, and profit ranges. There is, without a doubt, something to that insight, as those who command capital are much more influential than is commonly recognized, being able to shape not only the economy but also society, morality, and even the world of government and politics. Even many of the news media that have long touted their independence are now firmly in the hands of corporations and media moguls like Rupert Murdoch. Galbraith references the work of Carl Kaysen, who pointed out that the market power of "the giant corporation is the basis not only of economic power but also of considerable political and social power."[81] It seems as if there is another ultimate reality—manifest in large corporations and those who control them—that secretly shapes the reality of the market, which many economists consider ultimate.

What is the problem here? Myopia has been suggested as a problem of modern economics by self-described theists Herman Daly (an economist) and John Cobb (a theologian). Their project is based on the vision of a community in which all aspects of reality are related in an emerging "biospheric consciousness." The main problem with dominant economic paradigms, according to Daly and Cobb, is a myopia that leads to the destruction of communities and the separation of humans and the natural world. The lack of values that promote community and nature has led to the destruction of community and nature. Anthropological dualism and philosophical idealism are seen as main culprits in this state of affairs. Once this myopia is cleared up and a biospheric consciousness is adopted, Cobb and Daly argue, the principles of the free market can be put to more constructive use. In this approach, faith in God—a theocentric perspective—liberates us from the misdirected anthropocentrism of Western culture and economics. Faith in God also helps to interrelate concerns for the value of individual beings and for the holistic interrelation of all beings since both exist only in relation to God, Cobb and Daly conclude.[82]

But more seems to be at stake than just myopia. What if we were dealing not with shortsightedness but with a case of severely distorted vision? What if the problem with the images of the ultimate and of God were not that they are too narrow, in which case the problem could be solved by expanding them, but that they are headed in the wrong direction and are, thus, missing the reality of God altogether, promoting an anti-god that is shaped by the interests of capital? In this situation, faith in God is the problem rather than the solution. This brings us back to the problem of idolatry, an issue that has been explored by Latin American thinkers like Franz Hinkelammert, Hugo Assmann, and Jung Mo Sung. The problem with idolatry, as they point out, can be found in the pernicious nature of idols, as false gods demand sacrifices. The problem, thus, appears in sharp relief as a matter of life and death.[83] In this case, the problem cannot be solved by suggesting a freshened-up theism, or a broader image of God. In this case, the problem is one of rival "theisms," rival images of God, and rival understandings of the ultimate—and a decision needs to be made. The World Alliance of Reformed Churches has recognized this problem and has therefore called for a *processus*

confessionis, a process of confession, in regard to the issues of economic injustice and ecological destruction. This elevates the matter to the level of a
challenge to the basic faith commitments of the church; in the Reformed
traditions, it is the confession of faith with which the church stands or falls.[84]
The problem that needs to be addressed here is twofold: in exposing the false
gods, whose work is death, the reality of the true God will become clearer
and the questions of what is ultimate and who God is can finally be addressed
openly and decisively. We will come back to this in chapter 5.

For now, we need to admit that much of what has been declared ultimate and divine has failed large parts of humanity. Continuing to trust in
what failed us amounts to nothing more than trust in an idealistic, otherworldly, and unhealthy utopian hope that has so often had disastrous consequences in the past. Just as the classic supply-and-demand economics was
not able to anticipate the Great Depression, the economics of the ever-more-
deregulated free market was not able to anticipate the next big crash which
began to be felt in 2008. The argument in those days was based on trust in
something ultimate, arguing that if each person were free to pursue his or
her own interests within the market, some local imbalances might result, but
no overarching depression would materialize.[85] We have just passed a similar threshold in our own history, once again accompanied by the belief that
a crash of the market was impossible. Something is not working, with the
result that large parts of humanity get hurt, often beyond repair.

The question of God and the free-market economy raises important
questions that we will pursue further in the following chapters. Pastor Rick
Warren's prayer at the inauguration of President Obama touched on some
interesting issues in this regard.[86] But while Warren assumed that these topics were settled, we need to pose them as questions: Warren talked about
history as God's story, but which story is referenced here? The story of those
for whom the tide is high and keeps rising, or the story of those for whom
there is no rising tide? Warren also thanked God for "our prosperity." The
real question, of course, is whose prosperity is meant here, and which god
produced it. Only if we face the fact that prosperity has bypassed many, and
that this may not be God's will, can we develop alternatives.

Consuming Desire vs. Resisting Desire

4

That to Which Your Heart Clings

The notion of hope is not sufficient to grasp what it is that keeps us going when things do not go as anticipated. The notion of desire introduces another layer of reflection.[1] It takes up the question of hope and deepens it by investigating more closely the unconscious layers of reality that include repressions and hidden motivations. What is it that truly sustains us and keeps us going when everything else fails and when even our images of hope are challenged? Desire, in this context, refers to more than individual motivation. There is a collective quality of desire in free-market economies that needs to be examined as well. Both economic theory and theological reflection presuppose this collective quality of desire. Furthermore, the formation of desire in the free-market economy is tied closely to material objects, as the ultimate value of such objects is no longer based on their inherent nature or on their use value. This desire for material objects, however, goes deeper than the attachment of people to material things—a problem that is often overlooked in the common critiques of desire for material things found especially in religious circles. The desire for material objects ultimately points to the curious phenomenon that under the conditions of capitalism the relations between material things unconsciously shape the relations between human beings and, thus, human subjectivity at its deepest levels, including religion. The classic notion of commodity fetishism developed by Karl Marx—when related to Sigmund Freud's notion of the fetish as surrogate object of desire—might help to investigate this aspect of desire further.[2] This observation about the central role of material objects in the formation of desire is affirmed, from the other end of the spectrum, by economist Friedrich von Hayek, who noted that a progressive society "increases the desire of all in proportion as it increases its gifts to some."[3]

Lamentably, there is a lack of sustained reflection on desire both in theology and economics that is particularly problematic at a time when the economy has acquired the tools and the power to shape and reshape even our deepest desires. Desire is assumed to be a given in the textbook definition of economics—the allocation of scarce resources to infinite human desire—and neoclassical economics is typically not interested in examining its roots. Likewise, theologians often assume that desire is a general human category.[4] In this context, we need to take a closer look at how desires are at work and at possible alternatives.

The religious component of the notion of desire goes deep. Consider Martin Luther's response to the question, "What does it mean to have 'a god,' or what is 'god'?" God is, according to Luther, "that to which your heart clings and entrusts itself."[5] Luther realized that God is captured not merely by explicit images of the divine but also—and perhaps more importantly—by largely unconscious desires. In the realm of economics, it is the advertising industry in particular that is acutely aware of the importance of desire. The main concern for advertisers (in contradistinction to the self-understanding of most contemporary theologians and pastors) is not so much to communicate information—most people have a sense of the biased nature of advertising anyway—but to shape desire at a deeper, unconscious level that is more difficult to control. Unfortunately, the production of desire is mostly overlooked by many well-meaning critics of economics, especially by the ones who see consumerism as one of the key problems. What is overlooked here is the fact that while the desire to consume can seem to be almost universal, this desire is not natural but is produced to a large extent by economic mechanisms and reinforced by the advertising industry. It is those mechanisms that we will have to examine further. In this context, we also need to find out whether there are parallels between economic and religious desire, and what the alternatives are. Does the production of economic desire somehow shape our desire for the divine as well? And might our desire for the divine help transform economic desire? Unlike mainline theologians and economists, the Jesus of the Gospels appears to be aware that desire can be shaped by the production of wealth at the deepest levels and that this can interfere with our deepest convictions and ultimate values: "where your treasure is, there your heart will be also" (Matt 6:21). The problem of economics is, therefore, a genuinely theological problem.

If it is correct that who God is for us is not decided merely at the level of explicit confessions and statements but at the deeper level of desire, we need to add another layer of reflection. Some of the insights of psychoanalysis might help us here, insofar as they direct our attention to the unconscious, the level of reality which is often neglected both in mainline theology and mainline economics. While psychoanalysis reminds us that unconscious desires constitute a large part of who we are, this issue is often not only overlooked but methodologically excluded in both theology and economics. Economist Friedrich von Hayek for instance, one of the original architects of the current free-market logic, claimed that the task of explaining the source of people's actions was a matter for psychology but not for economics. Von Hayek's Austrian school of economics and the bulk of neoclassical economists agree that *de gustibus non est diputandum,* that is, that taste cannot and does not need to be discussed and disputed in economics.[6] Nevertheless, even von Hayek cannot disregard the matter completely. In a free-market society, he argues as we saw earlier, the desire of all grows in proportion to the growing wealth of some.[7] While he might consider desire to be natural and not to be disputed, he admits that the desire that is produced at the top levels of the free-market society takes on a special role in the formation of the desire of others.

Psychoanalysis has taught us that we are ultimately driven by our desires and that these desires cannot easily be controlled. Desires cannot be controlled, for instance, simply through mental processes or by thinking different thoughts. This is why the sort of ethical instruction and admonition that is so often found in religious communities is not very effective for the most part—it appeals to the mind and contributes little to the reshaping of desire at a deeper level. Of course, religious people and their spiritual advisors would be quick to admit that it is important that we direct our desires to God. But how can we do this is when we are bombarded by so many other influences, which seek to shape us unconsciously? In a situation where the success of the economy depends on the production of the desire to consume more and more, we have less and less control over our desires, and it would be illusory to think that we can intentionally direct them. Note that no one is exempt here: all of us are subject to the formation of desire by forces that are becoming more and more aggressive, due to an economic phenomenon called the "falling rate of profit." As profits keep falling in long downwards spirals,[8] the struggle for influence over people's desire must necessarily become more and more pervasive.

The question of desire goes very deep. It can no longer be addressed by assuming the sort of fairly straightforward choice of the object of desire, as Luther might have had in mind at a time when desire had not yet become such a battleground. Neither can desire be addressed by assuming spaces that are free from the struggle for desire; not even the church can provide such a safe space. This is not to deny that the church has an important role to play in the struggle for the influence over desire and that the Christian tradition may provide some viable alternatives, but we need to take a deeper look at how these alternatives emerge in the midst of churches and religious traditions that are themselves co-opted by the status quo.[9] In this context, the logic of downturn will both help us identify the places where desire has been co-opted and aid in the search for alternatives.

This common lack of awareness of how deep desire goes can also be seen in economics. Not only is desire taken for granted in neoclassical economics—"want" seems to be a natural human trait—the assumption is that markets work best when left to individual desires and, by extension, that when people follow their individual desires democracy is achieved. The tremendous naïveté behind these assumptions is perhaps best expressed in this statement from a team of Christian economists: "When business ventures succeed, consumers are signaling that they really like the ways in which entrepreneurs are using society's resources."[10] Desire is presupposed here not only as natural and unproblematic, but as that which deserves (without question) to shape the course of economics and, by extension, of life as a whole. The classic handbook on economics by Paul Samuelson and William Nordhaus points in the same direction when it addresses the question of power in a market economy: "The economy is ultimately ruled by two monarchs: consumers and technology. Consumers direct by their innate or learned tastes, as expressed in their dollar votes, the ultimate uses to which society's resources are channeled." While Samuelson and Nordhaus leave some room for "learned tastes," that is, desire that is not natural, this issue does not factor much into the equation, in which markets simply "reconcile the consumer's tastes with technology's limitations."[11] It is not hard to see what is missing here: a consideration of the power that is lodged in the production of consumer desires through advertising and other means, and the power that drives the production of desires in the first place, namely the production of products, including ideas and services. Only when this latter issue is discussed do we get closer to the bottom of this matter, and in this context we need to take another look at the role of workers broadly conceived—including both blue and white collar—which is not taken into account in any of these mainline formulas, the theological ones included.

If desire and the production of desire are thus taken seriously, we begin to realize that even the field of economics may have a god to which it clings and on which it depends (Luther). Here, the logic of downturn might help us to see more clearly: What is it that keeps us going when all else fails? It is curious that in situations of downturn CEOs and other executives get relatively little blame—any blame they might receive pales in comparison to the praise they receive in times of boom. While the decisions of CEOs may be scrutinized somewhat more than usual, it is rare that anyone calls for collective resignations: the leadership cannot be blamed for downturn, it seems. This means that the logic of the market is rooted at a deeper level than that of the leadership of CEOs. This deeper level has to do with desires—there is an assumption that the desire of consumers does not abruptly come to an end even in times of downturn and that it will eventually propel things forward again so that no dramatic restructuring or reorientation of economic principles is necessary. Reliance on desire thus creates some stability even in times of turmoil.

The free-market economy is, thus, safely rooted in the unconscious of our desires. This insight parallels an insight by Walter Benjamin, who reads psychoanalysis in terms of religion and capitalism rather than in terms of individual psychology, which is the challenge that is before us: "That which has been repressed . . . is in deepest analogy capital (still to be examined), which pays interest to the hell of the unconscious."[12] This can be demonstrated in terms of the logic of downturn. If the free market is rooted, consciously or unconsciously, in some deeper or ultimate reality, then the effects of actions and decisions taken by the leaders of the economy are relativized; they are not the ones who are ultimately responsible for what is going on in times of downturn (although, for some odd reason, they are the ones who reap the benefits when things are going well). Accordingly, we cannot hold them accountable for disappointing results, any more than we can hold priests responsible for acts of God such as earthquakes or tsunamis. This might help us understand the otherwise very strange fact that in cases of economic failure no one is really blamed—a fact that turned out to be true for the most part even in the disastrous downturn of 2008 and 2009. Not only are the leaders of the economy not held accountable for failure, they are rewarded for not giving up hope and for reassuring us of the deeper foundations of the market. Their usual message, repeated over and over again in slightly different words, is that the market has never been in a slump for very long periods of time and that progress is inevitable. The market becomes, thus, part of ultimate reality.

Is Consumerism Really the Problem?

When religious people discuss economic matters, one of the problems that is identified immediately is consumerism. People are too consumeristic, the charge goes. They identify their value by what they buy and how much they can buy, or so it is assumed. The related charge is materialism. People supposedly care about material things more than about spiritual things.

These charges overlook at least two basic problems and share one major blind spot. Even in a so-called consumer society, the will to consume more and more cannot necessarily be taken for granted. This may come as a surprise to many because it is commonly assumed that people always want more. Yet we shall see that the will to consume more needs to be produced, nurtured, and constantly revitalized if the economy is to grow. Those who run the advertising agencies know this best; the will to consume and the desire that drives it cannot be taken for granted, and this is what keeps them in business. Second, this so-called materialism is really a misnomer because it is not ultimately about material things. The things that we buy promise us much more: advertising thus directs us not towards materialism but towards ultimate things. We are promised that buying things results in happiness and fulfillment. The major blind spot that will need to be addressed in this connection—a blind spot perpetuated both by mainline economists and theologians—has to do with the role of production. There is no consumption without production. In order to deal with this issue, the logic of downturn will be once again helpful.

Economist John Kenneth Galbraith was one of the pioneers who contributed some initial clarification. In many ways, Galbraith's arguments are at least as relevant today as when they were first put forth over forty years ago. Unfortunately, they are still too often neglected. One of his most important insights was that consumers are not free agents. This leads to a crucial insight at the heart of this chapter: if consumers are not free agents, it may not make much sense to blame them for consumerism. Likewise, if consumers do not have exclusive control over their desires, it may not make much sense to blame them exclusively for distorted desires either. Both *consumerism* and *desires* are related to production. In his book, *The Affluent Society*, Galbraith notes the importance of production in mainline economics: "The interest of the economist is unique. The importance of production is central to his scheme of economic calculation. All existing pedagogy and nearly all research depend on it. Any action which increases production from given resources is good and implicitly important; anything which inhibits or reduces output is, *pro tanto*, wrong."[13] The weakness of this theory, as Galbraith notes, is the question of consumer demand, which is simply presupposed here as given and natural. In Galbraith's words: "The theory of consumer demand, as is now widely accepted, is based on two broad propositions, neither of them quite explicit but both extremely important for the present value system of economists. The first is that the urgency of wants does not diminish appreciably as more of them are satisfied." In other words, there is no concept of satiation in mainline economics, and so it appears as if production can continue without limits. "The second proposition," Galbraith continues, "is that wants originate in the personality of the consumer or, in any case, that they are given data for the economist. The latter's task is merely to seek their satisfaction. He has no need to inquire how these wants are formed."[14] This mistaken account of desire, we are beginning to realize, is at the core of all other problems.

The problem with these assumptions of mainline economics is that they misrepresent what is really going on. We are beginning to suspect that wants are not natural and that they are not sustained naturally. Galbraith, making the odd assumption that this should be common sense, notes a "diminishing urgency of ... wants," and a "diminishing urgency of consumption."[15] This fact is covered up in economic theory, he argues, because there is no distinction between important and unimportant goods. "This position ignores the obvious fact that some things are acquired before others and that, presumably, the more important things come first." Galbraith takes this observation to mean that there is not only a diminishing urgency of wants but also a "declining urgency of need."[16] It is, therefore, not universally true that people always want or even need more.

In all this, the role of production is central: "One cannot defend production as satisfying wants if that production creates the wants," Galbraith continues. And further: "Production only fills a void that it has itself created."[17] What drives consumption, therefore, is not primarily consumerism but the economic imperative of the production of goods, ideas, and services. Yet this engine is usually hidden from view, especially when consumerism is lamented as the problem. Galbraith points out the connection between production and consumption in no uncertain terms: "The even more direct link between production and wants is provided by the institutions of modern advertising and salesmanship. These cannot be reconciled with the notion of independently determined desires, for their central function is to create desires—to bring into being wants that previously did not exist." Galbraith concludes that "a broad empirical relationship exists between what is spent on production of consumer goods and what is spent in synthesizing the desires for that production." And, giving us a useful rule of thumb, Galbraith states: "Wants are dependent on production."[18]

As we begin to understand the link between production and consumption, consumerism and the problem of wants is no longer seen as a problem of individual ethics and cannot be solved, therefore, by moral appeals to individuals. To put it bluntly, too many critics of consumerism, theologians included, appear to be barking up the wrong tree. Economists William Dugger and Howard Sherman draw an interesting conclusion: "Galbraith made the simple point that consumers are not born with preferences for television sets. One must explain the emergence of these preferences from the rest of social relations. So ideas are not a final prime mover."[19] This is the key insight that we will need to develop further: the heart of the struggle is not located in the realm of independent ideas; neither is it located in the realm of individual desires that are freely movable in space. The heart of the struggle is located in ideas and desires that are produced socially and economically.

In Galbraith's assessment, it is economists who are not clear about the issues involved here, but we might add theologians to this list. Businesspeople and nonspecialist readers, on the other hand, will not be surprised by these arguments, he notes.[20] This is correct, of course, insofar as businesspeople in particular are aware of the importance of advertising, but it is not clear that they understand the link to production. While businesspeople are concerned about creating sufficient wants for their goods, it does not follow that they have any greater awareness of the created nature of desire and how it relates to production than economists.

In the production of wants and desire, the advertising industry has an important role to play. Advertisers know intuitively that their work is not primarily about putting out factual information about the nature of products, their cost, and where to buy them. Their role has to do with the shaping of desire and is, therefore, much more fundamental. For good reasons advertisers have been considered to be members of a "new high priesthood," the influence of which is crucial for setting the agenda in business and media—an influence that ultimately also extends to politics and religion. Paul Glasser, author of *The New High Priesthood,* expresses what mainline economists and theologians tend to miss. Glasser prefers to talk about desires rather than demands because "demand is not a settled economic fact of life, like a river, but is the resultant of latent desires, dreams, and aspirations that may be fostered or not. Marketing does not sell a product—it sells a dream, a dream of beauty, of health, of success, of power."[21] The role of advertising is to produce the desires that produce economic demand, and the high priests of advertising "use their key positions and means of persuasion to mould the natures and aspirations of their peoples."[22]

The desire promoted by advertising is not the simple desire for the product; desire is for something more transcendent, like a dream or the hope for happiness and a better life. Desire is, therefore, not aimed at a pearl necklace in and of itself, for instance, but at the related hope for greater self-confidence and even love. John Hood, building on Glasser's work, affirms this noble claim, pointing out that advertisement is what makes life meaningful: "The more advertising seeks to connect the brand names of tangible products to the intangible, the aesthetic, the social, and the individual, the more it accomplishes its underappreciated role of helping us infuse meaning and aspiration into what would otherwise be little more than the rote acquisition of basic necessities and the pointless accumulation of objects."[23] The task of advertising is, thus, to produce desire and to connect it with the transcendent—a truly religious task that points us to the deeper roots of consumerism.

At the same time, advertisers realize that their work has come under widespread criticism. While the advertising business is huge and advertisers need to advertise advertising, there are also sustained efforts to even play things down a bit in order to avoid challenges. Hood seeks to clear up what he calls "longstanding myths and misunderstandings." Seeking to defend the advertising industry, he claims that "ads are tools for enhancing competition and innovation, not propping up stodgy monopolies."[24] But what drives the industry? Is it really just the search for innovation and competition? Advertisers may have a hard time answering this question, since even the world of advertising does not yet reach to the bottom of the mechanisms that shape desire. Advertising itself is a symptom of broader shifts, piggybacking not only on cultural and religious dynamics but, more importantly, on the world of production. Hood also wants to deflect another critique, answering in the negative the question of whether advertising makes us "materialistic and take[s] away our freedom and choice."[25] Such an assessment would be way too simplistic, he claims, because the formation of personal values and preferences is complex and takes a long time. Advertising can, thus, at best only be one factor among many. With this argument he seeks to refute "the likes of John Kenneth Galbraith" and Galbraith's notion of "artificially created wants."[26] What this argument fails to take into account, however, is that a lot more is at stake here than the formation of personal values and preferences, since a whole economy rests on the back of the creation of new desire in large groups of people in order to keep demand for products flowing. Surely, Hood is too humble about the role of advertising.

The connection of advertising, consumption, and production has been identified by others who study advertising. In his book, *Consumerism in World History*, Peter Stearns points out that from the 1850s onward "the apparatus of consumerism changed, as shops and wordy advertisements were increasingly replaced by new retail outlets and a still-more manipulative advertising style."[27] Wondering why consumerism escalated so dramatically in this period, Stearns notes that "a key factor involved changes in methods of production and distribution. European and American manufacturers were now capable of expanding their output to the point that selling it became an increasing problem." Furthermore, he points out that "the range of goods themselves expanded . . . which could help explain new levels of desire."[28] The changes at the material levels of production and distribution brought about the production of new desires. A somewhat exotic example was the emergence of kleptomania as department stores began displaying goods and, in this way, facilitating desire. This relation of consumerism, desire, and production is absolutely crucial, and we need to return to this topic later; too often, the role of production is overlooked in these discussions and, with it, the role of labor.

Desire was also produced, the historian of advertisement tells us, by efforts of workers and middle-class people to make their lives more bearable. If the work could not be changed, the money made as a result could be used to make life a little more pleasant. In this context, consumerism provides both satisfaction and meaning.[29] This is another example for why consumerism is not primarily about acquiring material things. In addition, "Consumerism gives many people a sense of global belonging," Stearns states; "it also often stands for freedom and individual choice."[30] The religious undertones are hard to miss here: if a sense of belonging, of freedom, of satisfaction, of meaning, and of the fulfillment of dreams and hopes is supplied both by religious and by consumerist desires, we have to pay close attention to how these desires are related and distinct. Keep in mind that the engine that generates desire is not to be found in the ideal realm: the engine is tied to production, and so we will have to take a closer look at production as well.

It is hard to see how religion would be able to maintain pristine independence in this climate. While a rudimentary awareness of the relation of money and desire goes back as far as Aristotle,[31] we are dealing with a new intensity of this relation which is increasingly geared toward reshaping our innermost desires and reaching the deepest levels of our humanity that we cannot control at will. We are bombarded with thousands of images each day, all designed to shape our desires and to make us more perfect participants in the economic marketplace. With every breath we take, we are integrated into the market—be it through the workplace, the way we relax, the way we shop, the way we save money, the way we plan for our retirement, or the way we address social need; this list does not even mention the influence of media and entertainment. During most of our waking hours we are, therefore, more or less directly hooked up with the market economy.

Theologian and ardent supporter of mainline economics, Michael Novak has taken on earlier comments that I made to this effect: "It must be said that Rieger's description of Americans cringing under a deluge of seductive images (presumably from television) seems preposterous. Neither advertising gurus nor retailers feel anything like the omnipotence with which Rieger endows them: they sometimes experience abject failure and most of the time barely enough success to keep going on. A great many highly touted products, like the Edsel, just died. True, some products are so good that they are smashing successes, but rarely is it the advertising alone that brought them their good fortune."[32] After reading Novak's rebuttal, one might feel sorry for the advertising industry. He is right, of course, that advertisers are not omnipotent, but that is hardly the point. The problem lies deeper, with the fact that advertisers have access to a substantial array of tools designed to shape desire. Images on television are only the very tip of a growing iceberg since, in order to remain effective, advertising is constantly reinventing itself. As the media keep evolving, methods of communication become more refined, and are integrated more and more intimately into the shape of culture. A very cautious estimate says that each U.S. citizen is exposed to 245 ads daily:

108 from television, 34 from radio, and 112 from print media.[33] This number does not count cereal boxes on the breakfast table, billboards on the roads or on the side of buses, t-shirts, various kinds of computer use (computer games, web browsing, e-mails), or marketing calls. Nor does it include other methods of advertising that are less formal, like the use of certain products in movies, brand names that have been integrated into everyday language (like "Xeroxing" instead of "copying," or "Googling" instead of "searching the web"), and so on. Other estimates of daily exposure to advertisements go as high as three thousand ads per person per day. Even if the truth lies somewhere in the middle, advertising has an enormous presence in our lives, especially when compared with other forms of communication. But not even this information is sufficient to understand the reality to which we are exposed. The messages of advertisement go deeper than the slogans and statements that we perceive at the level of consciousness, where, for the most part, we can still be expected to put up some resistance: Who would really believe at the level of consciousness, for instance, that a soft drink is the "real thing"? Advertisement is aiming at associations produced in the unconscious: shaping desire, feeling good, and producing identity (what is called "branding" in advertising lingo—religionists might call it "initiation") are key.

This has implications for all other aspects of life. As we are being bombarded with messages that touch on the religious, how can theology and the church—even where they are trying to resist—escape being shaped by the capitalist market economy? Here is another parallel between mainline theology and economics, since both fail to investigate systematically what shapes our reality at the deeper levels. Just as theology needs to realize that it is dealing with more than religious ideas, so economics needs to understand that it is dealing with more than formal matters of finance and commerce. It is due to this lack of awareness of these deeper levels of reality that anything and everything can be blamed for what people perceive as leading to the much-discussed problem of a "loss of values"—except economics and religion. Theologians Paul King and David Woodyard, for instance, assume that capitalism becomes exclusive, dominating, and materialistic because it lacks religion and a god concept.[34] But what if capitalism promotes its own god concept—something that Martin Luther would have understood, because a god is "that to which your heart clings and entrusts itself"? And what if this capitalist god concept has an unacknowledged impact on how our visions of the Christian God shape up? Theologian D. Stephen Long operates under the assumption that only those theologians who intentionally make common cause with the economic status quo are endangered by it. Those who seek to be countercultural and cling to what he calls the "ancient traditions" appear to be safe.[35] Christian ethicist Max Stackhouse maintains that "Christian theology and theological ethics have the spiritual power and moral insight to comprehend, modulate, and guide" the powers that be.[36] But to assume that the church can work for the common good through transnational corporations without asking questions about its complicity, as both Long and Stackhouse claim in different ways, implies a strong belief in the independence of the church. If the production of desire aims at all of life, the church does not remain unaffected, and we need to take a much closer look at how it might develop the ability to resist.

As we have seen above, religion is frequently the ally of free-market capitalism. The Gospel of Prosperity is only the most blatant example. In this case, theology is assimilated to economic goals, endorsing the desires produced by the free-market economy and thus protecting them from being questioned. But the Gospel of Prosperity is not the only problem. Even those who resist such triumphalistic connections between theology and economics may still be influenced by the desires unleashed and produced by the free market. Long is right: even the language of "pluralism, inclusivity, individual freedom, growth and heterogeneity" is not unrelated to the "language of the market," at least in certain contexts. But what about Long's endorsement of theological virtues, including the Apostle Paul's ancient list of charity, faith, and hope?[37] Are those virtues today not also in danger of being shaped by the free market, if only unconsciously?

Even traditional faith language is not automatically safe. The idea of charity, for instance, is now at the basis of efforts to ensure the stability of the free-market economy because it involves taking care of the needs of those who otherwise might potentially destabilize it, if only through their suffering. Charity, the way it is mostly practiced today by the churches and others, helps reintegrate people back into the system—the so-called faith-based initiatives of the Bush years were designed to make this happen—but it rarely leads to a critique of the system. If the desires that got people into economic trouble are noticed at all, they are blamed on the victims themselves, who are "too consumeristic" and unable to limit themselves. To be sure, there is a theological surplus in the ancient notion of charity that pushes beyond the current embodiment of charity, but, for the most part, even theologians tend to think about charity in ways that conform to the system. Is this not also true for worship? The common expectation is that worship is uplifting, thereby contributing to the revitalization of tired minds and bodies on Sunday morning so that they will be able to be more productive and content in the marketplace on Monday. The theological surplus that exists even in this situation, cannot be measured in terms of whether people are enjoying the worship experience—the usual measure of ecclesial success—but in terms of whether it provides challenges and alternative inspirations. In this context, even traditional faith language, like the notion of "Christ's benefits" or talk about the "power of the Holy Spirit," needs to be examined for the difference that it really makes. Only when we begin to investigate what it is that shapes our deepest desires as Christians, can we start searching for alternatives.

Lamenting consumerism is the wrong approach in this situation, as it covers up the deeper reasons for the production of desire. It also covers up the fact that the problem is not primarily at the level of acquiring material things but at the level of our identity as a whole, which includes what people think, believe, and feel. People are lured into consuming to such a degree that their whole identity is reshaped—and this happens in order to guarantee growing production and increased profits even under the conditions of falling rates of profit. In this context, we can put to rest the old reproach that we have become too materialistic, since the consumption of goods is not primarily about material things but about achieving our dreams and our desires. Even the seemingly nonmaterialistic worlds of our beliefs and ideas are shaped by these processes and, thus, ultimately by the economic powers that be. Consequently, the appropriate response is not to become less materialistic and more spiritual, as if the spiritual world were safer and less impacted by capitalism than the material world. What we need is a different materialism coupled with a different spirituality, and here the Christian traditions might be helpful, as Christianity at its core has never been about playing material and spiritual things against each other. Neither is the appropriate response to be found in efforts to replace individualism with communitarianism. At a time when the logic of the free market shapes even our deepest desires, communities are not necessarily less influenced by status-quo thinking than individuals—the gated communities that have popped up in many of our major cities are perhaps the most vivid example, but the same thing might also be said of most mainline church communities. What is left? Is resistance still possible?

The Produced Nature of Desire

Confronted with the challenges of the economy—which shape not only the economic aspects of our lives but everything else, including our deepest desires—the most dangerous assumption is that the mechanisms of the free market and the desires connected with it are "natural." Indeed, most people who benefit from the economy tend to believe that the proverbial urge of "keeping up with the Joneses" is part of the natural human condition. This position claims that we are all alike: people always want more stuff; everybody wants a bigger car, a bigger house, and more money at the expense of everything else. Even economic globalization has been justified in this way.[38] If the mechanisms of the free market are natural, resistance is, indeed, futile.

Theologian Jung Mo Sung has noted a confusion between the concepts of desire and need in capitalist societies.[39] The difference, according to

Sung is that needs—the sorts of things that we require in order to live, like food, shelter, and clothing—have limits, while desires are unlimited. For our purposes, we might say that needs are more closely connected to natural functions of human life, while desires are not. And while desires are potentially unlimited, they are not natural, in the sense that they need to be produced and reproduced indefinitely. Furthermore, this production of desire is a component of the current free-market economy, necessary in order to keep things going. The mercantilist economists of previous centuries, for instance, did not seek to encourage desire and consumption. Just the opposite: for them, consumption was the problem that would force them to raise their payments to their servants and laborers. In free-market capitalism, on the other hand, desire and consumption are necessary in order to increase production and to make up for falling rates of profit. This is what ultimately drives the production of desire through the various methods that will be discussed here. Dugger and Sherman summarize what is going on from the perspective of the economic school of institutionalism: "In our current age, corporate researchers think up new things and new ways to produce them, then set about selling them to individual consumers and justifying the extravagance of some consumers in the face of real want for many others."[40]

The current free-market economy rests on the freedom to produce, sell, and consume, and it seeks to enhance production, sales, and consumption through the active promotion of desire. The role of the advertising industry has already been mentioned. Yet there are also other ways in which desire is promoted: at the most extreme end are the "economic hit men," whom John Perkins has described and outed in his book, *Confessions of an Economic Hit Man*. One of the functions of these active promoters of the benefits of capitalism is to spread the desires of the elite of the wealthy countries to the elite of other countries around the globe. Their mission is to make sure that "those leaders become ensnared in a web of debt that ensures their loyalty."[41] Desire is, thus, promoted at the highest levels of society in order to create a global elite. This sort of desire can be described as "mimetic desire," since it is aimed at the imitation of the desire of those who are better off.[42]

Another example of how this sort of mimetic desire is produced in less extreme ways has been explored by economist Robert Frank. Frank is concerned about the sinking living standards of the middle class. One of the problems that he discusses is how the lifestyles of the rich and famous affect the lifestyles and desires of everyone. While it is irrelevant for middle-class families that Bill Gates, the founder of Microsoft, has a 40,000-square-foot house, the existence of such houses still has an effect on society as a whole, as it shapes basic perceptions about how large of a house can be built, how many guests can be entertained at once, and so on. The concomitant increase in the size of everything can now even be seen in the growing value of gifts that middle-class people feel they have to give when invited to a party. Even the choice of a suitable spouse, an area of life that is rarely discussed in terms of economic logic, appears to be influenced by growing expectations of wealth and financial success.[43] In short, Frank's research demonstrates that increased spending at the top has changed the frame of reference for everyone.[44]

A traditional analysis of what is going on here might focus on people envying the rich or on their vain desire to keep up with the rich. But this is not the case, Frank argues.[45] The problem exists not just in the ideal realm, where it would just be a matter of people's self-image and of people being able to live out their dreams and fantasies. Rather, the problem is that not keeping up hurts people's real positions in life. Real disadvantages in life result from not keeping up with the developments at the higher levels of society. Children are not able to go to the better schools, for instance, if parents do not buy houses in more expensive neighborhoods. Frank even references consequences for people's health: in a British study, the rates of illness and death were many times higher among lower-ranking civil servants than among higher-ranking ones, indicating that making it to the top becomes quite literally a matter of life and death.[46]

Frank shows the problems that arise from this sort of produced desire. In a world where the rich keep getting richer, everybody is under pressure to work more and more in order to maintain their living standards. In the year 2009, American women were working about two hundred hours more at their jobs each year than they did in the mid-1970s; for men the number was one hundred hours more. There is a general rule which shows how this sort of mimetic desire impacts everyone: in countries where income inequality is high, people generally work longer hours than elsewhere in order to keep up.[47] Other social problems include the fact that countries with the largest increases in income inequality also have the highest divorce rates.[48] This is another indication that what is often lamented in the United States as the loss of moral values is perhaps more closely related to economic developments than to moral ones. The world of ideas and ideals, which comprises part of the world of religion, is much more closely tied to the economic world than most people realize.

None of these problems is taken into account in contemporary economics, Frank states, but he admits that he does not have an answer as to why this is the case.[49] This is where his project falters, since all that he can do is try to convince people at the top not to be so "greedy," and to spend their money more wisely so as to produce similarly wise desires in others. People at the top do have a choice, he notes, of whether they want to spend their money on more expensive wristwatches, or on better teachers and other things that would be beneficial for the community.[50] Frank also feels that the world of politics might help us in this regard,[51] but this a strange proposal from an economist, since it leaves economics completely off the hook. The problem with Frank's analysis is that, like other mainline economists, he does not go to the bottom of what it is that produces desires. While he provides an outstanding critique of the problems that emerge as desire is produced in the relation between those who are extremely well off and the rest—this is the relation that was praised by von Hayek as being the engine of all progress—he fails to ask what ultimately drives this desire for ever-more expensive products; here he joins von Hayek and neoliberal economics again. Frank shows how status objects matter more in the production of desire than objects that are less visible: thus, the possession of a larger house appears to be more desirable, for instance, than decent health care. But even in this case we might wonder whether the deeper reason for the production of desire for status objects has something to do with the unacknowledged need to ratchet up production.

While the production of desire does not necessarily make people happier or freer, it is essential in maintaining the status quo. The production of goods, ideas, and services can continue and grow only if the production of desire stays on track. And since desire is produced by such powerful means, it cannot be limited to the consumption of goods. The desire to consume goods itself is linked by the "new high priesthood" of advertising with loftier goals and dreams, as we have seen. This produced desire produces our gods, as Luther realized: the god of prosperity, whose existence is proved by economic gain; the god of the market, who claims to lift all boats; and the god of charity, who seeks to shape economically disadvantaged people in the image of their benefactors—as fellow consumers.

This produced desire also produces our images of humanity. In a strange reversal of cause and effect, economists tend to portray people not as the servants of the market (which they are), but as being in charge of the market. Assuming that the role of the market is to give people what they want, advertising scholar James Twitchell can claim that "consumers are 'the ones with the power, continually negotiating new sites for meaning.'"[52] In this context, consumerism is seen as an expression of the popular will; as a direct manifestation of democracy. Covering up the produced nature of desire, desire is now equated with what people really want and, ultimately, who they are. Human freedom is achieved in this model when people can live out every possible desire. Thomas Frank, reflecting back on the 1990s when this approach began to gain dominance, describes it in the following terms: "The market and the people—both of them understood as grand principles of social life rather than particulars—were essentially one and the same. By its very nature the market was democratic, perfectly expressing popular will through the machinery of supply and demand, poll and focus group, superstore and Internet. In fact, the market was *more* democratic than any of the formal institutions of democracy—elections, legislatures, government.

The market was a community. The market was infinitely diverse, permitting without prejudice the articulation of any and all tastes and preferences." This market, it appeared, "had no place for snobs, for hierarchies, for elitism, for pretense, and it would fight these things by its very nature."[53] This market, in sum, is seen as the exact opposite of the entity that seeks to manipulate people for the sake of increased production.

By masking the fact that desire is produced for the sake of the market, the market takes on the role of the servant of desire. In an odd reversal, the market is seen as the source of democracy, while politics is denounced as elitist.[54] As a result, any critique of the market can now be seen as a critique of common people. The list of the supposed critics of common people is now long: not only is politics elitist, organizations of common people like labor unions are even worse, since they supposedly interfere with people's freedom to follow their individual desires into the market. In this context, collective bargaining is no longer seen as the process by which workers who have no voice in the market gain some influence; collective bargaining is portrayed as an unfair interference in the market and as undemocratic. As the market takes center stage, the focus is directed away from the tensions under which desire is produced, and toward a harmonious image where the main concern is to make those who hold investments (where interest equals desire) happy. Frank quotes from a 1996 *New York Times* article, referencing a CEO who claims that "unionism is going down because corporations have changed their views. . . . We empower our people now. They work in teams with shared responsibilities. It's not management versus the workers in the plants now. We're all one for our shareholders."[55]

The image of humanity that develops here is one of human beings pursuing their natural and inborn individual desires in isolation from each other. Ensuring freedom means not interfering with this process, so that all can do as they please. What is overlooked, of course, is that if these desires are not natural but produced in the interest of growing production and profit, human beings are not free to begin with. What is commonly called "consumerism" describes, thus, not a situation of freedom where people can do as they please, but a lack of freedom that is twofold: not only is desire produced in us and for us, but when we are in a position to pursue our desires without impediment, we are even less free because we are really following someone else's script. Now we are at the heart of the issue.

The economy has become hegemonic to such an extent that the majority of humanity matters less and less, and consumerism has become a mode of existence that can no longer be contained by the individual will of the consumer. In this context, we need to rethink what it means to propose religion as an antidote—as the place from which resistance can be formed and alternative lifestyles can be developed. What if religion itself can no longer be considered to be free from the pull of the global market economy? What if even our most sacred notions of God have become tied into the ethos of the free market without anybody noticing? For many mainline Christians, Christianity and capitalism appear to be referring to the same reality. This problem has taken on such epidemic proportions that even alternative images of God are co-opted at an alarming rate. Even the God who lifts up the poor, for instance, now appears to be following capitalist principles. The God who empowers people appears to empower them to become capitalists: in a survey several years ago, most people thought that the phrase, "God helps those who help themselves," could be found in the Bible.[56] Even the recently rediscovered earthy and material qualities of God are being commodified in a growing market of nature-related travel, retreats, dietary supplements, exotic artifacts, and the principles of what is now called "free market environmentalism," which finds an odd sort of comfort in the self-healing powers of the economy.

Religion, Labor, and Resisting Desire

In a situation where desire is ravaging lives—particularly those of people who are unable to satisfy it—is resistance possible, and how? Biblical passages like Ps 23:1, "The LORD is my shepherd, I shall not want," have been referenced in recent theological debates in order to argue that God provides for us and, thus, overcomes scarcity and uncontrolled desires.[57] M. Douglas Meeks points out, for instance, that in the Christian perspective "the Holy Spirit is providing enough of what it takes for all to live and live abundantly."[58] Meeks is aware that this does not do away with insufficiencies, lacks, and shortages of goods, but he claims that this perspective challenges the modern economic definition of scarcity, which is based on the presumed insatiability of human nature and on efforts to block access to what is necessary for basic livelihood.[59] The Eucharist has been promoted as a resource from the Christian tradition that might inspire a sense that God is taking care of our needs—not only spiritually but also materially, in the elements of bread and wine—which results in Christians being able to share with others.[60] These insights are helpful to a certain extent, but they tend to assume too quickly that the church, or at least our traditional Christian imagery, is somehow exempt from the all-pervasiveness of the market. However, even images of care—gift-giving, sharing, and abundance—can be co-opted by the status quo to such a degree that they provide false hope. Part of the problem with these perspectives is that they often do not push for the deeper challenges. This problem manifests itself, for instance, in the fact that their focus is mostly on economic distribution without consideration of the realities of economic production.[61] Meeks, for instance, concludes his important book, *God the Economist,* by arguing that "the household of God is meant to be a peculiar sphere of distribution. . . . Its household rules of distribution are meant to conform to God's own distribution of righteousness."[62]

Keeping such alternative takes on Christian traditions before us while noting their limitations, we need to investigate the possibility of resisting desires and wants, and of developing alternatives that permit flourishing in the midst of downturn. The key issue in this regard is to forge relations to those whose existence has been severely damaged, if not wiped out, by the downturn; it is here that the whole scope of the problem can be seen, false hope can be filtered out, and the most pressing questions can emerge. On the one hand, this helps us understand the severe damage that has been done by the production of desire—as it has turned people to false gods and ruined their lives in the process. On the other hand, it is here that we can catch the first glimpses of possible alternatives that push beyond easy answers. What does desire look like in situations of severe economic downturn, when it is determined by real need rather than the desires dictated by the market? As desire is reshaped in this context, what alternative images of God and ultimate reality emerge? The study of desire in light of the logic of downturn points us to another kind of divine or ultimate reality, and here theology and economics intersect once again in the question of what it is that ultimately moves and motivates us.

Early critiques of consumerism in the eighteenth century focused on Christian moral themes, including attacks on greed, gluttony, and the pursuit of false gods. It seemed inappropriate in this context that lower social classes were coming to adopt lifestyles that seemed to be reserved for more advanced classes.[63] In the United States of the late nineteenth and early twentieth centuries, Americans also worried about "unmitigated materialism." This was shown, for instance, in their discomfort with the commercialization of Christmas—a mood that is still with us, although most churches have given in and many do not even offer services on Christmas morning so as not to interfere with the opening of presents. Environmental concerns were added in the early twentieth century, as well as a host of personal ethical concerns, including temperance, smoking, and sexuality and violence in the media.[64] Historian of consumerism Stearns notes, however, that such attacks rarely slowed down consumerism, whether in western Europe or in the United States. "From the eighteenth century onward, the forces propelling consumerism were stronger than those opposing it in the Western world."[65]

The consequences of consumerism cannot be underestimated: while it became increasingly accepted as normal, consumerism altered people's lives and imposed heavy burdens. Stearns points out that "for many people, particularly in the United States, the commitment to consumerism introduced a new precariousness to material life. By 2001, despite unprecedentedly high incomes, over half of all Americans had almost no savings and a third live[d] paycheck to paycheck, often in considerable consumer debt."[66] Yet lamenting consumerism does not help, as we have seen above. In fact, this lament may be one of the reasons why we are unable to put up any resistance to the dominant production of desire, because it points us in the wrong direction and makes us forget that desire has deeper roots. Theologians and others who have focused on consumerism have often reached an impasse exactly at this point.[67] If it is true, however, that "wants are dependent on production" (Galbraith), we need to take a closer look at economic production in our struggle to transform desires and ultimately consumerism. Resistance to desire needs to be rooted in understanding of production first, and only then can we take another look at consumption.

Stearns identifies three aspects that drive consumerism: "manipulation, fulfillment of social and personal needs, and habituation." The notion of manipulation is a subtle acknowledgement that other interests—the interests of production, to be exact—drive consumer desire. But how would it be possible to step out of this vicious circle? Stearns unwittingly points in a promising direction: "For the poor, consumerism is not the question; seeking adequate subsistence is."[68] This question, he notes, not only haunts large numbers of people around the globe, but also thirteen million children in the United States who live below the poverty line and whose numbers are growing. The distinction between needs and wants that we suggested earlier is helpful here: actual human needs have to do with the basic necessities of life, and many wants can be deconstructed when seen in relation to actual human needs. Galbraith approaches this matter from the other direction, showing that increasing production, on which the increase in wants is built, does not necessarily make a society better. From a certain point onwards, producing more stuff and wants does not increase welfare. He therefore concludes that production must not get stuck in private interests but should be liberated for the bigger challenges of humanity.[69]

The first step in producing the sort of desire that can put up resistance is, therefore, to reconnect with the real needs of people. This connection with real needs is what was lost when the free-market economy began to create the human being in its image. The free-market economy's fabricated human being is abstract; it knows only wants but has no real physical needs. Hugo Assmann and Franz Hinkelammert draw a parallel to certain spiritualizing theologies, which also function in abstraction from real human needs and from human life in general. In liberation theology, they point out, this spiritualization is overcome and attention is paid to real human need.[70] This is an important first step; yet more work needs to be done. As we become aware of real human need, we are able to see more clearly the constructed nature of desire. And it is this awareness of the constructed nature of desire that points us toward what is happening in production. Anne Cronin, a scholar of advertising, inadvertently affirms this approach to economics through the back door, as it were: "Whilst contemporary capitalism's web of institutions . . . and flows of finance, information and people are far too complex for most people . . . to grasp, advertising presents itself as a highly visible cipher for these formulations." No doubt, something of importance can be learned here, although we must not stop at this point. Cronin points out the limits: "In this context, the critique and regulation of advertising may offer a reassuring (if tenuous) sense that we have some control over capitalism's processes and development."[71] Attention to advertising, consumerism, and desire is only helpful if it points to the deeper and underlying reality of production.

While production seems to be a noncontroversial aspect of mainline economics that follows simple rules of supply and demand, the perspective of production changes when viewed from the perspective of labor. Here is a parallel to deep-seated Judeo-Christian traditions dealing with labor that have often been neglected in the history of theology and the church. This neglect cannot be seen as innocent, since these traditions are quite prominent in the biblical texts, which reminds us of the extent to which religious concerns are shaped by the economic status quo. While this is hardly discussed in mainline theology or the churches, the evidence shows that some of the key figures of the Judeo-Christian faith were involved in issues of labor and production firsthand. That Moses organized laboring slaves and that Jesus was a construction worker from a family of construction workers might sound cliché and trite, but these observations share deep levels of meaning and have had some impact in the history of the church. Why did God not chose to manifest divine power in favor of ancient empires like Egypt and Babylon? And why did God not become human in an upper-class family— especially since this would have had all sorts of advantages, "all other things being equal," as the economists say? Apparently, all other things religious are not equal if this social location changes.

In more recent history, the life and work of Claude Williams (1895– 1977), a Reformed pastor and founder of the People's Institute of Applied Religion, who spent much of his life engaged in labor issues, is an impressive example of the power of these traditions to reshape both the life and theology of Christians.[72] Williams, developing a "people's interpretation of the Bible" in the 1930s and 1940s in the south of the United States, studied the Judeo-Christian traditions in terms of an emerging group of leaders of the common people, to which he counted—in addition to those of Moses and Jesus—the stories of Abraham; the prophets Amos, Hosea, Jeremiah, Isaiah, Elisha, Elijah, and Jonah; John the Baptist; Jesus' disciples Peter and James; and later Stephen.[73] In recent research, Richard Horsley has offered a reading of Jesus' work and ministry, in solidarity with the peasants in Galilee and Judea who were under pressure from the Roman Empire.[74] The theological importance of the background of all these leaders, Jesus included, is that they were looking at things from the perspective of working people—and were, therefore, able to see more clearly what was wrong with the world and where the real problems were. Equally important was that from this perspective they were able to develop fresh visions of God, cutting through the many images of false gods which enslaved the people in their day—from the slaves in Egypt in the case of Moses to the peasants at the margins of the Roman Empire in the case of Jesus. In this process, desire was reshaped and readied for resistance.

The perspective of working people is crucial here. From the firsthand perspective of Jesus as someone who had experienced the life of a worker, it is not surprising to hear the following conclusion: "The kings of the Gentiles lord it over them; and those in authority over them are called benefactors. But not so with you. . . . For who is greater, the one who is at the table or the one who serves? Is it not the one at the table? But I am among you as one who serves" (Luke 22:25-27). According to this passage, Jesus understands himself and his work from the perspective of those who labor and produce. His reference to those who work and serve at the table is more than just a cheap analogy, which would further devalue them if it were simply used to make an abstract metaphysical point. When the mainline church has picked up such passages, by contrast, it has usually defused them by talking about "servanthood" in romanticized terms that are completely removed and abstracted from the everyday life of labor to which Jesus refers. From the secondhand perspective of Moses, who was raised in the upper class as an Egyptian prince, things become clear once he begins to listen to the experience of others: "One day, after Moses had grown up, he went out to his people and saw their forced labor. He saw an Egyptian beating a Hebrew, one of his kinsfolk" (Exod 2:11). This is the moment when Moses' troubles begin, as he sides with the Hebrew, kills the Egyptian, and is forced to go underground. It is precisely in the underground that God appears to him in unexpected and life-changing ways.

In these religious traditions, the view from the perspective of working people is indispensable. The legacy of Moses cannot be conceived without his solidarity with the Hebrew slaves—even though this does not mean that his killing is justified—and the legacy of Jesus cannot be conceived without his solidarity with working people of his own time. Jesus' parables—at the core of his message—are full of examples from the everyday life of work, including references to shepherds, who usually were not the owners of their flocks (Luke 15:1-7); working women (Matt 13:33, Luke 15:8-10); workers in vineyards (Matt 20:1-16; 21:33-46) and in fields (Mark 4:1-9, 13-20); fishermen (Mark 1:16-20); and service workers (Matt 18:23-34). One powerful example of the solidarity at the core of Jesus' message can be found in Matt 18:23-34, the so-called Parable of the Unforgiving Servant: a service worker, who experiences the rare forgiveness of his debt, fails to forgive one of his fellow service workers. The community of service workers notes the problem right away, and the worker is taken to task. In this parable, God is pictured as the employer and the one who owns the debt—but God as employer goes against all business logic by forgiving debt, the very thing that makes workers compliant to their bosses and that pits worker against worker. The resulting solidarity among workers that becomes possible on the basis of the forgiveness of debt—when debt is not pressing down on them—is so crucial that its breach has severe consequences.

That a story like this is told in the context of worker relations makes all the difference, and it can only be fully understood when interpreted from this perspective. This story could have conceivably been told from the perspective of the employers who lend money: in this case, the logic of the forgiveness of debt to others—that when one is forgiven one is also expected to forgive—would not necessarily hold up. This is a common story in the history of economics: the bailouts of the banking industry in 2008 and 2009, for instance, were not designed to lead to bailouts of those who owe money to the bank, and it occurred to hardly anyone that this should be the consequence. While it can be expected that desire would be reshaped in the life of the forgiven worker—the community is outraged when he resists this pattern—this expectation does not necessarily apply to the life of a forgiven banker. On this backdrop, the story of Zacchaeus, which only occurs in the Gospel of Luke, is all the more remarkable, but Zacchaeus's response would surely destroy his status among other wealthy chief tax collectors had he done as he says: "Half of my possessions, Lord, I will give to the poor; and if I have defrauded anyone of anything, I will pay back four times as much" (Luke 19:8).

In order to dig deeper into the creation of alternative desire, we need to understand the key role of workers in production—whether this be the production of goods, ideas, or services. This is what is most sorely missing in mainline economics, which emphasizes the creativity of CEOs and other business leaders but fails to consider the role of workers and their creativity. Clearly, there can be no production without labor, but what is the significance of this insight? To begin with, the goals of workers are different from the goals that mainline economics attributes to business leaders. The goal of workers, their deepest desire, is not the infinite maximization of profit for stockholders. Their desire points to processes of production that respect human dignity, that provide fair compensation and benefits, and that provide for the welfare of their families and the community. A process of production that respects human dignity will also give more room to the creativity of workers, who, even under current working conditions, often contribute significantly to improvements in the production of goods, ideas, and services. Including these considerations in mainline economic accounts would surely lead to major shifts. Note also that when seen from the perspective of workers, the idea of risk in mainline economics is reversed: while it is commonly assumed that the employers bear the bigger risk because they might go bankrupt if their business fails, the risk for workers is just as existential. They stand to lose their jobs, their livelihoods, and perhaps even their pensions. And while CEOs tend to have substantial personal resources, receive substantial severance packages, and often move on to other companies, workers tend to be stuck: if jobs disappear due to massive layoffs, this results in plummeting housing values, which then prevent them from selling their homes and seeking employment elsewhere. In the situation of large-scale recessions or depressions, risk is fundamentally different for large- and small-business owners. While the latter may indeed go bankrupt, those who run large businesses can count on bailouts or at least on public efforts to save their businesses through tax cuts and other incentives. In terms of the production of desire, we must also take into account that, in the current system, workers have to deal with a double burden: while production rests on their shoulders—profit is made based on their labor, as mainline economist David Ricardo demonstrated decades before Karl Marx—they are also the ones who are most needed when it comes to consuming the goods, ideas, and even the services that they produce. In other words, they are the targets for much of the production of desire, but for this reason they are also the ones who have the strongest interest in resisting desire.

The insights of psychoanalysis—especially when developed in terms of social analysis rather than in terms of individual analysis—might help us in further analyzing the problem and looking for another set of solutions. Jacques Lacan's distinction between realism and the real provides a first clue. What counts as reality—and that which realism picks up on—is what is commonly accepted as true by those who are part of the status quo. Statements such as "everyone knows" or "it is a commonly accepted fact" are based on the assumption that there is only one valid view of reality: the dominant one. The master narratives of a given culture and that which is perceived to be "common sense" belong to this realm of reality (which Lacan later would term the "symbolic order"). For our purposes, this may be considered the position of the mainline, based in the ways of production that underlie the current status quo. The real, by contrast, is that which escapes the realist perspective and cannot be captured by it. More specifically, the real is that which has been pushed underground and repressed by the realist perspectives.[75] As that which has been repressed, the real is not only invisible to realism; it becomes its alter ego, the back on which realism is built. Yet the fact that it is repressed does not mean that the real is gone: out of sight does not mean out of mind. The real is, therefore, something like the collective unconscious of the dominant positions. This collective unconscious is produced in analogy to the individual unconscious in moments of repression.[76]

The relation of employers and employees can be discussed in this framework as well. Mainline economics deals with what Lacan termed realism—that which is visible from the dominant perspective of the employers. No wonder that the situation of workers is hardly considered here in any depth. Although the system as a whole depends on labor, labor itself is not well understood by the dominant perspective. Those who work, on the other hand, see things from the perspective of that which has been repressed: what we have called the real. From this perspective, they are not unfamiliar with the dominant position of realism because it affects them in their repressed positions, especially the laws of supply and demand. Yet workers know better than anyone else what is really going on as production gears up to meet and produce demand, and—to the point of our discussion—they are in a better position than anyone else to understand the netherworlds of production through labor, which is at the core of the production of desire.

And while the worker's own desire is necessary to keep production going and is, therefore, subject to the control of the dominant powers—since without labor nothing would be produced—the desire of those who are engaged in production can never be completely co-opted and controlled. A first sense that desire cannot be co-opted completely grows out of an observation of the ambivalence of the status quo. Capitalism's power and influence is never absolute, and even its processes of production are never without ambivalence.[77] Alternative desire is at work in unexpected places; it emerges from those who are under pressure by the system but can never be completely controlled because they do not ultimately benefit from it. The challenge, therefore, comes from the "last" who "will be first" (Matt 20:1-16), and from the "least of these"; even the divine judgment ultimately depends on people's relation to the least of these, according to Jesus (Matt 25:31-46). This alternative desire may not seem like much, but free-market capitalism is challenged by any desire that is not in sync with its purposes and that does not play according to the rules and within the limits of its particular freedom. Worse yet, free-market capitalism is especially concerned about alternative desire that might organize itself to push for alternative goals, and this is the ultimate challenge of the labor movements.

In this connection, we can turn our view to alternative forms of production that develop as a result of the repressions of the status quo: factory workers, for instance, by having to collaborate and share time on the factory floor, can produce alternative means of solidarity and resistance. This might be possible for other working people as well, including those who traditionally consider themselves middle class: collaborative projects are also common in the work of those who produce ideas, and office workers who work in communal settings, for instance, can meet around the proverbial water cooler. Resisting desire can be organized and strengthened in these settings, whenever those who have access to some alternative desires meet. Michael Hardt and Antonio Negri may be too optimistic that such organization is now happening everywhere in what they call the "multitude," but their argument reminds us that we need to look more broadly for places where such organization takes place, with the expectation that transformations in the forms of production can lead to transformed forms of desire.[78] In the midst of a recession, we also need to add the alternative perspectives developed by the unemployed, especially by those who have never experienced this type of repression before and who would never have expected to end up in such a situation. In this situation, the differences between working class and middle class (as well as between the unemployed who come from these respective classes) matter less and less—and, thus, another space is emerging where solidarity can be practiced.

The most important thing to keep in mind is that desire cannot be changed easily, and that moralizing or sermonizing—the common responses of the system—will not work. In this context, it is important to dig deeper and to realize that desire is shaped in relationships and through repressions. Once this is clear, we will be able to see the tide of alternative desires that is already rising in a system that is becoming more and more repressive of more and more people. This alternative desire is thus truly a collective phenomenon, and it has the potential to create new ways of being human.[79] Yet this alternative desire also needs to be organized. Without organization, it disappears. This may be the wisdom embodied in alternative religious and other movements, particularly when they form on the underside of history. As Claude Williams noted in his "people's interpretation of the Bible": "the 'multitudes' who gather to hear the Son of Man do not appear magically but are the product of hard organizational work."[80] A middle road hardly exists in this polarized situation. Those in the middle are usually pulled into the defense of the powers and the desire of the dominant status quo, often without being aware of it. But those in the middle might also opt to step back from a system which does not allow them to form and maintain alternative desires, and join in the emerging production of desire from below.

In the present times, progress in creating alternative desires depends, therefore, on a return to situations of great pressure and the logic of downturn—similar to the situations in which many of the key events of the Judeo-Christian tradition took shape. Here, theological reflection and economic thought intersect in such a way that the contribution of theological and religious reflection to the further development of economics is not primarily that of providing another set of ideas or a new state of mind, but of finding glimpses into an alternative reality precisely where the pressures of the economic status quo become unbearable and are, thus, being questioned. This, rather than the closed realities of the status quo, points us to the ultimate and to the divine. Here, Christianity will be able to offer alternatives not where it represents the smug symbols of regulated religiosity (the kinds of symbols that are easily commodified by the commercial spin doctors' efforts at re-enchantment) but where it draws on the irrepressible energies emerging out of the undercurrent of its traditions, as they have developed and continue to take shape in the midst of the pressures of production and of life as a whole.

Resistance depends on the creation of alternative desires in this context, and here lies the biggest challenge. As desires function at an unconscious level, closely connected with that which we have repressed, desires cannot easily be controlled and redirected on the conscious level, neither through the well-meaning adoption of a new set of rules nor through the training processes that go into the formation of habits. Resistance based on moral rules and behavior, if it is possible at all and if the rules somehow manage to escape the almost irresistible pull of the status quo, will always remain a drag. No wonder burn-out is such a serious problem. In this context, theologian Sallie McFague's notion of "wild spaces" might be a first step in a more promising direction. A wild space is whatever does not fit the stereotypical human being in each of us—what some think is our "nature," which is really that which we have become as people produced by the demands of the free market. A wild space is created in rifts with the status quo, for instance in traumatic moments such as when a child dies, when having to deal with substance abuse, or when confronting clinical depression.[81] Such a wild space might also be created when the last of our economic safety nets crumble.

Yet this is only a first step at best. In order to truly resist the structures of a virtually all-powerful economy, we need to push beyond its rifts and move even further—all the way into the scary netherworld of its repressions. When we seek out not only the wild spaces but the repressed spaces created by the free-market economy, we will encounter the worlds of labor and, ultimately, even the growing worlds of those who are systematically excluded from the worlds of labor: the long-term unemployed, exploited children, commodified nature, and even parts of our own selves that we never knew existed. What if theology were to deal with the real—that is, the netherworld of our repressions—and, thus, move closer to those areas where desire is shaped and reshaped and power is unmasked?[82]

What we are dealing with here is not merely a rift with the status quo. We are dealing with a full-blown repression and the powers that cause it. Here is a parallel to the crucifixion of Jesus Christ. Like the crucifixion of Christ, the fate of people on the underside is not a mere accident, a rift having to do with bad luck or a combination of unfortunate circumstances. Like the crucifixion of Christ, the fate of people on the underside has to do with repression. As Christ experienced repression by the religious and political leadership of his time, working people often experience repression by the leadership of their own times, whose goal it is to profit as much as possible from the so-called free-market economy. The gap between the haves and the have-nots on the national and the global levels, and the power differentials between them, are exploited for economic growth—creating new desires and the belief that expansion is unlimited among the rich and even the middle class (our 401[k] retirement plans depend on this), while at the same time demanding full compliance from the vast masses of the lower classes, to the point of bodily enslavement.[83] Yet the Christian tradition also talks about a resurrection, which happens because God takes the side of the crucified Christ.

At the point where we begin to confront these kinds of repressions, a new thing happens and a different kind of resistance becomes possible. Desire—unconsciously produced on the backs of those who labor and produce, and normalized in the dominant economic values of the free market—is reshaped in unexpected ways. In this context, there is hope even for the middle and upper classes. Middle- and upper-class people, for instance, who have spent time with people in poorer countries, invariably report their conflicted emotions upon reentering our world of malls and supermarkets. Something has indeed changed in what they desire most, even if the shock is only temporary. Such transformation of desire, where we begin to cut through the many layers of the economic status quo, is at the beginning of a transformative process that opens up the way for alternative values and lifestyles that resist the control exercised by capitalist economic values. Here, more productive encounters with the alternative visions of the Christian traditions open up—and many aspects of these traditions are still waiting to be uncovered. Resisting desire no longer has to be self-generated but erupts from the underside where—to our never-ending surprise—Godself labors in solidarity with the people and resisting desire spreads from there.

To Each According to Their Need

How we view desire shapes how we view humanity, the world, and God. In mainline economic theory as well as in much of mainline theology, the view of desire is mostly static and fixed. Whatever desire is considered to be from these points of view, it is mostly seen as focused on the interests of the individual self. The rational self-interest promoted by economics is often interpreted as a close match with theological understandings of sin as self-centeredness.[84] Yet this interpretation is, at the same time, too strong and not strong enough. It is not strong enough because it does not account for sin in a deeper fashion. If sin were to be taken seriously in classical fashion as separation from God, the self-centered human being would not be guided by the rational self-interest of economic theory but by hunger for domination, lust, greed, anger, and envy.[85] If sin were to be taken really seriously in mainline economics, how could one maintain confidence that the capitalists who engage in the market were not merely out to kill and destroy one another? Is the mainline position too optimistic about human nature?

At the same time, this assessment of self-interest also seems to be too strong because it is too rigid. It is too quickly assumed that self-interest describes the reality of all human beings in all places and at all times. This assumption does not work on various levels. As economist Jim Stanford has noted, for instance, anthropologists argue that some sort of cooperative behavior—however limited—was an important factor in the emergence of humanity. Furthermore, there are many examples where monetary self-interest is not the only thing that moves people: Stanford names firefighters, scientists who work long hours, or parents caring for children and grandparents.[86] The commonly accepted assumption that people act selfishly in the marketplace and altruistically in the family has been shown to be false by feminist economists. If altruism were invariably at work in families, it would make little difference, for instance, if family allowance payments were made to fathers rather than to mothers. Furthermore, when males conspire to exploit women, they seem to engage in "selective within-sex altruism."[87]

What is missing in the mainline positions of economics is an assessment of human nature that is grounded in history, which includes the reality of economic production. This problem parallels a common problem in theology that occurs if sin is defined in abstract form without taking into account historical specificity. While the Augustinian definition of sin as pride does, in fact, fit some people—in our own context we might think of those in positions of great power like prominent CEOs and top investors—for others sin is better understood in the opposite way, for instance, as an unhealthy humility that leads people to underestimate their own capacity and power. In our society, this has been true especially of women who are taught to think of themselves as the "weaker sex," as submissive and subservient, and to put first not their self-interest but the interest of their husbands and families. Not surprisingly, this insight was first developed by feminist theology, yet it matches our logic of downturn. The problem of people underestimating their own power and, thus, failing to take themselves seriously may well be the bigger problem in our own situation for those for whom the tide is no longer rising. Desire may still be at work here, but it is the self-defeating desire that may, for example, play a role in obesity—a condition that is much more common in the lower classes than in the upper classes as well as in economically depressed areas of the country.

The economic and theological concept of self-interest can be terribly misused. Where people feel they have no choice but to pursue their own narrow self-interests (not realizing that these self-interests are based on produced desires), the free market succeeds at dividing and conquering. This approach has been quite successful, as our society is no longer structured by families, for instance, but divided into families that compete with each other, as feminist theorists Michèle Barrett and Mary McIntosh have pointed out.[88] Yet self-interest may not be altogether misdirected. Those who are forced to submit themselves to others in various ways—whether women of whom self-sacrifice is often expected as a matter of course or factory workers whose daily lives are determined by the presence of "lean and mean" production—deserve some relief. The last part of the second half of Jesus' love commandment talks about love of self: "Love your neighbor as yourself" (Mark 12:31). Viewed from the logic of downturn, which exposes the myth of individualism and reminds us of the connectedness of people, this phrase becomes clearer. At stake is not the promotion of individualistic self-love but the insight that the other is part of who we are: love your neighbor as being part of yourself. A kind of self-interest that understands that the other is part of who we are points in a whole new direction. Collective action and organization become possible on this basis.

What have been too quickly dismissed in this connection are the many streams of socialism. Unfortunately, these traditions have been widely misunderstood. Socialism is not about making everyone look alike, nor is it by definition about totalitarian government control, and neither is it naïve about the reality of human sin: its motto, "to each according to their need," allows for differences and human imperfection. And without the capitalist push to produce and expand desires infinitely, needs do not have to be infinite and impossible to meet. The biblical traditions point in the same direction. The following passage from the book of Acts does not sound so utopian anymore, if desire is not constantly produced and reproduced at ever-increasing speeds: "There was not a needy person among them, for as many as owned lands or houses sold them and brought the proceeds of what was sold. They laid it at the apostles' feet, and it was distributed to each as any had need" (Acts 4:34-35; see also Acts 2:44-45). Even the day laborers who were hired late in the day in Jesus' parable in Matt 20:1-16 are treated according to their need. The gracious gesture of the owner of the vineyard who pays them the regular wage for a day's labor will not make them rich; the wage they receive simply helps them to take care of their need and the needs of their families. It is interesting that there is no concern in this story that having their needs met will make them lazy. They have proven their willingness to work, and there seems to be a connection in this story between having their needs met and demonstrating a willingness to contribute. Human sinfulness is not neglected here, but it is expressed differently: sin is identified not with the infinity of human want but with situations of great inequality, where some have no access to the opportunity to live productive lives. Sin needs to be addressed by resisting this inequality and by supporting those who suffer from it so that their needs are met; otherwise this sinful situation of inequality can easily become a matter of life and death.

Nevertheless, the core concern of many of the socialist traditions lies even deeper, as it is not merely about sharing but about production. This is news to most people in the West. The first stance is not "to each according to their need," but "from each according to their ability." Distribution, like the production of desire through advertisement, follows production. The first question is not how things are to be distributed but how production can be organized so that all can participate according to the best of their abilities and make a living. In the current context, production is seen as a zero-sum game, where those who control large shares of the means of production make more profit if those who labor in production get paid less. As the call of Warren Buffet for "the small number of very large institutional investors [to] start act-ing like true owners and pressure managers and boards to do the same"[89] (see chapter 2) indicates, many more will be affected by the belt-tightening that is to come. That we are playing a zero-sum game is, of course, precisely what is denied by the statement that a rising tide lifts all boats. Yet this statement never amounts to much because it denies the radical nature of sin, which manifests itself not only in increased pressure on workers but also in the total exclusion of some from earning their livelihood. The game is indeed a zero-sum game if the basic economic assumptions are that wages need to be held in check, that self-representation of workers in unions is invariably harmful for business interests, that benefits need to be cut wherever possible, and that health care for everyone is out of the question. In this scenario, there may well be a rising tide, but there will be no lifting of the majority of boats.

Attention to what happens in production is key—not last of all in the kingdom of God where all are invited to participate in constructive work. The focus on distribution has too often covered up this insight. In the words of economist Jim Stanford: "The idea of socialism is not that rich people should share with poor people. Rather, the goal of socialism is to consciously manage economic activity with an eye to maximizing collective economic well-being, rather than individual profit. . . . That's a collective vision of self-interest—not a call for charity."[90] The underlying concern is for relationships of production which are just, and for the sort of self-interest that knows that the other is part of who I am; everything else follows from this, including the production and reproduction of desire and the fulfillment of human need. A famous saying of Jesus in the Gospel of Matthew makes more sense in this light: "Strive first for the kingdom of God and his righteousness [justice] and all these things [food, drink, clothes; mentioned in v. 31] will be given to you as well" (Matt 6:33). Relationships of production that are just, where all can contribute according to their abilities—the "kingdom of God and his justice"—create a situation where human needs are met and where human sin is addressed in realistic fashion.

When viewed from the perspective of production in terms of labor, scarcity as an absolute term in the sense of free-market economics turns out to be a pernicious myth. Economist Albert O. Hirschman makes an interesting distinction between goods, which are scarce based on their supply, and abilities, which increase with use. He notes the "confusion between the *use of a resource* and *the practice of an ability*."[91] Based on the doctrine of scarcity, mainline free-market economics assumes that an unemployment rate of at least six percent is necessary to maintain growth and keep wages in check. Milton Friedman considered this the "natural rate of unemployment."[92] But this scarcity of employment is an artificial one that results in increased pressure on workers and in the exclusion of others from production. "From each according to their ability" starts from the assumption that people do have abilities, however varied they may be, and that those abilities must not be blocked by an economic theory built on abstract notions of scarcity.

Hardt and Negri address the problem of scarcity in this way, pointing out an important shift which is presently occurring: "Some resources remain scarce today, but many, in fact, particularly the newest elements of the economy, do not operate on a logic of scarcity."[93] As Thomas Jefferson realized long ago, ideas are enhanced when they are communicated—an insight that could become key in the information age. Here a whole new understanding of economics emerges "from the underside," as it were: from the perspective of those who produce. In Hardt and Negri's terms, the "hegemony of immaterial labor" contributes to the fact that "the ruled become increasingly autonomous."[94] This insight would need to be deepened by a closer look at the subaltern character of "immaterial labor." What is the position of those who work in the production of ideas and services in the current economy? Nevertheless, traditional top-down models of domination and influence are challenged here, at least implicitly.

Alternatives to the capitalist production of desire are hard to detect on the surface of the current economy, because even the powerful are not really masters in their own house, no matter what they say or think. Their desire is distorted as well. In this situation, however, alternatives emerge from unexpected places—"from the underside," as classical Latin American liberation theologians would have said. Alternative desires that push beyond the pipe dreams of autonomy, unregulated economic power, and shapeless freedom emerge under pressure, forged as byproduct of the repressive powers of the status quo. While there is no one who is not affected by the production of desire based on the demands of economic production, people are affected in different ways. The logic of downturn helps us to realize that there are large numbers of people who benefit relatively little from the system as it is, and they have, therefore, less of a stake in the system. To be more specific, those on the margins of the global economy who are mostly excluded from it—the vast numbers of the unemployed, or even the casually employed for whom the economy has little use even in their capacity as consumers—have no stake in the system at all, except perhaps when they gather the crumbs that fall from its table. While "dumpster diving" has become a sport for some middle-class people in wealthy countries, millions of people are forced to survive on garbage. Further, neither mainline economists nor mainline theologians appear to be aware of the millions who have no choice but to live on the garbage dumps of this world, often with their families.

There is another vast group, however, of people who are also marginalized but on whose shoulders the weight of the economy rests—the workers who produce—in the broadest sense of the term—not just material goods but also ideas, who provide services, and who are essential for the production of profit and the overall movement of the economy. Their desire is strongly affected by the system, but, since they do not reap the majority of the benefits of the system, there are still limits to how much the system can control them. Once they begin to realize their limited stake in the system, these groups are free to push beyond it, not unlike the fishers, fieldworkers, and service workers of old who chose to follow Jesus.

Rethinking God and the World 5

Implicit and Explicit Theology: Beyond Ethics

In this book, we have challenged the idea that free-market economics is a neutral science that can be developed in a vacuum, as it were. Just as nature abhors a vacuum, there is no neutral position from which to start. Those who claim neutrality, whether in economic theory or in theology, forget this simple truth. Our social locations, our values, and our beliefs cannot be turned off at will, and neither can we ever completely escape the powers that be. If those things are not accounted for and addressed, they will come in through the back door and haunt us. This was Antonio Gramsci's point about what he called the "traditional intellectuals": they may consider themselves neutral and independent, but they always end up supporting the status quo because this is the context that shapes us by default.[1]

While it is increasingly recognized that values matter in economic discourse, in this book we have dug deeper: our values have complex roots, as they are shaped by our hopes and desires, which are tied to a sense of ultimate reality. It is here that theology can be of help. Understood as self-critical reflection on images of ultimate reality or God,[2] theology helps us to address two significant questions: Where do images of God come from, and where do they lead us?[3] In addition, theology might help us identify alternatives that are often repressed. In this context, arguments about values often tend to short-circuit the debate. The notion of self-interest is a case in point: while economists in the tradition of Adam Smith have regarded self-interest as a positive factor which drives the economy and contributes to common interest and progress,[4] in common ethical opinion and in most ethical debates self-interest is usually portrayed as a negative value that can only lead to selfishness. Robert Nelson notes that such general ethical prejudices are among the biggest hurdles for students of economics. The first task of economics, which strongly depends on the concept of self-interest, is, therefore, to overcome such common ethical short circuits. Free-market economists do this, for instance, by trying to demonstrate that free markets work successfully and are, thus, able to channel self-interest in support of common interest and the common good.[5] In this context, the question is not whether economics has values or not—even self-interest can be seen as a positive value—but which values are affirmed based on the bigger picture. Here we enter the realm of theology.

The work of Nelson supports my argument when he points beyond the ethical to the religious dimensions of economics. The free-market economy, in his opinion, is based not only on ethics but also on a religion, which is able to provide the larger framework for the pursuit of self-interest.[6] Nevertheless, Nelson does not raise the question of God. Going beyond Nelson, we need to ask what images of God and ultimate reality are presupposed in such a religion. What are the foundations of our hope, and where are our desires rooted? The tools of theological reflection will help us in this search, allowing us to dig deeper, and to investigate how solid those foundations are. As we have seen in the previous chapter, theological reasoning can contribute to fresh perspectives on issues such as self-interest, pushing beyond the common ethical demonizations as well as the unilateral economic endorsements of the concept. Theology will only be of help, however, if we keep in mind its contextual nature. Even seemingly abstract and general dogmatic theological statements and confessions of faith are rooted in particular contexts. When 1 John 4:16 claims that God is love, for instance, the reference is not to love in general but to a particular history of love that is closely connected to how the authors of the passage experienced God's love in their own world. When the context of theological statements is neglected, we end up with absolute images of God that can no longer be debated and corrected, and that are, therefore, easily misused. Church history is full of examples of such misuse of absolute images of God—usually in the interest of the powers that be.[7] The most severe trouble emerges when such images of God operate implicitly and below the surface, without being recognized.

Once both our implicit and explicit images of God are uncovered and brought out into the open—the work that is done in the previous chapters of this book—theology can engage them, debate them, and propose alternatives. German theologian Ulrich Duchrow and a team of German-speaking theologians have sought to addresses these theological underpinnings in a context that is usually confined to a debate of ethics and values. Duchrow observes that in addressing ethical issues like, for instance, the moral responsibility of CEOs and other business leaders, bigger problems are often hidden, and the system itself is endorsed or at least goes unchallenged.[8] Rather than limiting the discussion to the ethical performance of representatives of the system, we need to take a deeper look at the system and the theology that grounds it. Duchrow's comments are made in the context of a position paper by the Evangelische Kirche in Germany (EKD), which emphasizes the ethical responsibility of CEOs while explicitly endorsing the system of corporate profits and economic competition.[9] To be sure, the ethical critique leveled here is stronger than most public pronouncements by prominent Christian leaders in the United States in the new millennium: Wolfgang Huber, the presiding bishop of the Evangelische Kirche, made national headlines with his ethical critique of CEOs. In a case that drew much media attention in Germany, he challenged the chairman of the Deutsche Bank, Josef Ackermann, for focusing too much on profits and not enough on his responsibility for the common good in times of financial crisis. Huber, moving beyond the realm of ethics into the realm of theology, went on to compare this attitude to worshiping a golden calf.[10]

While Huber makes reference to idolatry in the context of a particular overemphasis on profits, he does not question the system that produces profits. Duchrow, on the other hand, identifies a full-fledged theological problem with the system itself that has reached the status of a confessional issue for the church.[11] Reminiscent of the struggles of the European Reformation in the sixteenth century, economics is identified in this latter position as a confessional issue that cuts to the heart of what the church believes. As a result, theologians and the churches are challenged to take a confessional stance that challenges the implicit theology of the free market, which is becoming more and more explicit. Unlike many theological arguments that remain confined to the realm of the academy, this argument has been picked up by large international church bodies—in particular, by the Lutheran World Federation (LWF) and by the World Alliance of Reformed Churches (WARC), which have developed theological statements that address the theology of the market.

The Tenth Assembly of the LWF in 2003 formulated the challenge in this way:

> Through our diverse experiences, we are facing the same negative consequences of neoliberal economic policies (i.e., the Washington Consensus) that are leading to increased hardship, suffering and injustice in our communities. As a communion, we must engage the false ideology of neoliberal economic globalization by confronting, converting and changing this reality and its effects. This false ideology is grounded in the assumption that the market, built on private property, unrestrained competition and the centrality of contracts, is the absolute law governing human life, society and the natural environment. This is idolatry

and leads to the systematic exclusion of those who own no property, the destruction of cultural diversity, the dismantling of fragile democracies and the destruction of the earth.[12]

The theological problem is clearly stated here: it is the full-fledged idolatry of the free market as false god, which is characteristic of the system as a whole and goes beyond individual ethical missteps. This problem is compounded by its results that, as the document states, can be observed particularly in the global South and in Central Eastern Europe. The assembly further notes the results of what it denounces as the results of the idolatrous worship of false gods: a growing gap between the rich and the poor that especially affects women, youth, and children; the marginalization of Indigenous people; the growing international debt; unemployment and underemployment; and free trade of capital and goods without free movement for people.[13] This analysis leads to a renewed commitment by the church to assume its prophetic role by promoting justice and human rights; raising awareness of these problems; and taking concrete action through ecumenical partnerships between the churches, multifaith cooperation, and participation in social alliances like the World Social Forum.[14]

The WARC in 2004 took an even clearer theological position, after providing the following analysis of the problem:

> In classical liberal economics, the state exists to protect private property and contracts in the competitive market. Through the struggles of the labour movement, states began to regulate markets and provide for the welfare of people. Since the 1980s, through the transnationalization of capital, neoliberalism has set out to dismantle the welfare functions of the state. Under neoliberalism the purpose of the economy is to increase profits and return for the owners of production and financial capital, while excluding the majority of the people and treating nature as a commodity. As markets have become global, so have the political and legal institutions which protect them. The government of the United States of America and its allies, together with international finance and trade institutions (International Monetary Fund, World Bank, World Trade Organization) use political, economic, or military alliances to protect and advance the interest of capital owners.

This analysis, which makes explicit reference to the working class and the ownership class, leads to the following theological statement: "Speaking from our Reformed tradition and having read the signs of the times, the General Council of the World Alliance of Reformed Churches affirms that global economic justice is essential to the integrity of our faith in God and our discipleship as Christians. We believe that the integrity of our faith is at stake if we remain silent or refuse to act in the face of the current system of neoliberal economic globalization and therefore we confess before God and one another." Thus, what is at stake is not just an economic matter but the heart of the Christian faith itself.

From this crucial insight, the WARC pronounces a series of confessions and rejections that are modeled after the Barmen Declaration in which the German Confessing Church pronounced its resistance to Nazi Germany in 1934. Here are some examples: confessing God as Creator and Sustainer of life and Jesus' mission to bring the fullness of life (reference to John 10:10 and Ps 24:1), the WARC rejects "the current world economic order imposed by global neoliberal capitalism and any other economic system, including absolute planned economies, which defy God's covenant by excluding the poor, the vulnerable and the whole of creation from the fullness of life," as well as "any claim of economic, political, and military empire which subverts God's sovereignty over life and acts contrary to God's just rule." Confessing God's covenant with all of creation as gift of grace, which includes the poor and marginalized as "preferential partners" (reference to Gen 9:8-12; Isa 55:1; Matt 25:40; and Hos 2:18; and the following), the WARC rejects "the culture of rampant consumerism and the competitive greed and selfishness of the neoliberal global market system, or any other system, which claims there is no alternative." Confessing that human beings are called to choose God over Mammon, the WARC rejects "the unregulated accumulation of wealth and limitless growth that has already cost the lives of millions and destroyed much of God's creation." Confessing that God is a God of justice and the God of the destitute, the poor, the exploited, the wronged, and the abused (reference to Ps 146:7-9), the WARC rejects "any ideology or economic regime that puts profits before people, does not care for all creation, and privatizes those gifts of God meant for all," as well as "any teaching which justifies those who support, or fail to resist, such an ideology in the name of the gospel." Based on the confession that God requires us to do justice, love kindness, and walk in God's ways (reference to Mic 6:8 and Amos 5:24); the WARC rejects "any theology that claims that God is only with the rich and that poverty is the fault of the poor. We reject any form of injustice which destroys right relations—gender, race, class, disability, or caste," and "any theology which affirms that human interests dominate nature."[15]

I am referencing these two documents so extensively because, in the United States, it is not very well known that churches have taken explicit theological stands on these matters. There are other examples as well, including some statements by the United States Conference of Roman Catholic Bishops and by the United Methodist Church. In their Pastoral Letter "Economic Justice for All," the Roman Catholic bishops state, for instance, that "our faith calls us to measure this economy, not by what it produces but also by how it touches human life and whether it protects or undermines the dignity of the human person." On this basis, the bishops suggest "that the time has come for a 'New American Experiment'—to implement economic rights, to broaden the sharing of economic power, and to make economic decisions more accountable to the common good."[16] The United Methodist Church states in its Social Principles that "all economic systems" are "under the judgment of God no less than other facets of the created order," and claims support for "measures that would reduce the concentration of wealth in the hands of a few."[17] All these statements provide important starting points as they raise the implicit theology of the market to the level of consciousness, begin to engage it, and suggest alternatives. More work needs to be done, however, as the systematic nature of the theology of the market needs to be explored further and analyzed more succinctly. This chapter will provide additional suggestions for how theology matters in economic discourse.

Religion and Economics, Upside Down

The problem with religion and economics is not that there are overlaps and that economics shapes religion—just as religion impacts economics. The problem is that mainline religion and mainline economics cover up these connections, and, by doing so, they endorse the status quo. This sense has grown stronger throughout the chapters of this book and is confirmed by a comment of Robert Nelson on the importance of Adam Smith: "The greatest significance of Adam Smith to the economic history of the world was not in any power of economic explanation but in offering a 'scientific' doctrine by which the many losers from all this radical change could be persuaded to accept their faith without active revolt."[18] From the Christian perspective, we are dealing here with a theological distortion that puts at risk the Christian faith itself, which cannot be reconciled with any logic that keeps down the "losers" and the lost.

There is something odd about Christianity when it seeks to move from the top down, although this has become a common mode of operation over the centuries. From the German perspective, sociologist Dirk Baecker has pointed out that free-market capitalism now functions like the spirits and gods of old: one has no choice but to submit to its tempers and decisions—ambivalence is eschewed, and no critique is permitted. Baecker doubts that the critique of religion will help much, as capitalism, itself, has turned into religion, equating money and the divine.[19] Another German scholar, Christoph Deutschmann, argues that, in such a situation, replacing one myth with another may not help anymore: "disenchantment" and "weaning" should be the next steps.[20] Religion, itself, needs critique and demystification.

Yet there are alternatives to capitalism, which are often overlooked, some of them as old as capitalism itself. Only twelve years before the publication of

Adam Smith's *The Wealth of Nations,* John Wesley, the founder of Methodism, wrote in his journal: "Religion must not go from the greatest to the least, or the power would appear to be of men."[21] This statement anticipates much of the nineteenth-century critique of religion, which argued that religion was, for the most part, a projection of people's ideals.[22] Yet Wesley's statement also contains what is missing in the nineteenth-century critique of religion: namely, a sense that this critique may not apply to religion in general. Rather, we are dealing here with the critique of the religion of the powerful who are accustomed to shaping everything in their image: their workers, their colonies, the political system, the world of the intellect, and also religion. Religious projection is primarily (although not exclusively) the problem of the powerful, and so it is not surprising that these processes are still at work when we imagine God in terms of all those who operate from the top down: the superrich, the superpowers, and so on. Such images of God may indeed be not much more than the projections of wealth and power.

From this perspective, we can observe an odd aspect of Smith's account that is missed by all those who praise Smith's "realism," economists and theologians alike: due to his belief in the balancing effects of the market, he does not perceive the dangers of a position of top-down power. These dangers can only be seen from the perspective of those who do not benefit from the market—the kinds of people with whom John Wesley was in ministry, like the members of the newly emerging working class, as well as those who were even worse off due to dismal poverty, crippling sickness, imprisonment, or slavery. If the religion that goes "from the greatest to the least" is easily unmasked as a human construct—the construct of the powerful, to be precise—the religion that goes the other way around may have more promise. This type of religion from the bottom up cannot be explained quite so easily. No one will be surprised if those who are in control of great fortunes and who command positions of power are successful at imposing their own interests on whatever they choose—religion and images of the divine included. This is the default mode of how things work, for even those who occupy less powerful positions usually turn to those who are in positions of power in order to make things happen. Mainline churches, for the most part, tend to function in this way: they build their budgets on the contributions of the biggest donors and model their programs accordingly.[23] The construction of anything from the underside, however, follows a different process.

In the previous chapter, we mentioned that Moses organized a band of slaves and that Jesus was a construction worker. Many other traditions in the Bible follow this bottom-up logic: when Israel demands a king after a long history of alternative forms of rule, God pronounces a severe warning that kings will take people's sons for their armies and their daughters as servants, demand the best of their fields, and ultimately enslave everyone (1 Sam 8:10-18).

When God finally gives in to the will of the people and appoints a king, things take a turn for the worse—and, when God appoints the next king, God chooses not the tallest and strongest but the youngest son of a family, who did not even count in his own father's eyes (1 Sam 16:1-13). When Christianity was tempted to adapt to the Roman Empire, the Apostle Paul noted that "God chose what is foolish in the world to shame the wise; God chose what is weak in the world to shame the strong; God chose what is low and despised in the world, things that are not, to reduce to nothing things that are" (1 Cor 1:27-28). In these passages and many more like them, a deep logic of the Judeo-Christian traditions is anchored. The ancient confession that Jesus Christ is both fully divine and fully human, which unites most Christian denominations, adds another wrinkle to this logic that is hardly considered by most contemporary Christians. In Jesus Christ, Godself not only takes the side of construction workers, but becomes a construction worker; this is the reality to which the often mystified term *kenosis* (God's self-emptying in the incarnation) refers. When Christians affirm that "the Word became flesh and lived among us" (John 1:14), we must no longer overlook the fact that Christ became flesh in a particular body, in a particular place and time, and in a particular social location—as the son of a construction worker and an unwed mother at the margins of the Jewish world, which, itself, was merely at the margins of the Roman Empire.

Christianity has too often repressed these facts, and the commonly re-cited creeds, the Apostles' Creed and the Nicene Creed, make no reference at all to the life and ministry of Christ. Fortunately, this tendency of spiritualiz-ing and generalizing Jesus has never gone uncontested, and it can be argued that the Gospels of the New Testament were written in order to combat it. Mainline Christian theology has had a hard time admitting to the particular-ity of the person of Jesus throughout its two-thousand-year history; even at the Council of Chalcedon in 451, when the fullness of Jesus' humanity was asserted together with his divinity, this issue was skirted, as both Jesus' humanity and his divinity were asserted in general terms, without reference to the kind of person that Jesus was. The result of this oversight was not the affirmation of generic humanity, as is often believed; the result was the affirmation of dominant humanity at the time and of dominant humanity ever since. Since there is no generic humanity (just like there can be no theo-logical vacuum), if nothing is specified and no particulars are mentioned, the top-down position becomes the default position.

For Christianity, it is the incarnation of God in the construction worker Jesus Christ, born in a stable rather than a palace, in the company of service workers who tended other people's sheep (Luke 2:1-20), which turns things upside down. The typical religiosity that goes from the greatest to the least comes to a halt here and is turned around. This has implications for our images of God and, ultimately for Godself. If this Jesus was really God—"of the same substance" with God, as the Nicene Creed states—there must be something to God's substance that is overlooked in mainline religion. Even the pre-Christian story of Moses becomes clearer when seen in this light, as it now makes more sense why God would speak the following sentences: "I have observed the misery of my people who are in Egypt; I have heard their cry on account of their taskmasters. Indeed, I know their sufferings, and I have come down to deliver them from the Egyptians" (Exod 3:7-8). The theological grounding of what we have called *the logic of downturn* is now established even more firmly. As the incarnation of God in Jesus Christ turns things upside down, we might say that the incarnation is the logic of downturn. This position has deep roots in the Christian traditions.

In recent theological history, Dietrich Bonhoeffer suggested that we need to "follow God where God has already preceded us,"[24] and even the mature Karl Barth of the *Church Dogmatics* stated clearly that God takes the side of those who are oppressed: "God always takes His stand unconditionally and passionately on this side and on this side alone: against the lofty and on behalf of the lowly, against those who already enjoy right and privilege and on behalf of those who are denied it and deprived of it."[25] More recently, liberation theologians have developed similar insights further in ways that have still not yet been fully digested by contemporary theology.[26] All these voices remind us, in their own ways, that the problem with failing to look on the underside where God is at work in the world is not merely that we are losing an important aspect of the image of God; the problem is that we might miss the reality of God altogether. This insight cannot be overemphasized.

The story of what has been called "urban ministry" offers an example of what is at stake here. Current efforts by churches to engage in ministry in urban areas are commonly built on the presupposition that we need to bring God back into these places: it is implicitly assumed that God left the cities when middle-class churches moved to the suburbs as a result of white flight and growing affluence. According to this logic, God moves with those whose fortunes and wealth are increasing, and the increase in fortune and wealth is seen as proof of the presence of God, just like the decrease of fortune and wealth in urban areas is seen as proof of the absence of God. In this situation, the task of the church is seen as bringing God back into these places of struggle. Based on what we have found so far, however, there is another option that is hardly considered: What if God did not leave the city when the churches left? Such a thought would not only imply a different approach to the praxis of urban ministry, it would also imply a different theology, which would take the notion of God's incarnation at the underside of history seriously.

From this perspective, not all of religion is necessarily a projection. If Christianity moves the other way around—according to its own inherent

logic, not "from the greatest to the least," but from the least to the greatest—new perspectives open up where projection is not the major concern
due to a lack of power and incentives to project. This is true not just for
theology and religion but also for economics. If economics is too often the
projection of those who benefit from it—with all the resulting problems
of the creation of bubbles based on wishful thinking such as we have seen
in recent history—things change when economics is seen from the bottom
up. The persons who end up homeless and on the street, for instance, may
have some important insights, of which the CEOs are not aware, about how
the economy functions. The workers whose wages and benefits are slashed
know something about the economy that differs from the insight of mainline economists. These insights counter common-sense epistemology, which
assumes that the clearest view is either from the top or from a neutral position—the latter of which, as we have seen, does not exist. Furthermore,
these insights push beyond the sort of projections and wishful thinking that
prevent those on the top from seeing what is really going on where the rub-
ber hits the road. A fundamental challenge emerges here that goes beyond
the regular sort of challenges, which merely seek to add another perspective
on top of conventional perspectives. Conventional perspectives in both theology and economics, which are usually top-down perspectives, need to be
rethought from the bottom up.

Context thus becomes an important aspect of theological and economic
reflection—but not any context will do. In the Judeo-Christian theological traditions, what matters is the context that is chosen by the divine: this
context, as it is described in many parts of the Bible, is with an insignificant
people in the Middle East, rather than with the established empires of the
Egyptians, Assyrians, Babylonians, or Persians; with people in exile; with the
poor and downtrodden of whom the prophets of the eighth century BCE
spoke; with the "least of these," who are the companions of Jesus; with the
persecuted churches of early Christianity; and with struggling people ever
since (Matt 11:28). In addition, this bottom-up context is also for the most
part the context of the religious leaders in these traditions (a fact which is
often overlooked): patriarchs, prophets, kings, the priests, bishops, elders,
apostles, and Jesus' disciples are all located in bottom-up contexts to varying
degrees.

Economists might find this structure attractive because it could contribute to creating the sort of economy from which everyone would benefit, not
just the chosen few. There is now an alternative to operating from the top
down, to trusting without evidence that a rising tide will lift all boats and
that the growing wealth amassed at the top will eventually trickle down. As
these mainline models are failing us, considering the plight and the struggles
of those on the bottom of the system could lead to a new beginning. Pay-

ing attention to those on whose shoulders the current economy rests—workers, in particular, but also all others who bear an inordinate share of its burdens, including those who get stuck in what economists consider the necessary quota of unemployment—would make a tremendous difference. What if economists understood that bankers, stock brokers, stockholders, CEOs, CFOs, managers, presidents, and board members are all located in this bottom-up context as well, whether they realize it or not? This is not to say that theology has all the answers and that it could provide neatly detailed blueprints for economics; but theology can help rethink fundamental matters of perspective and of that which ultimately matters, thus sparking some new research both in its own field and in the field of economics.

These reversals—moving from the bottom up rather than from the top down—do not require a naïve understanding of human nature or unbridled optimism. The energy for change does not have to be produced by some heroic leader but exists already at the bottom, produced in the processes of repression discussed in the previous chapter. This energy at the bottom is often missed, not only because those on the top fail to recognize it, but because it cannot easily be harvested for their projects. People may drag their feet when they get the impression that their work produces results mostly for others' benefit, rather than for that of themselves and their families. If workers do not benefit from their work, their energy goes elsewhere. However, when people begin to reap more of the benefits of their work, they are willing to put more effort and creativity into their work. While free-market economics has understood this phenomenon, to a certain extent, at the level of economic leadership—most leaders are highly motivated because they reap some benefits from what they do—this insight has not "trickled down" to the level of the workers, whose wages and benefits continue to be slashed, increasingly robbing them of motivation.

This is not to mean that a few mild concessions to workers would suffice. The levels of motivation, effort, and creativity will rise according to the levels at which workers are able to truly participate in their work and benefit from it, to the point that ownership of the means of production may have to be reconsidered in economic theory. When that latter question is broached, of course, it is commonly assumed that the ruling class and management must be the losers, but this is not necessarily true. The biggest surprise of a bottom-up movement may be that it benefits everyone: if all contribute their best efforts, the project as a whole will benefit. Such a dynamic could be seen, for instance, when Argentinean workers took over some of the factories that were supposed to be closed in the early 2000s: by increasing their efforts, by collaborating, and by assuming roles of leadership, they were able to save some of their factories. Unfortunately, owners and management often returned after the workers had saved their businesses, and refused to acknowledge the accomplishment of the workers.[27] What if the owners and the management of a factory that was saved by its workers had entered into a new relation with the workers, where workers gained some level of leadership and ownership, and what if the owners had made their expertise available for the good of all?

As noted earlier, the basic problem at the intersection of theology and economics is not that both espouse hopes and desires, and that both presuppose images of God and of ultimate reality. The basic problem has to do with the question of whether or not those hopes and desires are adequate and support life not just for a few, but for everyone. No matter what the prophets of prosperity may say, God does not guarantee the unlimited economic success of God's people in a capitalist system. In fact, faith that follows Jesus leads in a different direction, not "up" but elsewhere: "out into the roads and lanes" (Luke 14:23). Religion and economics, turned upside down, bring us back to the logic of downturn, which provides a new perspective on God that is more in touch with the God of the Bible because it is in touch with the people on the underside. The hope and desire that grow from this alternative view of God produce resistance and open up alternatives that the current economic elites do not want us to see.

In the midst of long-term downturn, the top-down view of God becomes questionable. In Europe, for instance, members of the working class, who have collectively experienced the pressures of the system since the beginning of industrialization, are often atheists. What they reject, however, are not necessarily all images of God, in general, but certain well-established forms of theism manifest in the established churches, which have a long history of backing up the status quo and of identifying God with the powers that be. Here is an interesting parallel to early Christianity, where this situation was reversed. Early Christians were considered atheists as well, and for good reasons. Not only did they refuse to affirm the gods of the Roman Empire; their God who died on a cross clearly did not match the requirements of classical theism. From the Latin American perspective, Assmann and Hinkelammert affirm this sort of atheism, arguing that it is necessary when dealing with the god of the market; only by declaring themselves atheists in terms of the god of the market can people believe in the Christian God.[28] This was also the reality of the workers in a small industrial town in Switzerland in the early decades of the twentieth century, and this reality changed the history of Christian theology when it led theologian Karl Barth, as their pastor, to the insight that God is indeed "Wholly Other": not the god of the theism of the status quo but the God who transforms the world from the bottom up in Jesus Christ. In Barth's somewhat mystifying language: "He whose nature and essence consist, whose existence is proved, in His descending into the depths [in Jesus Christ], He the Merciful, who gives Himself up for His creature to the utter depths of the existence of His creature—He is God in the highest. . . . the highness of God consists in His thus descending."[29]

The perspective from below challenges a tendency towards spiritualization that exists in both theology and economics. Michael Hardt and Antonio Negri are right when they argue that "economics, if it is to be a science, has to return to something closer to the ancient Greek meaning of the term and take *all of social life* into consideration." This includes taking into account, for instance, "the new common anthropology and the intellectual and affective power of productive labor."[30] In addition, the view from the bottom up needs to take into account not just management and workers, but also those forced to live in abject poverty and those who are now completely excluded from the global economy because they have nothing to contribute. In Christian theology, a similar argument can be made for taking *all of social life* into consideration, since the reality of God relates to all of life, including the interests of economics.[31] A deep concern for the material world is a common, though often neglected, thread in Christian theology; it goes back to the Jewish traditions, where Godself creates heaven and earth and reaffirms this commitment to the material world and its rhythms once and for all after the Great Flood (Gen 8:21-22). It is often overlooked that, in the Hebrew Bible, the concern of theology is not the divine as it relates to nonmaterial realities or an afterlife (an idea that appears only very late in the history of this literature) but life in this world and its well-being. Spirituality, in this context, is inextricably bound up with the material at every turn, and this is the ground on which Christianity rests as well.

Justice in Economics and Religion

As we have seen, the success of the market is not just based on the exploits of capital; labor makes much more significant contributions than mainline economists acknowledge. Capital, itself, is ultimately produced through labor, a fact that the bubble economies of recent years have increasingly covered up. Unless labor is honored for its contributions to the economy, wealth keeps trickling up, not down. This raises the question of justice.

In neoclassical free-market economics, *justice* is often applied as a formal principle. Arguments against a progressive tax, for instance, according to which the wealthy are taxed at higher rates, are based on a formal understanding of justice as fairness. Those who follow this model of justice tend to prefer a flat tax or flat-rate tax, which treats everyone equally, so that the wealthiest and the poorest would pay exactly the same percentage of income as a tax. Free-market economics is often based on this particular understanding of justice, as well, as exemplified by economist Friedrich von Hayek's critique of the notion of "social justice." Justice, according to von Hayek, means "the fair and impartial application of legal, moral and perhaps customary rules." If this kind of fairness is not guaranteed, according to von Hayek, the world is turned upside down: "Precede [the word 'justice'] with the word 'social' and everything changes. Social justice may require redistributing property and treating people unequally. In this way the word 'social' empties the nouns it is applied to of their meaning."[32] At first sight, many people would agree with von Hayek that "treating people unequally" cannot promote justice—only fairness can do that, by "treating everyone exactly alike."

The free market can be understood as the ultimate arbiter of this sort of justice, since here everyone appears to be treated the same. Everyone needs to compete, and, in the ideal state of the market, there are no special conditions for anyone. All participants in the market are considered to be equal. This is not the case, of course, in the real world. There is a substantial difference between large and small participants in the market. Not all participants in the market are equal, for instance, if the government steps in as a matter of course when large corporations are in trouble in order to save them. This is not only the case with the bailouts of the largest corporations, which began with the financial sector in 2008 and 2009. Some worry that this will be part of a new set of policies adopted by the Obama administration, but similar steps were taken under previous administrations as well. In the aftermath of September 11, 2001, for instance, the Bush administration endorsed substantial support to embattled corporations, like the airlines and others which were affected by the fallout of the terrorist attacks. In addition, large corporations often get special deals, like tax breaks and governmental subsidies for their projects. It may seem paradoxical, but proponents of the free market have been among the strongest supporters of such programs. Even the so-called free-trade agreements, like the North American Free Trade Agreement (NAFTA), contain many stipulations intended to boost the position of the most powerful players in the market. Chapter eleven of the NAFTA agreements even allows corporations to sue the governments of Canada, the United States, and Mexico for compensation if any of their policy decisions have a negative impact on their investments.[33] Liberalization of the trade of agricultural products with Mexico, to name another example, was skewed in favor of U.S. farmers, who receive substantial subsidies from the U.S. government. The result was substantial downward pressure on the price of corn in Mexico, which is often produced by small farmers. There does not appear to be much of a level playing field for all participants in the market.

Yet even if market relations were fair and balanced, and no special deals were made that give preferential treatment to the more powerful participants in the market—this is the situation that Adam Smith envisioned and that the textbooks presuppose—significant problems remain. The equal treatment of unequals may well be the greatest injustice of all, especially in situations of severe power differentials.[34] When, in the ideal situation of the free market, unequals are made to compete on level ground, the outcome can easily be predicted. Children perhaps understand this problem better than adults, especially those who are in a position to view things from the perspective of the disadvantaged. A five-year-old child, for example, intuitively understands why a race where the same rules apply to a five-year-old and an eleven-year-old cannot be considered to be just; treating a five-year-old and an eleven-year-old exactly alike in a competitive situation would indeed be the greatest injustice of all. Based on this simple insight, it is not hard to see why a free market, in which significant differentials of power and wealth exist, cannot lead to greater justice for all—certainly not without a strong belief in some invisible hand of the market. This insight is especially important in a situation where large corporations dominate the economic scene. When Wal-Mart Stores, Inc., moves into a community, for instance, small businesses often cannot survive, and they are not supposed to survive; this is part of the business plan. In this case, the free market does not work for small-business owners, due to the advantage of large corporations, which is often intentionally boosted by lowering prices initially until the competition is ruined. What is true in the world of business—as large businesses increasingly take over the territory of small businesses—is also true in the world of labor. In a situation where workers have nothing to sell but their labor, and where they have little other support, the corporations who employ them have a tremendous advantage. This advantage is compounded under the conditions of globalization, when workers are played off against each other on the global scene.

Justice defined as fairness is, therefore, not a helpful concept in situations of grave power differentials. An alternative perspective emerges from those who are the losers in the current situation, like workers, small business owners, and the growing masses of those who cannot find or keep a job in an economy where jobs are increasingly under pressure. This brings us back to the logic of downturn. Here, theology in the Judeo-Christian tradition can make a significant contribution, as many of the traditions on which it builds adopt the perspective of people under pressure and find the divine there.

From the perspective of those who are affected the most by downturn, justice might be redefined as being in solidarity with those who experience injustice and as taking the sides of those who have been marginalized and excluded from the community and from relationship. This is precisely the notion of justice that is most common in the texts of both the Old and the New Testaments. In many biblical texts, justice refers not to the notion of fairness but to a covenant—that is, to a relationship between God and humanity which is dynamic and responsive. This relationship is expressed in terms of God's faithfulness, which implies God's special concern for those pushed to the margins of the covenant and for those who are excluded by some who are under the mistaken impression that their way of life is closer to God.[35] Justice in the Judeo-Christian traditions has to do, therefore, with a particular concern for the restoration of relationship with those who are excluded from relationships and pushed to the margins of the covenant: the proverbial widows, orphans, and strangers of the Old Testament; and the fishermen, prostitutes, tax collectors, and the sick of the New Testament. In this context, restoration of relationship with the marginalized is not simply a social issue or the moral consequence of faith; rather, the quality of faith, itself, and the relationship with the divine are closely connected to the restoration of relationships among the people, since distortions in relations to others get reproduced as distortions in relations to God, and vice versa.[36] This revised notion of justice reshapes the relation of theology and economics in the following ways:

First, justice is now linked to a detailed account of the kinds of pressures that people who do not benefit from the free-market economy have to endure in their lives.[37] Viewed from the perspectives of those pushed to the margins, there can be no illusion of equality or a level playing field. As a result, a structural understanding of injustice emerges. From this perspective, there cannot be a grand theory of justice—whether theological or economic—based solely in the world of ideas. This attention to the pressures that people have to endure requires a very close look at the claims of individual achievement in the current economy. Individualism is questioned at the most fundamental level here. Is the wealth of corporate America built single-handedly by a few prominent CEOs, as their compensation packages seems to indicate—or is it, rather, tied to the labor of billions in a globalizing economy who are forced to work under constantly worsening conditions? From the perspective of workers who are pressed to sell their labor for less and less money, the individualism displayed by top-level CEOs is easily exposed as fraud. The challenge for the system is, thus, not to become less individualistic but to become aware of the relationships already in place, to put an end to the cover-up, and to form less asymmetric relationships. This insight has important implications for the relationship to God as well, and here a revised notion of justice holds an important lesson, especially for those in positions of power and control: as they misrecognize their relationship to other people, they are also prone to misrecognize their relationship to God. Neither a well-meaning communitarian approach nor the insistence on equal rights makes much of a difference here—in fact, both communitarianism and equal rights might be harmful since both discourses often cover up the differences in power that produce unjust relationships.[38]

Second, justice that is aware of power transcends the common focus on distribution and takes into account productivity. Injustice is tied not just to unequal distribution but to the dramatic differences in the valuation of productivity. Thus, justice provides an adjustment of the value attached to various forms of productivity. Such justice is the opposite of the giving of alms, and neither is it primarily concerned about social programs supposed to level the playing field, nor about advocacy for the marginalized. Justice in touch with the lives of those under pressure in a free-market economy leads to a new awareness and valuation of their productivity—and, thus, it might lead also to a new awareness of God's own mysterious productivity in places where we least expect it, even on a Roman cross. Once the free market's myth of individualism and fairness gives way to an awareness of actual relationships, the location of true productivity with those who do the actual work in the global economy can be seen. This productivity bears a certain family resemblance to the kind of energy that is set free at the personal level once persons connect with their repressions. Below the surface, at the level of what has been repressed, lie tremendous energies that push toward transformation and justice—not primarily in justice's punitive or redistributive forms but in the form of creating a space for alternative productivity. It should go without saying that these energies must not be romanticized or idealized.[39] We must not forget that our desires are ultimately formed in moments of repression, as Freud noted; any hope for transforming desire needs to take into account these repressions. Elsa Tamez reinterprets Paul's doctrine of justification by faith in a parallel way, as focusing on productivity: "Insofar as it is by faith and not by law that one is justified, the excluded person becomes aware of being a historical subject and not an object."[40] Such alternative productivity is one of the things that mainline religion is unable to deal with, because it never realizes that the divine is at work from below rather than from above; for similar reasons, mainline economics misses this alternative productivity as well.

Third, justice that takes the sides of those pushed to the margins of the economy is concerned about broken relationships. The restoration of relationships also precedes the more common concern for distribution. The initial step in the context of broken relationships is a search for solidarity. Economic pressures tend to weld together people who are vastly different—including those white-collar employees (often white and male) who are now also experiencing the economic squeeze firsthand. Theologians could be ahead of the game if they realized that the distortion of economic relations is a central issue in both Christianity and other religions—once again, not merely as a social or ethical issue, but also in terms of the distortion of our relation to the divine.[41] Community needs to be rebuilt in response to the particular forms in which it has broken down and in terms of where the pressures fuse us together—thus the need to pay close attention to economics as one of the primary matters of life and death, although this is obviously not the only reality that matters. This is the context of the preferential option for the poor, a notion initially developed by Latin American liberation theologians, which has often been misunderstood as a special-interest concern which neglects the interests of the rich. Yet, this was never the intention. A preferential option for the poor includes the rich—those who benefit most from asymmetries and distorted relationships—but it reminds us that they are faced with a particular challenge; the rich are the ones who need all the help (or *grace,* to use a theological term) that they can get, since they are the ones most beholden to the system and unable to step out of it. The energy and productivity that bubble up from the underside of the economy—God's own location in Christ's ministry, death, and resurrection—provide some help by pushing toward justice, not in punitive or retributive ways, but by initiating the transformation of relationships.

Finally, justice understood as solidarity and as taking sides throws new light on our vision of ultimate reality and, thus, on images of the divine. The biblical sources, although not lacking in diversity, converge in various important ways. What many of the biblical notions of justice have in common is their focus on relationship. The Hebrew verb *ṣdq* means to be faithful to the community established by the covenant.[42] The Greek term *dikaiosynē,* as used in the New Testament, has not eclipsed this emphasis on relationship. Although there is no uniform notion of justice in the New Testament, justice tends to include both the relations between human beings and the relation to God; here is a significant difference to the classical Greek notion of *dikaiosynē,* which focuses exclusively on the relations between human beings.[43] In the works of the prophets of the Old Testament, the term justice specifically addresses the distorted relationships between the rich and the poor, caused by oppressive actions of the rich, who "trample on the poor" (Amos 5:11), an action that also distorts their relationship with God.[44] This distortion of relationships by oppression is a concern in various parts of the Bible—the Psalms come to mind as another prominent example[45]—and can also be found in Jesus' sayings and other parts of the New Testament. Justice in all of these cases aims at the restoration of relationships with others and with God, and at putting an end to oppression. The primary concern of justice is, thus, not so much helping those in need but overcoming oppressive relationships and learning how to relate differently—both to other human beings and to God. The Apostle Paul's notion of justification can be seen in a similar light: not simply as a religious transaction but as a manifestation of God's justice, which resists injustice and reconstructs distorted relationships.[46]

As a result, justice, as restoring broken relationships, needs to address the power differential between oppressor and oppressed, and is partisan insofar as God sides with those who are trampled underfoot. Gustavo Gutiérrez's reflections, published three decades ago, match these more recent reflections: "To deal with a poor man or woman as Yahweh dealt with his people—this is what it is to be just." And: "To be just is to be faithful to the covenant. . . . Justice in the Bible is what unites one's relationship with the poor to one's relationship with God."[47]

The image of the divine emerging here is dynamic. A God who favors those whose relationships have been violated can never be pinned down in terms of an abstract notion of fairness. God takes sides for the benefit of all. Christians sometimes get sidetracked by wondering whether we are talking about "spiritual" or "social" processes here: Is this a matter of "social justice" or some other sort of justice? This question is moot, as the biblical traditions do not operate with this division: there is only one justice. If the Judeo-Christian God is God of all things, there is no way to separate those realms.

Religion, Freedom, and Private Property

One of the pillars of the free-market economy is the notion of private property. Freedom is often seen in conjunction with it, defined as the freedom to own private property and the freedom to do with it as one pleases. While the notion of freedom might have the potential to open things up and to relieve both economics and religion of some of their stuffiness, in the context of free-market economics the notion is mainly limited to the freedom of those who own property. This is reflected in the voting laws enacted early on in the United States of America, as only white men who owned property were allowed to vote and, thus, to participate in the budding democracy. Economic status and political rights were seen as related, and democracy was located at the intersection between the two. This situation was remedied in part as voting rights were successively granted to all white men, to African American men, and to women—of course not without substantial struggles. What were never addressed in these developments, though, were the implications a broadening political democracy might have for economics. This has led to a situation wherein economics and politics have drifted apart: while politics has moved in the direction of increased democracy, economics has become less and less democratic. Even the organized voice of workers, which used to uphold some semblance of democracy in economics, has come under increased attack in the past decades.

Some of the problems that are faced in the political arena are related to this lack of economic democracy in obvious ways, like, for instance, matters of campaign financing, which have a significant impact on politics, as the level of funding helps determine the outcome of elections. More worrisome, however, are the problems that are less visible, beginning with powerful political lobbyists and ending with "economic hit men," who further the causes of economic power concentrated in the hands of a few, not only abroad but—how could such massive power possibly be contained?—at home as well.[48] A sense of the challenge of the interests of large corporate property owners to democracy developed early in the United States and was expressed by Thomas Jefferson: "I hope we shall . . . crush in its birth the aristocracy of our moneyed corporations, which dare already to challenge our government to a trial of strength and bid defiance to the laws of our country."[49]

Karl Marx has described the ideal realm envisioned by the free-market economy with great clarity:

> This sphere . . . is in fact a very Eden of the innate rights of man. There alone rule Freedom, Equality, Property and Bentham [individualism]. Freedom, because both buyer and seller of a commodity, say of labour-power, are constrained only by their own free will. They contract as free agents, and the agreement they come to, is but the form in which they give legal expression to their common will. Equality, because each enters into relation with the other, as with a simple owner of commodities, and they exchange equivalent for equivalent. Property, because each disposes only of what is his own. And Bentham, because each looks only to himself. The only force that brings them together and puts them in relation with each others, is the selfishness, the gain and the private interests of each.

This is the ideal conception of the market and of freedom, which still dominates contemporary economics almost a century and a half later. Unfortunately, this ideal realm, which is "on the surface and in view of all men," is not the whole of reality. Something else is going on when we look at the relationship of power that is in place here. In the words of Marx: "He, who before was the money-owner, now strides in front as capitalist; the possessor of labour-power follows as his labourer. The one with an air of importance, smirking, intent on business; the other, timid and holding back, like one who is bringing his own hide to market and has nothing to expect but—a hiding."[50] This scenario depicts an important difference between employers and employees that is not taken into account in the ideal world of mainline economics and that we need to investigate here.

Milton Friedman fervently believed that the introduction of economic freedom—by whatever means necessary—would lead to political freedom and probably to religious and cultural freedom as well.[51] The basis of it all is the freedom of the market. Friedman reproduces and endorses the same image that Marx had already identified as an ideal existing only on the surface, without posing deeper questions:

> So long as effective freedom of exchange is maintained, the central feature of the market organization of economic activity is that it prevents one person from interfering with another in respect of most of his activities. The consumer is protected from coercion by the seller because of the presence of other sellers with whom he can deal. The seller is protected from coercion by the consumer because of other consumers to whom he can sell. The employee is protected from coercion by the employer because of other employers for whom he can work, and so on. And the market does this impersonally, and without centralized authority.

According to Friedman, the market must be trusted here, because "underlying most arguments against the free market is a lack of belief in freedom itself."[52] The history of the past thirty years of pursuing this logic tells, of course, another story, as more and more pressures have been put on the shoulders of workers and consumers whose "free choice" is increasingly an illusion. The freedom of which Friedman dreamed rings hollow now.

Friedman sees the enemy of freedom in "the power to coerce, be it in the hands of a monarch, a dictator, an oligarchy, or a momentary majority." Freedom, in his opinion, is established "by removing the organization of economic activity from the control of political authority," so that "the market eliminates this source of coercive power."[53] This argument is a common one now in popular discourses in the United States: there is a deep-seated distrust of government and its power. Yet, while the public sector is actively distrusted, trust in the private sector appears to know hardly any limit, even in situations of downturn. Friedman, himself, supports this idea, arguing that political power is centralized in a way that economic power is not, as "there can be many millionaires in one large economy" but not many truly outstanding leaders in politics.[54] Several things are overlooked here, however: the current popular sense, supported by Friedman, that governmental power is generally undesirable while private power is generally desirable, is odd. Why should people trust leaders of private business more than leaders of public policy? If anything, the argument should be reversed, since the basis of leadership in private business is diametrically opposed to the basis of leadership in public office: politicians are democratically elected by the people, while business leaders are not. And if one were to accuse a politician of having bought an election by using private funds, this accusation describes what is commonly accepted and seen as desirable in the world of business, where private funds translate directly into leadership and power without public elections. Moreover, those who level the common accusation of corruption in political circles hardly ever investigate who is doing the corrupting. Who might have an interest in corrupting politicians, and possess the means to do so?

In this context, ownership of property and command of capital is the foundation on which everything else rests, but which is neither discussed nor questioned. Theological arguments are often used in support of this situation. Adam Smith, for instance, assumed that the ownership of private property was given directly by God—a sort of deist theological argument, where God made the world once upon a time and then retreated and left things in the hands of humanity. Duchrow and Hinkelammert note other theological foundations: "The absoluteness of modern property does not derive directly from Roman law, but from the secularization of the idea that God is the absolute owner of creation." Neoscholastic theologians in the sixteenth and seventeenth centuries argued that God's absolute right over property could be conferred on humans. This notion was further developed in the seventeenth century by natural-law theorists like Hugo Grotius.[55] Thomas Frank notes the pressing need for divine sanctification of large differentials in property ownership and acquisition: "There is no social theory on earth short of the divine right of kings that can justify a five-hundred-fold gap [in salary] between management and labor."[56]

Nevertheless, modern economists following Milton Friedman do not have to make such explicitly theological assumptions. Friedman understands the constructed nature of property rights—a matter that gets more complex when intellectual property is considered from cultural production to biotechnological knowledge, which was not even an option when Friedman initially put his ideas to paper. Today, we should think about property in even broader terms, including the notion of "access."[57] Nevertheless, in Friedman's discussion of property and freedom, he takes the matter of property for granted, and thus another theological assumption comes in through the back door, as it were: property rights can be assumed to be absolute and nonnegotiable. The examples that Friedman uses presuppose property rights and merely consider cases where these rights are in conflict; for instance, whether one can "deny to someone else the right to fly over *my* land in *his* airplane. Or does *his* right to use *his* airplane take precedence?"[58] When the matter of property becomes problematic—for example, in the creation of a monopoly, which Friedman defines as a situation "when a specific individual or enterprise has sufficient control over a particular product or service to determine significantly the terms on which other individuals have access to it"—Friedman simply shrugs off the problem. Admitting that competition is never perfect, he concludes that "as I have studied economic activities in the United States, I have become increasingly impressed with how wide is the range of problems and industries for which it is appropriate to treat the economy as if it were competitive."[59] Worrying mostly about political coercion as the problem, and playing down the sort of coercion that is connected to the ownership and control of property, Friedman overlooks or hides the problem of what I called, in chapter 1, the "postcolonial empire," where power is mostly soft rather than hard, and where power is rooted in economic processes that are mostly invisible and under the surface.[60] A similar dynamic can be observed in the thought of Friedrich von Hayek, who, as we have seen, defines liberty as "that condition of men in which coercion of some by others is reduced as much as possible in society."[61] In this context, von Hayek states that liberty is more important than democracy. What is overlooked both by Friedman and von Hayek is not only the problem of economic coercion, but the fact that their definition of economic liberty based on property implies coercion—both economic and political—by default.

In this debate, the Judeo-Christian traditions present an alternative to mainline presuppositions about property and freedom once we cut through the distortions. Too often capitalist notions of ownership and freedom are projected onto the divine, and this presents a perfect example of how free-market economics undermines and reshapes Christian theology. Nevertheless, notions of God's ownership of the world, for instance, are not necessarily seen as rigid in the Judeo-Christian traditions, as the logic of free-market economics would lead us to expect. In the beginning of the Gospel of John, for instance, the statement is made about Jesus that "the world came into being through him," and that "he came to what was his own, and his own people did not accept him" (John 1:10-11). While ownership is not disputed here, it is not enforced coercively. The notion of God's freedom also takes a surprising turn in these traditions, as it does not necessarily entail the freedom to do anything. Medieval theologian Anselm of Canterbury, for instance, developed a sense of the limit of God's freedom: once God creates the order of creation, God is bound to it. When something goes wrong and this order is violated, God cannot arbitrarily choose to act as if nothing had happened. Unlike in the later work of Thomas Aquinas, Anselm's God is not free to do as God pleases; this implies that God is unlike a tyrant, whose power is arbitrary and unrestricted.[62] A similar dynamic can be seen earlier, in the biblical records themselves: when God strikes covenants with the people in both the Jewish and the Christian traditions, God limits Godself. Divine freedom in the context of a covenant is not the freedom to do anything; it is, rather, the freedom to maintain constructive covenantal relationships and to live within their boundaries; and it is the freedom to resist the coercion of those who seek to destroy these relationships and who wield power in ways that contradict these relationships because they pursue their own power and profit.

Another alternative tradition is presented by the "year of the Lord's favor," which Jesus announces in the Gospel of Luke (Luke 4:19), and during which good news is preached to the poor, release proclaimed to the captives, recovery of sight granted to the blind, and liberation granted to the oppressed (Luke 4:18). This Christian tradition is rooted in ancient Jewish traditions, laid out in the book of Leviticus in the Hebrew Bible, which establishes ground rules for the community that come as a surprise to those of us who think of the free-market logic as ultimate rationality: "You shall hallow the fiftieth year and you shall proclaim liberty throughout the land to all its inhabitants" (Lev 25:10). The liberty proclaimed in this "year of jubilee" implies a radical reversal of contemporary economic interpretations of liberty, which protect those who own property. The liberty of the year of jubilee protects those who have been deprived of their property, and it implies a reversal of property rights: "the land shall not be sold in perpetuity, for the land is mine; with me you are but aliens and tenants," the author of

Leviticus has God say (Lev 25:23); land that had to be sold because someone fell "into difficulty" "shall be released" after forty-nine years, "and the property shall be returned" (Lev 25:25-28).[63] Divine claims to ownership in this context do not model human claims to ownership, as is often assumed in the theology of the free market, but limit it. This tradition poses a fundamental challenge to mainline notions of private property and freedom, as property is always provisional and preliminary and subject to redistribution in situations of grave imbalances, while freedom only exists when all are free, including those on the bottom of society.

John Wesley pushes the matter even further in his interpretation of the Christian understanding of stewardship. Wesley calls into question a position that claims that God has entrusted private property to us. In fact, he even rejects understanding what God has entrusted to us as a loan, because even such an arrangement does not put enough emphasis on our ongoing relationship with God. In this regard, Wesley's position is in direct opposition to the later deist defense of private property by Adam Smith. Wesley develops an alternative model that he calls stewardship, which means that "we are . . . indebted to [God] for all we have; but although a debtor is obliged to return what he has received, yet until the time of payment comes he is at liberty to use it as he pleases. It is not so with a steward: he is not at liberty to use what is lodged in his hands as *he* pleases, but as his master pleases."[64] As a result, no human being can ever be the absolute owner of anything; not even the analogy of a debtor is appropriate here, because debtors have control over the loan that they have taken out until it is to be repaid. The only basis for having anything, according to Wesley, is an ongoing relationship with God, which constantly provides the focus for the use of what Christians have.[65] This implies that those who have things (one hesitates to use the term *ownership*) do not enjoy the sort of freedom promoted by contemporary free-market economics. Wesley's interpretation sets clear limits—something that might have been easier two centuries ago when private property did not yet come in the form of the extensive monopolies now represented by large transnational corporations—but it is precisely because private property has taken on such absolute forms and is held in such large pools that Wesley's reflections are now more relevant than ever.

This train of thought can be extended to God and the notion of divine freedom, pushing beyond Wesley's statement: Godself is not free to do anything God pleases, as the image of the master might falsely imply. Godself is bound by the covenant, which is concerned about productive relationships that resist exclusion by the dominant groups. The doctrine of the Trinity is helpful here, because it models a relationship of three equals—without hierarchy, oppression, or exploitation.[66] But there is more: God's faithfulness to the covenant implies not only equality but support of those who are excluded or pushed to the margins of the relationship, as we have seen in the previous section on justice. This is the part that is usually left out by those who emphasize the doctrine of the Trinity as a solution to economic problems.[67] The surprising conclusion is that, according to core Judeo-Christian traditions, private property and the freedom to do anything one pleases with this property do not even exist at the level of the divine and of ultimate reality.

What are the consequences of such alternative notions of property and of freedom for economic thought? Questioning the common presuppositions about private property and freedom creates new possibilities. If ownership of private property is seen as conditional rather than as absolute, things change. An example of a minor change along these lines might be the German constitution, which states that "property imposes an obligation," and that property is supposed to serve the common good.[68] Freedom, in this case, is not absolute either but is directed toward the common good. Consequently, freedom is only freedom if it results in something that benefits the community. Friedman's sense that political and economic freedom are closely related, explicitly stated by President Ronald Reagan in the 1982 Economic Report of the President,[69] is indeed correct, but in a different way than Friedman and Reagan assumed: if true economic freedom is available only to a few select people at the top, political freedom is skewed as well. If, however, economic freedom is broadened in such a way that it includes everyone, even the poorest of the poor, political freedom benefits as well.

This has implications for property. The property that mattered in the book of Leviticus was land, on which the livelihood of an agrarian society depended. In our situation, land is still important, but it is the ownership of means of production, more broadly conceived, on which the livelihood of people depends. In other words, private ownership of personal items, including cars and even houses, is not the problem here. Private ownership of means of production becomes problematic where it becomes so absolute that it allows for the exploitation of the many by the few who hold it. In this context, one of the most common justifications of the ownership of the means of production needs to be mentioned. If it is not claimed that this ownership is given directly by God, ownership is often justified on the basis of superior performance: those who own substantial shares of the means of production supposedly have earned their ownership. But, as Michael Parenti asked over a decade ago—as if foreseeing what would ensue in the recession in 2008: if this were true, "why must [this ownership] be provided with so many artificial privileges under the law, so many bailouts, subsidies, and other special considerations—at our expense?"[70] And why would this ownership class seek advantages in unfair competition or deteriorating conditions of workers, including the systematic destruction of unions?

Too often, even the slightest question about private ownership of the means of production raises the specter of state planning and state-driven communism.[71] But this is not the only alternative to what we now call free-market economics. However this situation is resolved, it does not follow that the ownership of means of production must pass from one absolute claim to another. Things begin to change when the relative nature of any form of ownership becomes clear. In this vein, collective ownership of the means of production—or at the very least, more public accountability for those who control the means of production—does not have to be a recipe for totalitarianism; the opposite is the case. If political and economic freedom are indeed related, as all sides in this debate claim, a more open system of ownership can model a more open system of politics that is more truly democratic, and vice versa. If democracy is to be viable in the political arena, some form of democracy also needs to be viable in the economic arena. The problem is that our current mainline economic notions of private property and freedom work against democracy, and that the representatives of these positions blame the political arena rather than the world of economics for a lack of democracy. Two Christian economists, Victor Claar and Robin Kendrick Klay, model this misunderstanding and its implications for various topics: "When a government can take anything it wants from its citizens, there is no incentive to work hard to create anything. Christians should continue to work for economic freedom and social justice throughout the global economy."[72] First of all, why would "government" want to take just anything from its citizens, and who is "government" in a democracy if not the citizens? Second, whose incentive "to work hard" are we talking about? And third, whose freedom is at stake here, and how is this related to social justice?

In searching for alternatives, the free market's resistance against top-down coercion, which Friedman emphasized, must not be overlooked. Yet, too often this resistance leads to another form of domination that is less visible. The libertarian doctrine for which Friedman stood, and liberal tendencies among economists, in general, trust in the liberating powers of the market. This was perhaps most clearly seen in the 1990s, but will probably be reappearing soon after the rigid Bush years and Obama's emergency bailouts. Thomas Frank shows, for instance, how in the 1990s the market was seen as a liberating force, which assisted in overcoming stuffy hierarchies. Here, the market is no longer seen as a top-down authoritarian mechanism but as the place of active interchange, diversity, and mutual challenge. This market even integrates diversity and multiculturalism, and there is no predetermined outcome.[73] This emphasis on liberty, however, hides the fact that the goal of the free-market economy is the defense of the liberty of the big players in the market, those who own or control the means of production and command capital, rather than the liberty of everyone. This is, ultimately, also the liberty for which U.S. soldiers have fought most recently in Afghanistan and Iraq. This notion of liberty is, however, ultimately an illusion because not even the biggest players are absolutely free: even they need to play according to the rules of the market. Liberty as independence can never be fully achieved.

The freedom that is tied to a covenant, which liberates those who are forced to endure bondage and oppression, is different. It liberates even the divine from the need of absolute control because it is tied to the common good. True freedom does not imply independence, but freedom for a new life in relation with God and other people—including those whom we had not noticed before because our so-called independence was built on their backs.

Gaining New Hope

We cannot do without hopes and dreams. As the hope for the rising tide that lifts all boats vanishes, alternative hopes are emerging in the midst of severe economic pressures. These images of hope include what theologian Johann Baptist Metz (following Walter Benjamin) has called the "dangerous memories" of the church.[74] One example of such a dangerous memory, which holds out a different hope, is Jesus' radical reversal, according to which "the last will be first, and the first will be last." One of the contexts of this saying, which occurs in various places in the Gospels, is Jesus' parable of the workers in the vineyard (Matt 20:1-16). This parable delivers both a critique of an economic status quo that gives little consideration to the hope of the workers, and provides fresh hope for those affected by the pressures of downturn—a dangerous memory indeed.

What might be the basic hope, the most basic image of God in this global economy, and what is its context? In the work of Adam Smith, self-interest points in the direction of basic ideas of growth and progress. Taking up the standard, Nelson notes that scientific progress is the most vital religion of modernity and that economists are the modern priesthood of the religion of progress.[75] While the image of God as the one who guarantees progress can be found in fewer and fewer people's experience as the free-market economy keeps failing them, this particular experience is still universalized in economic theory and applied to humanity as a whole.[76] Even in a situation of downturn, there are still some people who appear to have been richly endowed by the grace of the god of progress and who substantially benefit from the meanderings of the free-market economy. The stories of those people, of the economic elites, and of those who enjoy economic success at any given moment, are well known and also well publicized by the media for good reasons. Even the representatives of the middle classes of the so-called first world are still supposed to believe that the free-market economy works for them, and are taught to gaze admiringly upward rather than to the side at their struggling peers—much less down to their drowning fellow citizens.

Nonetheless, we cannot suppress the rising flood of doubts, as new generations of the middle class gain awareness of the fact that their own standard of living is, and most likely will remain, significantly below that of their own parents. If we look below the middle class, things are much worse yet. The economic progress of the last century has not benefited most of humanity as much as one would expect, not even in the "first world." The considerable economic progress of the 1990s has not eased the problem, as those who believe in the universality of progress would have expected, but exacerbated it. This is true for many of the so-called developing countries, as globalization has benefited some, but hardly the great masses, yet the fallout can also be observed at home. Economic disasters for the working and even the middle classes rapidly increased during those years—exemplified by a steady downward trend for the weaker members of society, and represented in the trauma of falling real wages, growing debt, growing rates of child poverty, and increasing rates of child homelessness.[77]

Hope, thus, appears to be a scarce commodity for many people in the contemporary world. Business consultant Peter Senge tries to recapture it with reference to the well-known saying of Jesus about the camel and the needle's eye, which follows the story of the rich young man who is unable to leave behind his privileged status. In Jesus' own words, "it is easier for a camel to go through the eye of a needle than for someone who is rich to enter the kingdom of God" (Matt 19:24). According to Senge, this saying refers to a gate in the city wall of Jerusalem called "the needle," which "was so narrow that when a fully loaded camel approached it, the camel driver had to take off all the bundles before the camel could pass through." No real challenge is involved here, just a little effort. Senge does not even address the question of wealth; what needs to be unloaded is just inner "baggage we've acquired on our journey."[78] This approach to the story of camel and the needle's eye is common in Christian circles. Some would add that the camel would have to get on its knees to get through the gate. But this misses the point of the story and the reason for hope. The shock of Jesus' disciples at this saying, expressed in their question, "Then who can be saved?", is reflected in Jesus' answer: "For mortals it is impossible" (Matt 19:26). This story is not about a little more humility, or about being less beholden to wealth and letting go. This story is about things that are impossible: camels cannot go through the eyes of needles and rich people cannot be part of God's kingdom. Yet that is not the final word. Jesus concludes that "for mortals it is impossible, but for God all things are possible" (Matt 19:26). The passage ends without any further comment. Hope is, thus, rooted in God and not in the actions of rich people. The next paragraph ends with another affirmation that "many who are first will be last, and the last will be first" (Matt 19:30). This hope is not utopian because it is realized in the life and ministry of Jesus and his movement, which is larger than the twelve disciples and includes a variety of people, including some wealthy women (Luke 8:1-3 is the only reference to them), who appear to be living this reversal of last and first.[79]

While the hope of the free-market economy is rooted in the hope for the ongoing production of economic surpluses—the sort of thing that is produced by labor but today is often hidden in the bubbles created by the market—it might help to talk about another kind of surplus, which finds expression in the traditions of the oppressed, and of which Jesus, Paul, and many others who struggled against the status quo of power and wealth must have been aware.[80] Jacques Lacan's notion of "surplus-enjoyment" refers to a sort of energy that is available only to the repressed—at the underside— and not to those who are part of the status quo.[81] Hardt and Negri talk about a similar phenomenon in this way: "The production of the common always involves a surplus that cannot be expropriated by capital or captured in the regimentation of the global political body. This surplus, at the most ab- stract philosophical level, is the basis on which antagonism is transformed into revolt. Deprivation, in other words, may breed anger, indignation, and antagonism, but revolt arises only on the basis of wealth, that is, a surplus of intelligence, experience, knowledges, and desire."[82] In other words, the oppressed and marginalized are not limited to a role as the ones who are ex- cluded, fragmented, and confronted with a lack; they have their own sort of wealth. To be sure, this wealth is not recognized by the system, and so there is a certain niche or safe space that opens up. Based on this alternative sur- plus, the way resistance and activism are conceived changes substantially. A substantial part of the work of resistance happens in the context of everyday work and in the networks in which we live our daily lives—the sort of ad- ditional meetings during people's spare time on which much activism today depends are still important, but their focus needs to be on the better organi- zation of resistance in daily life rather than on an extraordinary number of extraordinary activities.[83]

At this point, a religious surplus comes into view. If God is not forced into the role of the guarantor of private property or of the surplus of the free-market economy, God can be conceived in alternative ways. If the divine cannot be controlled by the free market, its manifestations keep bubbling up despite the system's best efforts to subdue them. In my book *Christ and Em- pire*, I talk about a "theological surplus" or a "christological surplus." If peo- ple cannot ultimately be controlled, does it not make sense to consider the possibility that there is a divine reality that cannot be controlled either? The difference, of course, is that this alternative kind of surplus is produced on the underside. It is linked to particular acts of repression in a repressive system. The theological surplus is produced in the context of top-down repression, which generates not just the commonly acknowledged pressure but also a surplus from which resistance grows. The economic empire, itself, without being aware of it, thus creates the conditions for a new thing. For good reasons, union organizers have a saying that "the boss is our best organizer." This alternative surplus emerges precisely in those places where the free market least expects it. But once these places are recognized as genuine places for the creation of alternatives, new energies and resources are discovered.

This perspective challenges us to question the images of God presupposed by the global free-market economy one last time. The most important question has to do with our blind spots.[84] What is repressed and overlooked when we follow the god of economic progress? This is the place where theology needs to enter into a critical dialogue with economics. Of course, theology cannot render judgment out of nowhere, as if it existed in a vacuum or in a realm of ethereal bliss; rather, theology, itself, needs to be judged according to its own embodied forms, in communities that are interconnected with growing global experiences of downturn and the all-pervasive logic of free-market economics.[85] Even the kind of theology which intends to be purely "traditional," working exclusively with classical concepts, needs to be examined for how it is now shaped by the current ideology of the market. Of course, since these influences are located mostly at the subconscious level, theologians are not usually aware of them. Even the most classical theological confessions—for instance, such as the confession that "Jesus is Lord"—can become confessions of the market; the notion of Jesus' lordship is easily subverted and assimilated to the images of those who rule the free-market economy, without anyone noticing the heresy. Absolute and abstract images of God that cannot be questioned—the kinds of images that are produced from the top down, from positions of power and control—create problems both in the life of the church and in the life of the free-market economy. Not only can they not be critiqued, they commonly function as Trojan horses that introduce and activate their cargo in secret, which makes them even more powerful and dangerous. As a result, absolute images of God lead to an absolute church; an absolute market; an absolute surplus, which is calculated as the bottom line; and, thus, to institutions that can no longer be questioned and challenged. Images of God produced from the bottom up, on the other hand, tie into a different surplus—not the one that can be calculated as the bottom line and controlled, but the one that knows that it is born in a particular struggle and under particular pressures, always fragile and limited, but also full of energy and passion.

At the end of this chapter, reenvisioning the lordship of Christ opens up new perspectives both on God and on the world, and on the connection between the two. The early Christians knew just as well as the Roman

Empire that there could not be two lords: Caesar and Jesus. A decision had to be made between the two, and hence between two fundamentally different ways of being lord. The difference was not between spiritual and material but between different forms of power: top down vs. bottom up (Matt 4:8-10); between different forms of relating to others: mutuality and service vs. control (Mark 10:35-45); between different ways of being effective: collaboration vs. domination (Mark 9:38-41); and between different ways of relating to the divine: modesty vs. pride (Luke 1:46-55). And, since the alternative politics of Christ's lordship cannot be separated from economics, a different form of economics takes shape from these attitudes: fulfilled labor that parallels God's own redemptive work vs. exploited labor (Matt 11:25-30); cooperative labor vs. competitive labor (Mark 10:35-45); regard for all labor vs. preference for management (Mark 9:33-37); solidarity with others who labor vs. solidarity based on kinship and privilege (Mark 3:31-35); labor that addresses need vs. labor that follows the rules of the status quo (Mark 2:23-28); regard for those who work and, thus, walk the walk vs. regard for those who merely talk the talk (Matt 21:28-32, 25:31-46).

To be sure, these alternatives cannot always be had without conflict, as Mary, the mother of Jesus, knew. In her own words, spoken at the beginning of the Gospel of Luke and based on an even more ancient source,[86] she claims that the God who "has looked with favor on the lowliness of his servant"—an unwed mother who had to produce her own livelihood—has "lifted up the lowly." This is as far as mainline religion usually takes things. Lifting up the lowly, and, perhaps, accepting those who are different to some degree, is only one side of this struggle, however. In conjunction with lifting up, Mary also notes that God "has brought down the powerful from their thrones." And, as if this were not enough, this God has also "sent the rich away empty" as he "has filled the hungry with good things" (Luke 1:48; 52-53). God, thus, takes a stand once again on the side of the lowly, reversing mainline political, economic, and theological logic.

What about the powerful and the wealthy, then? What about those who own major shares of the means of production and who command capital? Is there no hope for them? There is hope if we understand how things are connected in the global free-market economy—to a degree that might have surprised the ancients. The current situation harms not only those pushed to the margins but everyone. In relationships of oppression, not only the oppressed but also the oppressors are damaged. This is, of course, true for any situation of oppression, and Mary is aware of this in her own ways—but this insight is even more crucial in our own time, when oppression has become so blatant that more than twenty-five thousand children continue to die every day of hunger and preventable causes[87] while the oppressive structures become not only less and less visible but are celebrated in terms of the rising tide that will lift all boats. How can the humanity of the wealthy, who build their enormous fortunes on the back of large parts of humanity, not get damaged in this context? How can the humanity of employers who keep reducing the wages and benefits of their workers in order to increase their margins of profit not be affected? If this is correct, it may be a good thing for the powerful to be brought down from their thrones. This may be their only chance to learn how to become fully human. Perhaps it is also a good thing for those who are full to be sent away empty in order to be forced to think about what really matters in life.

My students often draw the conclusion that if God deals with the powerful and the wealthy, as Mary says in the Gospel of Luke, God does not really care about them. But that is a mistake. The opposite is true: God cares so much about the powerful and the wealthy that God takes some unpopular steps in order to bring them back to the right way. That's what it takes to make sure that new hope can truly flourish for everyone.

Conclusion: The Turning of the Tide: Theology, Religion, and Economics

Alternatives

Free-market economics—capitalism—is in crisis. A rising tide does not lift all boats, and wealth flows up rather than trickling down. This insight is independent of economic cycles, or whether we find ourselves in bear or bull markets. It is true not just in times of downturn, but the logic of downturn helps us see better what is going on all around us. Yet, although free-market economics is in crisis, it continues to shape everything. This is not just true for how we do business or politics but also for how we think and feel, and even for what we believe. It is for this reason that we must address economics, theology, and religion together. For theologians, this means that we can no longer do our work without taking into consideration what is happening in the economy and how it affects us; before religion can become part of the solution we need to understand how it has become part of the problem.[1] As we take into account what is going on in the economy, we will not only be better able to understand what is happening to us, but, out of this understanding, we might also be able to provide alternatives and to contribute to a turning of the tide.

As the market takes over all areas of life and the flow of money determines who we are, those who do not benefit from the market are at an ever-greater disadvantage. Those without employment or funds are the worst off, but any workers who have nothing to rely on but their labor power cannot expect to fare well in this system. Even the middle class will need to reevaluate itself along those lines. The ruling classes, who command capital and control or own substantial shares of the means of production, on the other hand, have every reason to assume that the system is working in their favor, to the point that they often deeply identify with the system. As a result, all classes are in need of an alternative vision that points beyond this system, rooted in an initial sense that not everyone benefits from the market equally and that this system cannot provide a true home for anyone if it does not provide a home for everyone. Religion can support or sabotage this alternative vision in various ways. There is a sense of not belonging at the core of Christianity that finds expression in Jesus' recognition that "he has nowhere to lay his head" (Luke 9:58), and in an early Christian understanding that "here we have no lasting city, but we are looking for the city that is to come" (Heb 13:14). At the same time, there are also calls to conform in Christianity that have often been used to keep in line those who are in positions from which alternative visions tend to develop—and who might become a threat to the status quo. These calls to conformity include reminders to wives to obey their husbands, to slaves to obey their masters, or to church members to follow their leaders.[2] As we have seen, those who are thus conditioned to follow religion blindly are the ones most likely to follow economics blindly as well. The results of much of this faith throughout history have been destruction and even death.

In this context, a first step is to realize the ambiguity and ambivalence of this situation. Those whose lives are being ruined by the market—literally and figuratively—have a deep sense of this ambiguity and ambivalence, no matter how much the system tries to cover it up. Those who are forced to subordinate themselves to the powers that be have the opportunity to see these powers in ways that these powers cannot see themselves. The truth about an oppressive system is best seen from the positions of the oppressed.[3] Yet, even those who feel that they benefit from the system can become aware of the ambiguity of the situation, if they develop an awareness of what the free-market economy is doing to the majority of humanity. This demands taking sides, however, as such an awareness does not come naturally and cannot be developed simply by taking in the relevant information; the awareness of what is going on at the underside of the market economy needs to be developed in solidarity with real people whose lives are being destroyed.[4] This will take time and effort, and this is one thing that this book cannot accomplish. All that can be done here is to extend an invitation to spend some time in the world of downturn that affects more and more of us: to push beyond secure positions, and to get in touch with those most affected. A deepening sense of ambiguity and ambivalence will be the result. Without this sense, no alternatives—whether theological or economic—can be envisioned, and everything will remain as it is.

The Common Good

While free-market economics claims that it has in mind the common good—the rising tide that will lift all boats—we are not able to identify this common good in the real world. Free-market economics, it appears, promotes an eschatology which resembles those misguided Christian eschatologies that promise a pie in the sky. If we wait just a little longer, we are assured, things will improve for everyone. Even John Maynard Keynes, whose approach Milton Friedman and other neoclassical free-market economists sought to overturn, affirmed this point in his reflection on "economic possibilities for our grandchildren." Some day in the future, Keynes states, we will "return to some of the most sure and certain principles of religion and traditional virtue—that avarice is a vice, that the exaction of usury is a misdemeanour, and the love of money is detestable." That day, however, we should not be surprised to hear Keynes state, has not arrived yet: "For at least another hundred years we must pretend to ourselves and to every one that fair is foul and foul is fair; for foul is useful and fair is not. Avarice and usury and precaution must be our gods for a little longer still."[5] Even if Keynes were right with this assessment, made in 1930, we still would have to wait another twenty years—and, as Keynes himself said so well: "In the long run, we'll all be dead," a statement that even Milton Friedman saw fit to use.

If the realization of the common good is, thus, pushed further and further into the future, the common good loses its character. The question of what will happen to our grandchildren is not unimportant; but what will happen to these grandchildren if our generation and the generation of our children cannot survive as human beings? The common good also loses its character and turns flat if it does not take into account differentials of power and the deep divisions between human beings that have been created by the free-market economy. These sorts of divisions are not "natural"—as we are often made to believe. Only in the current economic system does it appear to be possible that one person (a top investor) can earn twenty-thousand times what another person (an average worker who may own a house and a car) makes, and many more times more than what informally employed or unemployed people make. Faced with these grave imbalances, which no free market could possibly balance until the end of time, we need to think about the common good in fresh ways.

Our reflection on the common good gains depth if we take into account the logic of downturn. The common good cannot be perceived by identifying some statistical middle ground, it can only be perceived by identifying the weakest members of society. As Ulrich Duchrow and Franz Hinkelammert have pointed out, only if these weakest members of society can live, all can live.[6] This perspective on the common good is deeply rooted in the Judeo-

Christian traditions. The rejoinders in the Hebrew Bible to respect widows, strangers, and orphans are not moral rules that protect special interests. Just the opposite: concern for widows, strangers, and orphans is tied to the well-being of the community as a whole. Only when they can live can everyone live. Conversely, if their humanity is disrespected, everybody's humanity is disrespected. In this perspective, it is quite meaningful that the first bill that President Obama signed into law was on equal pay for women. In light of our broadening understanding of the common good, a matter like this can no longer be considered special interest, and Obama made this clear in his own way when he noted that this new law addresses not just a women's issue but a family issue. We might broaden the picture further and note that this is an issue that also relates to the interests of communities and of the globalizing economy as a whole. Consequently, if the good of women—or of any other marginalized group—is not taken into consideration, it becomes meaningless to talk about the common good.

Yet the common good is about more than equal distribution. The common good also needs to be considered in relation to productive participation in life. Do all people have the opportunity to develop and employ their creativity for the common good? The opportunity to employ one's creativity is usually seen as one of the privileges of those who occupy higher-level jobs in politics, industry, or intellectual production through the academy and other outlets. But the notion of the common good reminds us that this is not enough, and that no one should be deprived of the opportunity to labor creatively, so as not to stifle the creativity of work as a whole. Such a situation might be considered true progress, as opposed to a situation where only a few really get to participate, while all others are told to hold their hopes and to defer their dreams into some future that may never come. Here, the focus on production rather than on distribution is crucial. While it may be argued that more people have color television sets now than fifty years ago, opportunities for creative and productive labor have not increased at the same rate, if at all. The fact that so many people around the world have no televisions and no employment only makes matters worse.

What has been said so far also applies to the question of common interest, discussed in chapter 2. Common interest is best constructed from the bottom up rather than from the top down. This may sound odd, for in the ideal realm of economic and theological thought, common interest is considered to be just that: common, without up and down. In the reality of economic life, on the other hand, up and down are quite real, and it is the top that shapes not only the order of things but also that which is commonly accepted as valid; religious life shows little difference here, as the mainline tends to be shaped by the ideas and expectations of those who are in charge and those who fund it. This top manages to project its interests in terms of common interests and, thus, to cover up its special interests: tax cuts to the wealthy, for instance, are presented as beneficial to everyone and rising tides are eulogized. But little hard evidence for these beliefs has been produced. The economic formula $S = I$, that tax savings (S) translate directly into investments (I), on which part of this top-down view of common interest is based, does not hold up to investigation and has not propelled the economy forward as much as was hoped.

While the mainline considers questions from below as special interest, the reality is the reverse. In economic reality, neither workers nor small-business people—and certainly not the vast armies of the unemployed and underemployed—benefit much from tax cuts at the very top and from government subsidies to the largest corporations, since these often fail to trickle down below a certain level: both workers and small-business people, however, share an interest in resisting the monopolies that are formed at the top.[7] In this regard, the Keynesian shift to subsidies for workers and middle class, a limited form of which is now becoming economic policy again with the Obama administration, brings some relief, as it draws the circle of common interest broader—recognizing that subsidies are more likely to trickle up than down. Here, common interest is, indeed, supported from the bottom up to a certain degree. Nevertheless, the top is not challenged here, and the lion's share of profits ultimately ends up at the top again. While Keynesianism was particularly successful in Europe, where large industries were often nationalized and public health care and welfare were established so firmly that they have lasted until today, common interest needs a stronger foundation yet, rooted in the biblical concern for the "least of these."[8]

Constructive Critical Theology and Economics

If faith images are, indeed, at work in economics, interdisciplinary conversations between theology and economics assume a new level of urgency. Theology, understood as constructive and self-critical reflection on faith and ultimate reality, can make important contributions, since it cultivates investigations into where different images of God and ultimate reality come from and where they might lead us.

Absolute claims of faith—images of God and of ultimate reality—that operate below the surface or that cannot be questioned, even in situations of downturn and great pressure, result in problems for both theology and economics. The challenges faced by a growing number of us who now experience economic downturn firsthand push us to take another look. In this context, an approach to theology that refuses to see its interconnectedness with economic realities, and that conceives of theology as an autonomous discipline, not only deceives itself but reinforces unconscious dependencies. Exploring economic structures in terms of the pressures of real life can enable theology to take into account its own formation by the now all-pervasive forces of the economy, and to develop a more self-critical perspective.

In regard to economics, the question, as should be clear at this point, is not whether there are images of ultimate reality and the divine in economics and whether this is appropriate or not. Like it or not, such images pervade and support our economic system. The question is whether those images are supporting life. For Christians, the question is also whether these images match Christian notions of the reality of God as the one who offers life to all, including the "least of these" and those members of the economy on whose shoulders it rests: the workers, broadly conceived. Does the current economic theology of the free market merely sanction and sanctify the status quo, or does it contribute to a better life for all? At stake is not the question of honest belief in the market, but whether there is an awareness of the vast numbers of people who at present do not benefit from the market, and what role this awareness plays in economic theory. We do not need to doubt that many economists honestly believe that they have found solutions for the problems of the world and that they trust that at some point in the future everything will be fine. Such faith in the free-market economy keeps them on track even if the economic reality looks dismal for more and more people and—this matter should give us pause—even if millions of lives are lost. What happens, though, when the question of divine and ultimate reality is posed not from the perspective of the economic status quo but from a broader perspective that includes all of humanity? What happens when the economy is viewed not primarily from the perspective of the select few at the top but from a perspective that includes the billions of people on the underside? What gives hope and comfort to all those who are being crushed by the economic success of a relatively small group of people? The theology that trusts in the "invisible hand of the market" has had little to offer to the majority of people, who do not benefit from free-market economies.

An alternative perspective might take a cue from alternative theological approaches that—in the midst of the catastrophes of the early twentieth century, which included two World Wars and the Holocaust—have developed resistance to the theology of the status quo and its endorsements of top-down power. These theologies of resistance talked about God as the "Wholly Other." God was described as "Other" not because God is located in some isolated transcendent realm, far removed from the world, but because the true God is Other than the familiar gods of the status quo. God is Other than the authority and power of those on top—the elites, those whom we commonly consider to be in control and who seem to determine the order of things. This God comes as a surprise, because this Other God is in solidarity with those who suffer; with the weak, the widows, and the orphans of the Old Testament; and with those on the margins of society in the New Testament. It is often overlooked that even Karl Barth, the most prominent theologian of otherness, saw God not as an abstract "Wholly Other," but as the Other who locates Godself alongside the oppressed and against the oppressors. In this context, transcendence does not first of all refer to what is otherworldly. Rather, transcendence means a break with certain kinds of immanence in favor of other kinds of immanence—the sort of immanence where Jesus Christ is found.[9] The contemporary Roman Catholic theologian Jung Mo Sung, arguing from a different perspective, arrives at a similar insight. Sung notes the transcendence of the cry of those who suffer from the market, because it breaks through the totality of the oppression and transcends the boundaries of the system. Those who do not hear this cry, Jung observes, are unable to grasp the work of God in the world.[10] Here is one of the most crucial challenges posed to economics by Christian faith—a challenge deeply rooted in many of the voices that come together in the biblical sources, from the Old Testament to the Apostle Paul; the latter even includes an awareness of the suffering of non-human creation.[11]

There is one more step, however, that constructive and critical theological and economic reflection needs to take. It is not easy for those of us who still benefit from the economy, or who feel, at least, that we have a stake in its future through personal investments and retirement plans, to step outside the theology of economics. This is true not only for professional economists but also for professional theologians and for the members of mainline Christian churches. In order to resist the almost inevitable accommodation to the status quo of those who benefit in some ways from the free-market economy, the awareness of God as Other will have to be tied very closely to an awareness of other people, and anchored there. Those other people, in this case, are particularly the ones who are designated as "other" by the logic of the free-market economy, perhaps because they cannot compete in the market or because they are prevented in various ways from performing at what counts as superior levels of success. In building relationships and ties of solidarity with these others, we have an opportunity to gradually developing greater respect for that which is other, the sort of respect that ultimately will also shape our images of God as Other.[12]

The main goal of this constructive critical theological reflection is to discover and make use of new impulses and energies that can reshape our images of God and ultimate reality—whether those subconsciously held by economists or those consciously held by theologians—and lead us in new directions.[13] What guides and reinforces our hope in this new paradigm is no longer an absolute and ideal image of the free market, as held by many economists and theologians, but a tangible world of real people that includes the least of these, a world in which all can not only survive (this, in itself, would be a significant improvement over the current situation, when over twenty-five thousand children die every day of hunger and preventable causes[14]) but also live productive lives. In this new paradigm, the now virtually ubiquitous preference for individual wealth would be replaced by a preference for those who have been severely crushed by the economy.[15] This new type of preference is related to biblical notions of God's own concern for those who suffer and are crushed by the powers that be—from the oppressed poor and the crushed needy mentioned by the Prophet Amos (Amos 4:1) to the "low and despised" mentioned by the Apostle Paul (1 Cor 1:28). This preference emerges also as the central issue when we consider the question of whether all can survive and live.

These theological considerations lead us back to economic matters. One of the biggest surprises in this respect might be that we can now claim a new place for self-interest, one of the key terms in free-market economics since Adam Smith. Rather than demonizing or sanctifying self-interest, as both ethicists and economists are wont to do, we need to realize that self-interest is part of life and of survival. When we encounter God as Other, however, we begin to see self-interest in a new light. Self-interest that is becoming aware of the challenge of otherness does not necessarily have to lead to the exploitation or the exclusion of the other; it can also lead to new kinds of relationship with the other and to the other's inclusion. Even in the logic of free-market economics, of course, self-interest includes some awareness of the other—but what if self-interest came to include particularly those others whom we do not notice at present and those who, in terms of the dominant economic system, do not seem to be of much value to us? Jesus' commandment, "love your neighbor as yourself" (Mark 12:31, with roots in the Old Testament), reminds us that self-interest is always tied to others, whether we notice them or not. At stake here are not primarily special acts of support or the distribution of alms, but the recognition that the neighbor is a part of who we are, even when are not aware of it. This flies in the face of mainline economic (and theological) wisdom.

That the neighbor is part of who we are is not religious idealism or wishful thinking. This is the (still mostly hidden) truth of the economy, which produces its profits mostly by extracting the surplus from the labor process on which trade and, ultimately, even financial capital rest. That our neighbors are part of ourselves today often means, first of all, that we are developing our own economic advantages on their backs; they are part of us because we benefit directly or indirectly from their exploitation—if only because we can buy certain goods very inexpensively and because certain services are cheap since labor costs are being pushed lower and lower. In these very particular ways, our neighbors are always part of us, even though we may never know them and even though we often prefer not to get to know them. In the midst of these oppressive relationships, however, other connections are created that produce an unexpected kind of "surplus," which cannot be measured with current economic tools. This different kind of surplus has nothing to do with what is considered the "bottom line" of economic profit, but with a potential for alternative relationships among people who are brought together by the economic system, often against their will. These relationships can lead to new kinds of solidarity that typically emerge only under pressure, when people begin to realize their true common interests, and to new kinds of economic exchanges. In the words of the Apostle Paul, "If one member suffers, all suffer together with it" (1 Cor 12:26); or, in the language of the trade unions, "an injury to one is an injury to all." Only when we become aware of these connections already in place can we realize the true complexity of our relationships and move beyond the crippling myths of individualism on which much of contemporary mainline economics and theology is built.

Without seeing this complexity of our connections to other people, including the severe distortions in these connections, we will never be able to transform them in life-giving ways. In this regard, seeing the complexity of our connections to the divine Other might be of help, too; more hopeful and life-giving alternatives emerge where the pressure is greatest and where the divine Other enters into our predicament and shares in it, rather than being envisioned at the lofty tops of this world. Is this not part of the Christian message of the incarnation of Jesus Christ—in a manger and under severe threat of persecution and annihilation (Luke 2:7; Matt 2:16)? When we realize our complex location between other people and the divine Other more fully, we have a better chance of becoming fully human and—herein lies our hope for the future—of developing a more humane economy.

Notes

Preface

1. Will Deener, "Working?" *The Dallas Morning News,* July 13, 2009, 4D, notes that, unlike in the previous four recessions, more than half of the layoffs will be permanent.

2. See Joerg Rieger, *Christ and Empire: From Paul to Postcolonial Times* (Minneapolis: Fortress Press, 207), 11 and 21, n. 38.

3. One recent exception is Sean McCloud, *Divine Hierarchies: Class in American Religion and Religious Studies* (Chapel Hill: University of North Carolina Press, 2007).

4. See, for instance, Robert H. Nelson, *Economics as Religion: From Samuelson to Chicago and Beyond* (University Park, Pa.: Pennsylvania State University Press, 2001), and Duncan K. Foley, *Adam's Fallacy: A Guide to Economic Theology* (Cambridge, Mass.: The Belknap Press of Harvard University Press, 2006).

5. In this context, Economist Foley's efforts to write an "economic theology" should be welcomed as a helpful first step, as he raises some critical questions about the weaknesses of capitalism. Of course, Foley attempts to rescue capitalism for a new day and age.

1. No Rising Tide

1. The median income was $2010 lower. These numbers are based on figures released by the U.S. Census Bureau in August 2008. In addition, the inflation-adjusted incomes of median households rose by 1.3 percent in 2007 from the previous year, from $49,568 in 2006 to $50,233 in 2007 (2007 dollars), while the overall poverty rate increased slightly, from 12.3 percent to 12.5 percent. Jared Bernstein, "Median Income Rose as Did Poverty in 2007; 2000s Have Been Extremely Weak for Living Standards of Most Households," August 26, 2008, Economic Policy Institute, http://www.epi.org/publications/entry/webfeatures_econindicators_income_20080826/ (accessed 7/1/09).

2. Wage growth repression was accomplished to a substantial degree through the Federal Reserve's efforts at raising interest rates. See Robert Brenner, *The Economics of Global Turbulence: The Advanced Capitalist Economies from Long Boom to Long Downturn, 1945–2005* (New York: Verso, 2006), 255. According to Brenner, Tobin's Q, indicating the ratio of companies' stock value to their net assets, was at 130 percent in 1998, the highest value since 1920 (251). Brenner predicted the unsustainability of this scenario already in 1998 and foresaw "a serious turn downward of the world economy" (266). The other part of the bubble in more recent years was, of course, the housing bubble. Brenner notes it in a 2006 afterword to his book (313–17). Housing, through equity withdrawals and other gains, accounted for 27.1 percent of the GDP

between 2000 and 2005 (319). On this topic, see also the work of Dean Baker of the Center for Economic Policy Research (CEPR).

3. "WTO Chief Warns of Looming Political Unrest," AFP Report, February 7, 2009, http://www.channelnewsasia.com/stories/afp_world_business/view/407470/1/.html (accessed 7/1/09).

4. Thomas Friedman, "Elvis Has Left the Mountain," *The New York Times,* January 31, 2009, http://www.nytimes.com/2009/02/01/opinion/01friedman.html?th&emc=th (accessed 7/1/09). A version of this article appeared in print on February 1, 2009, on page WK9 of the New York edition.

5. See special report on Forbes.com, "The Forbes 400," ed. Matthew Miller and Duncan Greenberg, September 7, 2008, http://www.forbes.com/2008/09/16/richest-american-billionaires-lists-400list08-cx_mm_dg_0917richintro.html (accessed 2/28/09).

6. This is the lowest tax rate since the IRS began tracking the four hundred largest taxpayers in 1992. "Under Bush, Tax Rate of Richest Averaged 17.2 Percent," *The Dallas Morning News,* February 3, 2009, 4D.

7. Tom Hertz, *Understanding Mobility in America* (Washington, D.C.: Center for American Progress, 2006), ii, http://www.americanprogress.org/kf/hertz_mobility_analysis.pdf (accessed 2/28/09).

8. Claire Prentice, "'Econocide' to Surge as Recession Bites," BBC News, March 11, 2009, http://news.bbc.co.uk/1/hi/business/7912056.stmhttp://news.bbc.co.uk/1/hi/business/7912056.stm (accessed 4/29/09).

9. Some of these stories are described by Nick Turse, "The Human Costs of the Economic Crisis," January 28, 2009; the number of calls rose to 568,437 in 2008, compared to 412,768 in the previous year. http://brechtforum.org/human-costs-economic-crisis?bc= (accessed 2/28/09).

10. Steve Keen, *Debunking Economics: The Naked Emperor of the Social Sciences* (New York: Zed Books, 2001), 9.

11. Kathryn Tanner, *Economy of Grace* (Minneapolis: Fortress Press, 2005), x, feels that works on theology and economics have too often started with this insight, but we should add that at this point none of the mainline discourses of theology have been influenced in substantial ways. Tanner's own effort to link the discourses of theology and economics from the other end—via economy rather than theology, of course—also ends up forging a link between religion and economics.

12. Paul Tillich, as is well known, talked about matters of God as our "ultimate concern."

13. Fredric Jameson has talked about the "political unconscious." See Fredric Jameson, *The Political Unconscious: Narrative as a Socially Symbolic Act* (Ithaca, N.Y.: Cornell University Press, 1981).

14. Between 1997 and 2001 the top 10 percent of U.S. earners received 49 percent of the growth in real wages and salaries, and the top 1 percent got 24 percent of the total, while the bottom half of workers received less than 13 percent. William K. Tabb, "Wage Stagnation, Growing Insecurity, and the Future of the U.S. Working Class," *Monthly Review* 59 (June 2007): 2, http://monthlyreview.org/0607wkt.htm (accessed 3/6/09). One of the most notable things about the economic growth of the 1990s was that only the elites truly benefited from it. The compensation packages of CEOs, for instance, increased at incredible rates. Even though some still contend that many people have never been as well off as now, starting in the 1990s in the so-called first world more and more people, including significant numbers from the middle class, began to take significant economic hits. See also William Wolman und Anne Colamosca, *The Judas Economy: The Triumph of Capital and the Betrayal of Work* (Reading, Mass.: Addison-Wesley, 1997).

15. Hugo Assmann and Franz J. Hinkelammert, *Götze Markt,* trans. Horst Goldstein (Düsseldorf: Patmos Verlag, 1992), first published in Portuguese as *A idolatria do mercado: ensaio sobre economia e teologia* (Sao Paulo: Vozes, 1989); see also Franz J. Hinkelammert, *The Ideological Weapons of Death: A Theological Critique of Capitalism,* trans. Philip Berryman (Maryknoll, N.Y.: Orbis, 1986); and Jung Mo Sung, *Desire, Market and Religion* (London: SCM, 2007).

16. Of interest is also the work of Arend Theodoor van Leeuwen, perhaps the only professor of economic theology, formerly at the University of Nimwegen. His major work is in Dutch: *De Nacht van het Kapitaal: Door het oerwoud van de economie naar de bronnen van de burgerlijke religie* (Nimwegen: SUN, 1984).

17. M. Douglas Meeks, *God the Economist: The Doctrine of God and Political Economy* (Minneapolis: Fortress Press, 1989).

18. The afore-mentioned book by Hinkelammert and Assmann, for instance, was first published in Portuguese and is available in Spanish and German but not in English. See also the work by Alexander Rüstow, *Die Religion der Marktwirtschaft,* 2nd ed. (Lit Verlag: Münster, 2001) (German).

19. John Kenneth Galbraith, *The Culture of Contentment* (Boston: Houghton Mifflin, 1992), 82.

20. Robert H. Nelson, *Economics as Religion: From Samuelson to Chicago and Beyond* (University Park, Pa.: Pennsylvania State University Press, 2001); and *Reaching for Heaven on Earth: The Theological Meaning of Economics* (Lanham, Md.: Rowman and Littlefield, 1991).

21. Nelson, *Economics as Religion*, xiv, "The Interior Department was often a battleground for a modern form of religious disputation." "Economists played their most important role in American society in the twentieth century as theologians and preachers of a religion" (8).

22. Paul Knitter and Chandra Muzaffar, eds., *Subverting Greed: Religious Perspectives on the Global Economy*, Faith Meets Faith (Maryknoll, N.Y.: Orbis, 2002), 10.

23. "I do not mean to employ theological reflection as an argument for or against any form of political economy. My aim is more modest. The point of Incarnation is to respect the world as it is, to acknowledge its limits, to recognize its weaknesses, irrationalities, and evil forces, and to disbelieve any promises that the world is now or ever will be transformed into the City of God." Michael Novak, *The Spirit of Democratic Capitalism* (New York: American Enterprise Institute, Simon & Schuster, 1982), 341. The third part of the book, from which this quotation is taken, is titled "A Theology of Economics." Novak's titles speak for themselves. See also his book *Toward a Theology of the Corporation*, rev. ed. (Washington, D.C.: AEI Press, 1990).

24. One discussion of this problem was put forth in Linda J. Bilmes and Joseph E. Stiglitz, "The Iraq War Will Cost Us $3 Trillion, and Much More," *The Washington Post*, March 9, 2008, http://www.washingtonpost.com/wp-dyn/content/article/2008/03/07/AR2008030702846.html (accessed 7/1/09).

25. Meeks, *God the Economist*, xi.

26. This is discussed, for example, in *Christianity and the Culture of Economics*, ed. Donald A. Hay and Alan Kreider (Cardiff: University of Wales Press, 2001). The book contains contributions from a team of European economists. Donald A. Hay, dean of social sciences and professorial fellow of Jesus College in Oxford, points out the tensions between Christian values and the values of the free-market economy and considers them in light of the personal ethical dilemma of the individual economist (166 and the following).

27. *Handelsblatt*, April 9, 2003, 1.

28. Sarah Anderson and others, *Executive Excess 2007: The Staggering Social Cost of U.S. Business Leadership* (Washington, D.C.: Institute for Policy Studies and United for a Fair Economy), 9, www.ips-dc.org (accessed 2/28/09).

29. Anderson and others, *Executive Excess 2007*, 10.

30. See the article by Jaqueline L. Salmon, "Most Americans Believe in Higher Power, Poll Finds," *Washington Post*, June 24, 2008, http://www.washingtonpost.com/wp-dyn/content/story/2008/06/23/ST2008062300818.html (accessed 7/6/09). Thirty-nine percent attend religious services at least once a week, and 33 percent attend once or twice a month. Nearly 80 percent of Americans believe in miracles. In one of the largest polls on religious beliefs ever conducted, the Pew Forum interviewed more than thirty-six thousand adults.

31. With the "church-growth movement," a whole branch of the church is busy applying the insights of mainline economics. The way capital campaigns are run provides another example of this trend.

32. Assmann and Hinkelammert, *Götze Markt*, 23.

33. The privatized German Postal Service might be considered an exception to this rule, as things are going fairly well at the time of this writing, especially for the largest customers. However, many services to individual customers have been eliminated, and the Postal Service receives government subsidies for those parts of its work that are not lucrative, like sending mail carriers to remote settlements or to islands in the North Sea.

34. Beverly W. Harrison, "The Fate of the Middle 'Class' in Late Capitalism," in *God and Capitalism: A Prophetic Critique of Market Economy*, ed. Norman Gottwald, Mark Thomas, and Vern Visick (Madison, Wis.: A-R Editions, 1991), 53.

35. Nelson, *Economics as Religion*, xv.

36. See Dirk Baecker, ed., *Kapitalismus als Religion* (Berlin: Kulturverlag Kadmos Berlin, 2003), 7.

37. Neoclassical and neoliberal theories "have been able to sustain themselves for more than a hundred years without any fear of contradicting reality." Ulrich Duchrow and Franz J. Hinkelammert, *Property for People, Not for Profit: Alternatives to the Global Tyranny of Capital*, trans. Elaine Griffiths and others (New

York: Zed Books, 2004), 142. The importance of the Chicago School is undisputed; this school has housed more Nobel Prize winners and John Bates Clark medalists (the two most prestigious prizes in economics) than any other.

38. While my description may be seen as somewhat of a caricature, this is also the way in which the standard economic textbook of Paul Samuelson and William D. Nordhaus, *Economics*, 13th ed. (New York: McGraw-Hill, 1989), 828, describes the Chicago School. Named in particular are economists Frank Knight, Henry Simons, Milton Friedman, and Friedrich von Hayek.

39. White House Briefing, July 10, 1987. Reference on the Web: http://www.nationmaster.com/encyclopedia/Reaganomics (accessed 1/7/09).

40. Keen, *Debunking Economics*, xiii.

41. Samuelson and Nordhaus, *Economics*, 39. The authors define economics as "the study of how societies use scarce resources to produce valuable commodities and distribute them among different groups" (5).

42. Here is another definition along the same lines: "Man acts to maximize utility in consumption and production. Such behavior establishes the impersonal forces of supply and demand that determine prices and quantities. Price is the governing parameter to which entrepreneurs respond, being guided by the rational behavioral principles (a) marginal cost equals marginal revenue and (b) the price of labor (and each other factor) equals the value of its marginal product. If markets should operate in a reasonably effective manner, the greatest allocative and technical efficiency will result, leading to Paretian optimality and maximum economic welfare." William R. Waters, "Social Economics: A Solidarist Perspective," in *Why Economists Disagree: An Introduction to the Alternative Schools of Thought,* ed. David Prychitko (Albany: State University of New York Press, 1998), 186. Another standard definition describes economics as "the science which studies human behaviour as a relationship between ends and scarce means which have alternative uses." Keen, *Debunking Economics*, 9, reference to Lionel Robbins.

43. Stiglitz made this statement in the context of the development debate, arguing that development advice should be tailored to the specific requirements of each country. Joseph E. Stiglitz, "Towards a New Paradigm for Development: Strategies, Policies, and Processes" (Prebisch Lecture, UNCTAD, Geneva, October 19, 1998), 9, emphasis in original, http://siteresources.worldbank.org/CDF/Resources/prebisch98.pdf (accessed 2/28/09).

44. Keen, *Debunking Economics*, 2.

45. Joseph E. Stiglitz, "Towards a New Paradigm," 9. Stiglitz, of course, is a critic of applying these principles unilaterally and argues that this has led to failure. The "Washington Consensus," a term coined by John Williamson, lists ten basic principles for the economic relationship to Latin America upheld by the three most influential Washington institutions: the U.S. government, the World Bank, and the International Monetary Fund. These basic principles, in turn, reflected the "common core of wisdom embraced by all serious economists." During the 1990s, this position became popularized as "let's bash the state, the markets will resolve everything." "Redefining the Role of the State, Joseph Stiglitz on Building a 'Post-Washington Consensus,'" an interview with introduction by Brian Snowdon, *World Economics* 2 (July–September 2001): 3, 47, http://www2.gsb.columbia.edu/faculty/jstiglitz/download/2001_World_Economics.pdf (accessed 2/28/09). The term has clearly taken on a life of its own, but Williamson clarifies: "Some of the most vociferous of today's critics of what they call the Washington Consensus, most prominently Joe Stiglitz . . . do not object so much to the agenda laid out above as to the neoliberalism that they interpret the term as implying. I of course never intended my term to imply policies like capital account liberalization . . . monetarism, supply-side economics, or a minimal state (getting the state out of welfare provision and income redistribution), which I think of as the quintessentially neoliberal ideas." John Williamson, "Did the Washington Consensus Fail?" speech, Center for Strategic and International Studies, November 6, 2002, http://www.iie.com/publications/papers/paper.cfm?ResearchID=488 (accessed 3/3/09).

46. One-page advertisement in *The Dallas Morning News*, February 9, 2009, 13A.

47. George Soros, *The Crisis of Global Capitalism: Open Society Endangered* (New York: Public Affairs, 1998), xxii.

48. Soros, *Crisis of Global Capitalism*, 126–28. Soros points out that this is based on a mistaken logical dualism, which believes that if there are problems with state intervention in economics, the opposite must be the right approach: complete noninterference by the state.

49. Beverly W. Harrison, "Fate of the Middle 'Class,'" 54–55.

50. James Callaghan, speech to Labour Party Conference, September 28, 1976, quoted in Milton Friedman, "Inflation and Unemployment," (Nobel Memorial Lecture, The University of Chicago, Chicago, Ill., December 13, 1976), 274–75, http://nobelprize.org/nobel_prizes/economics/laureates/1976/friedman-lecture.pdf (accessed 7/6/09). What better way to impose economic ideas than by quoting those under one's own influence?

51. Friedrich von Hayek, referenced in Robert Lekachman and Borin Van Loon, *Capitalism for Beginners* (New York: Pantheon Book, 1991), 151.

52. John Kenneth Galbraith, "Change and the Planning System," in *The New Industrial State* (Princeton: Princeton University Press, 2007), http://press.princeton.edu/chapters/s8389.html (accessed 2/28/09).

53. Galbraith, "Change."

54. Galbraith, "Change."

55. Lekachman and Van Loon, *Capitalism for Beginners*, 61.

56. "Neoliberalism named a strategy that sought to place capitalism clearly back on the track of its still incomplete development by accelerating the drive to commodify, and therefore open every aspect of life to profits and the social discipline imposed by profits. This was not just a matter of the extension of markets spatially ('globalization'), but of deepening the domestic penetration of markets into any social, personal, or cultural space." Sam Gindin, "Anti-Capitalism and the Terrain of Social Justice," *Monthly Review* 53:9 (February 2002), 6.

57. Joerg Rieger, "Christian Theology and Empire," in *Empire and the Christian Tradition: New Readings of Classical Theologians*, ed. Kwok Pui-lan, Don Compier, and Joerg Rieger (Minneapolis: Fortress Press, 2007), 3.

58. A German study, for instance, shows that social background rather than personal achievement decides who is at the very top. See the book by sociologist Michael Hartmann, *Der Mythos von den Leistungseliten* (Frankfurt: Campus Verlag, 2002). What matters most for entering the highest levels of the professions in law, economics, and engineering are family roots in the upper-middle class or the upper class. Making educational opportunities more broadly available, Hartmann concludes, has not led to opening equal opportunities for top positions.

59. "Milton Friedman: Greed," Phil Donahue interviews Milton Friedman, video on YouTube, http://www.youtube.com/watch?v=RWsx1X8PV_A (accessed 2/28/09).

60. Assmann and Hinkelammert, *Götze Markt*, 21; they reference Giovanni Battista Vico, who realized this paradox early on (80–81). Another root of this thought is in the work of the British philosopher Bernard de Mandeville, who saw the beehive as paradigmatic for this reversal (82).

61. Adam Smith, in *An Inquiry into the Nature and Causes of the Wealth of Nations*, 5th ed. (London: Methuen and Co., Ltd., 1904), bk. 1, chapt. II.

62. Assmann and Hinkelammert, *Götze Markt*, 97.

63. Assmann and Hinkelammert, *Götze Markt*, 99.

64. See Sheila C. Dow, "The Religious Content of Economics," in *Economics and Religion: Are They Distinct?* ed. H. Geoffrey Brennan and A. M. C. Waterman (Boston: Kluwer, 1994), 195.

65. John Maynard Keynes, *The General Theory of Employment, Interest and Money* (New York: Harcourt, 1964), 381; see also Waters, "Social Economics," 180; Keynes goes a little too far when he states, "I am sure that the power of vested interests is vastly exaggerated compared with the gradual encroachment of ideas."

66. See Thomas Frank, *One Market Under God: Extreme Capitalism, Market Populism, and the End of Economic Democracy* (New York: Doubleday, 2001), ch. 6.

67. See Joerg Rieger, *Christ and Empire: From Paul to Postcolonial Times* (Minneapolis: Fortress Press, 2007), chs. 4 and 5.

68. Reference in Lance E. Davis and Robert A. Huttenback, *Mammon and the Pursuit of Empire: The Economics of British Imperialism* (New York: Cambridge University Press, 1986), 318.

69. See Ellen Meiksins Wood, *Empire of Capital* (New York: Verso, 2003), 115–16.

70. For a trenchant critique of the misleading nature of this hope, see William Wolman and Anne Colamosca, *The Great 401(k) Hoax: Why Your Family's Financial Security Is at Risk, and What You Can Do about It* (Cambridge, Mass.: Basic Books, 2002 and 2003).

71. See "Opting for the Margins in a Postmodern World," my introduction to *Opting for the Margins: Postmodernity and Liberation in Christian Theology*, ed. Joerg Rieger (Oxford: Oxford University Press, 2003).

72. In an earlier article, "Theology and Economics. The Economy is Expanding: Theology to the Rescue," *Religious Studies Review* 28 (July 2002): 3, 215–20, I discussed several books on theology and economics whose authors do not appear to be particularly worried that the economy might have the ability to take over the inner sanctum of theology. The solution, therefore, comes at the level of theological ideas. One author claims that if the church can get ahold of the imagination of the business world and the corporations, we can turn things around. A deeper analysis of the complicity of the church is not necessary since change will come "by the *ecclesia* through the corporation without the state." D. Stephen Long, *Divine Economy: Theology and the Market* (New York: Routledge, 2000), 260.

73. A whole book has been dedicated to this topic from the perspective of world religions: Knitter and Muzaffar, eds., *Subverting Greed*. Knitter and Muzaffar claim that all world religions agree that "greed is not an admirable human trait" (ix). In his chapter, titled "Conclusion," Muzaffar notes that "the contemporary world has legitimized, sanctified, and normalized greed as no other epoch before us has done" (157). In this context, the "root cause" of economic liberalism is seen as the pursuit of unfettered self-interest (158).

74. Muzaffar, "Conclusion," 160.

75. Muzaffar, "Conclusion," 163.

76. See a more systematic exposition of this problem in Joerg Rieger, *Remember the Poor: The Challenge to Theology in the Twenty-First Century* (Harrisburg, Pa.: Trinity Press International, 1998), chapt. 3.

77. For the methodological details on this approach, see my book *Remember the Poor.*

78. Prychitko, *Why Economists Disagree,* 4. Note that Prychitko considers himself a follower of the Austrian school of economics, which is close to the neoclassical mainstream.

79. Keen, *Debunking Economics,* 312.

80. "Context is that which hurts," I stated in my chapter, "Developing a Common Interest Theology from the Underside," in *Liberating the Future: God, Mammon, and Theology,* ed. Joerg Rieger (Minneapolis: Fortress Press, 1998), 129. This was said to sharpen contextual theology.

2. The Logic of Downturn

1. William Wolman and Anne Colamosca, *The Judas Economy: The Triumph of Capital and the Betrayal of Work* (Reading, Mass.: Addison-Wesley, 1997), ix, 9, 24.

2. In a court ruling of the Michigan Supreme Court in 1919 (Dodge v. Ford Motor Company), the brothers John Francis Dodge and Horace Elgin Dodge, owners of 10 percent of Ford stock, challenged Ford's decision to cut dividends in order to invest in new plants and grow production and numbers of workers, while cutting prices. Henry Ford stated: "My ambition is to employ still more men, to spread the benefits of this industrial system to the greatest possible number, to help them build up their lives and their homes. To do this we are putting the greatest share of our profits back in the business." The court ruled in favor of the Dodge brothers, arguing that a corporation is organized primarily for the profit of its stockholders, rather than for the benefit of its employees or for the community. I thank Ph.D. student Meredith Minister for calling my attention to this case. See also the brief entry in *Wikipedia,* "Dodge v. Ford Motor Company," http://en.wikipedia.org/wiki/Dodge_v._Ford_Motor_Company (accessed 3/3/09).

3. See, for instance, the account of Michael Zweig, *The Working Class Majority: America's Best Kept Secret* (Ithaca, N.Y.: ILR, 2000).

4. Walter Benjamin, "Theses on the Philosophy of History," in Walter Benjamin, *Illuminations: Essays and Reflections,* ed. and introd. Hannah Arendt, trans. Harry Zohn (New York: Schocken Books, 1969), 257.

5. Reference in: Christoph Deutschmann, "Die Verheißung absoluten Reichtums: Kapitalismus *als* Religion?" in *Kapitalismus als Religion,* ed. Dirk Baecker (Berlin: Kulturverlag Kadmos Berlin, 2003), 160. They are said to infuse creativity through rationalization, new technology, new products, and advertising.

6. See also Deutschmann, "Die Verheißung absoluten Reichtums," 161.

7. This logic of downturn is an extension of my earlier studies of the Lacanian notion of the real and the "turn to the other" in my books *Remember the Poor: The Challenge to Theology in the Twenty-First Century* (Harrisburg, Pa.: Trinity Press International, 1998) and *God and the Excluded: Visions and Blindspots in Contemporary Theology* (Minneapolis: Fortress Press, 2001).

8. For the notion of "theological surplus," and in particular "Christological surplus," see my recent book, *Christ and Empire: From Paul to Postcolonial Times* (Minneapolis: Fortress Press, 2007).

9. This is what the Greek term *tektōn* refers to; the word describes the line of work of Joseph and Jesus, and is often translated as "carpenter."

10. See Theodore W. Allen, *The Invention of the White Race: The Origin of Racial Oppression in Anglo-America* (London: Verso, 1997). Allen has chronicled the origins of the history of the use of racial categories in the cover-up of class differentials.

11. A television series titled "Lifestyles of the Rich and Famous" ran from 1984 to 1995.

12. John Kenneth Galbraith in *The Affluent Society*, 40th anniversary ed. (Boston: Houghton Mifflin, 1998), xi, noted this increased tendency to blame the lower classes for their own misfortune in 1998: "Forty years ago I did not fully foresee the extent to which affluence would come to be perceived as a matter of deserved personal reward and thus fully available to the poor, were they only committed to the requisite effort. . . . Given such social attitudes, it could be better to be poor in a poor country than poor in an affluent one."

13. Zweig, *Working Class Majority*, 10, 34–35. The middle class has limited authority and includes professionals, small business owners, managers, and supervisors; college professors are included in the middle class because they have considerable freedom, although corporate-management practices penetrate more and more deeply into this class. Many physicians are now in the process of unionizing, and even the Association of University Professors (AAUP) is adding a collective bargaining unit. For an update, see also Michael Zweig, ed., *What's Class Got to Do With It? American Society in the Twenty-First Century* (Ithaca, N.Y.: ILR, 2004).

14. See, for instance, the book by Jack Good, *The Dishonest Church* (Scotts Valley, Calif.: Rising Star Press, 2003). Good appears to be too optimistic, though, about theological independence in the seminaries.

15. Marion Grau, *Of Divine Economy: Refinancing Redemption* (New York: T&T Clark International, 2004), 27, 185, makes a valiant effort to challenge "starkly crystallized binaries, oppositions between rich and poor, exploiters and exploited." Grau later argues that "most of us experience some degree of exploitation as well as profit from our entangled place in transnational trading." Yet this approach overlooks that degrees of exploitation do in fact matter, that the economic problem is not just one of trade but, more fundamentally, one of production, and that it matters in what part of the production process people find themselves and how they relate to the means of production. Even when grey zones are acknowledged, the binaries produced by the free-market economy cannot be so easily overcome.

16. A new study, along the lines of H. Richard Niebuhr, *The Social Sources of Denominationalism* (New York: Meridian Books, 1957), showing the class-based nature of denominations, might be quite enlightening in this regard. The matter today, however, might be more complicated and less defined by denominational borders.

17. See, for example, John Russo and Sherry Lee Linkon, eds., *New Working-Class Studies* (Ithaca: ILR, 2005).

18. While following this basic definition, I do not mean to downplay the complexity of class. Sean McCloud, who is one of the few others who argue that class has a role to play in religious studies, makes his contribution in this regard. Seeking to combat reductionistic definitions of class, he suggests understanding the notion of class in terms of "socially habituated subjectivities," picking up Pierre Bourdieu's term of "habitus" and developing it further. Sean McCloud, *Divine Hierarchies: Class in American Religion and Religious Studies* (Chapel Hill: University of North Carolina Press, 2007), 168. McCloud is especially concerned about deprivation theories, which argue that religious expressions are directly tied to experiences of lack and deprivation. Clearly, such theories are too narrow, as they investigate only one aspect of the matter of class. Yet the emphasis on complexity can also be misleading, and McCloud's notion of "putting some class back into the study of religion" may not be sufficient to grasp the problem (70). The problem is that without a clearer understanding of the notion of class and the role it plays, scholars will end up picking and choosing social issues mainly based on their own personal tastes and preferences. The list of potential issues is long: in addition to class, there is race, gender, sexuality, age, and so on.

19. Barbara Ehrenreich, *Bait and Switch: The (Futile) Pursuit of the American Dream* (New York: Metropolitan Books, 2005), 70–71.

20. Ehrenreich, *Bait and Switch*, 73.

21. Ehrenreich discusses some of the work of religious communities along these lines in *Bait and Switch*, 121–47.

22. Ehrenreich, *Bait and Switch*, 146.

23. Ehrenreich addresses the problems tied to the peculiar lack of professional credentials in the business world. See Ehrenreich, *Bait and Switch*, 213–38.

24. Beverly W. Harrison, "The Fate of the Middle 'Class' in Late Capitalism," in *God and Capitalism: A Prophetic Critique of Market Economy*, ed. Norman Gottwald, Mark Thomas, and Vern Visick (Madison, Wis.: A-R Editions, 1991), 60.

25. As David M. Brennan has found: "Productive employees are often invested in 401(k)s with defined contributions. Hence, current workers have an interest in increasing surplus-value extractions from other current workers. Specifically, current workers have an interest in increasing the rate of exploitation in the firms in which their 401(k) funds are invested. This causes a significant division among those who are currently working." David M. Brennan, "'Fiduciary Capitalism,' the 'Political Model of Corporate Governance,' and the Prospect of Stakeholder Capitalism in the United States," *Review of Radical Political Economics* 37, 39 (2005): 47. I thank Professor Christopher Roberts for calling my attention to this study.

26. There are some efforts to organize smaller shareholders and their vote, but, in most cases, alternative views are overruled easily. And since many 401(k) plans are invested in mutual funds, this option does not apply anyway.

27. For a very astute critique, see William Wolman and Anne Colamosca, *The Great 401(k) Hoax: Why Your Family's Financial Security Is at Risk, and What You Can Do about It* (Cambridge, Mass.: Basic Books, 2003).

28. Sweden is ranked 1st, with a poverty rate of 6.3 percent. See Kevin Watkins and others, *Fighting Climate Change: Human Solidarity in a Divided World*, United Nations Human Development Report 2007/2008 (New York: United Nations Development Programme, 2007), 241, http://hdr.undp.org/en/media/HDR_20072008_EN_Complete.pdf (accessed 3/3/09).

29. In Germany, by comparison, the ratio of the richest 10 percent to the poorest 10 percent was 6.9, and the Gini coefficient was 28.3. Watkins and others, *Fighting Climate Change*, 281.

30. Amy K. Glasmeier, *An Atlas of Poverty in America: One Nation, Pulling Apart, 1960–2003* (New York: Routledge, 2006), 3.

31. Watkins and others, *Fighting Climate Change*, 281.

32. Arthur F. Jones Jr. and Daniel H. Weinberg, *The Changing Shape of the Nation's Income Distribution 1947–1998* (Washington, D.C.: U.S. Census Bureau 2000), 2, http://www.census.gov/prod/2000pubs/p60-204.pdf (accessed 3/3/09). The report concludes wisely: "Whether the trend toward increasing income inequality the country has seen in the 1970s and 1980s will continue, or whether it has stopped or even reversed itself, remains to be seen" (10).

33. Jones and Weinberg, *The Changing Shape*, 1.

34. The reasons for this arbitrary cutoff are unclear. Is it perhaps because these numbers are considered statistically irrelevant? But why would they be, if another significant change in numbers would be the result? Michael Parenti reports that a Census Bureau official told his research assistant that "the bureau's computers could not handle higher amounts." Michael Parenti, *Blackshirts and Reds: Rational Fascism and the Overthrow of Communism* (San Francisco: City Lights Books, 1997), 130, n. 4.

35. These numbers are reported in Robert Frank, *Falling Behind: How Rising Inequality Harms the Middle Class* (Berkeley: University of California Press, 2007), 9–10.

36. Glasmeier, *Atlas of Poverty*, 3.

37. See *Overview: Growth for Human Development*, United Nations Human Development Report 1996 (New York: United Nations Development Programme, 1996), 2, http://hdr.undp.org/en/media/hdr_1996_en_overview.pdf (accessed 3/3/09).

38. Richard Jolly and others, *Globalization with a Human Face*, Human Development Report 1999 (New York: United Nations Human Development Programme, 1999), 3, http://hdr.undp.org/en/media/HDR_1999_EN.pdf (accessed 3/3/09).

39. Jolly and others, *Globalization with a Human Face*, 3.

40. Philip Alston and others, *Human Rights and Human Development*, Human Development Report 2000 (New York: United Nations Human Development Programme, 2000), 82, http://hdr.undp.org/en/media/HDR_2000_EN.pdf (accessed 3/3/09).

41. Kevin Watkins and others, *International Cooperation at a Crossroads: Aid, Trade and Security in an Unequal World*, United Nations Human Development Report 2005 (New York: United Nations Human Development Programme, 2005), 4, http://hdr.undp.org/en/media/HDR05_complete.pdf (accessed 3/3/09).

42. See Frank, *Falling Behind*, 13.

43. Tom Hertz, *Understanding Mobility in America* (Washington, D.C.: Center for American Progress, 2006), i, http://www.americanprogress.org/issues/2006/04/Hertz_MobilityAnalysis.pdf (accessed 3/3/09).

44. Hertz, *Understanding Mobility*, i. "Children born to the middle quintile of parental family income ($42,000 to $54,300) had about the same chance of ending up in a lower quintile than their parents (39.5 percent) as they did of moving to a higher quintile (36.5 percent). Their chances of attaining the top five percentiles of the income distribution were just 1.8 percent."

45. Watkins and others, *Fighting Climate Change*, 352.

46. According to the United Nations Universal Declaration of Human Rights, article 23, paragraph 4: "Everyone has the right to form and join trade unions for the protection of his interests," http://www.un.org/en/documents/udhr/index.shtml#a23 (accessed 5/20/09). The Social Principles of the United Methodist Church state, for instance: "We support the right of all public and private employees and employers to organize for collective bargaining into unions and other groups of their own choosing." *The Book of Discipline of the United Methodist Church 2008* (Nashville: United Methodist Publishing House, 2008), paragraph 163, B, 119.

47. See Michael Payne, "Unionization: A Private Sector Solution to the Financial Crisis," *Dissent* (Spring 2009): 59. The AFL-CIO estimates that 60 million workers would like to be organized in unions, while opponents of the Employee Free Choice Act reduce this number to a still sizable figure of 25 million workers. For religious positions on the organizations of unions, see *What Faith Groups Say about the Right to Organize*, compiled by Interfaith Worker Justice (IWJ) (Chicago, IL: Interfaith Worker Justice), http://iwj.org/template/page.cfm?id=62 (accessed 5/20/09).

48. Sam Stein, "Bailout Recipients Hosted Call to Defeat Key Labor Bill," *The Huffington Post*, January 27, 2009, http://www.huffingtonpost.com/2009/01/27/bank-of-america-hosted-an_n_161248.html (accessed 3/3/09).

49. The common argument that allowing workers to vote for a union through "card check" (that is, by voting without secret ballot) would be undemocratic is distorted. The "card check" option exists already, but it is the choice of the employer whether it can be used or not. The Employee Free Choice Act would afford this choice to the employees as well, as they are the ones who would be voting.

50. Heather Boushey, *Equal Pay for Breadwinners: More Men are Jobless While Women Earn Less for Equal Work* (Washington, D.C.: Center for American Progress, 2009), 1, http://www.americanprogress.org/issues/2009/01/pdf/gender_paper.pdf (accessed 3/3/09).

51. Boushey, *Equal Pay*, 4.

52. Glasmeier, *Atlas of Poverty*, 1.

53. Glasmeier, *Atlas of Poverty*, 1.

54. Glasmeier, *Atlas of Poverty*, 1, 28.

55. This is according to 2006 numbers, the most recent data available. See *Facts on Health Insurance Coverage* (Washington, D.C.: National Coalition on Health Care, 2009), http://www.nchc.org/facts/coverage.shtml (accessed 3/3/09).

56. Rik Kirkland, "The Real CEO Pay Problem," *Fortune* (June 30, 2006), http://money.cnn.com/magazines/fortune/fortune_archive/2006/07/10/8380799/ (accessed 3/3/09). The Muncer and Bush quotations can be found there as well.

57. Tom Gardner, "Hundreds Should Go to Jail," *The Motley Fool* (January 29, 2009), http://www.fool.com/investing/general/2009/01/29/hundreds-should-go-to-jail.aspx (accessed 3/3/09).

58. Zweig, *Working Class Majority*, 75.

59. Religion is left underanalyzed even in terms of currently popular cultural-linguistic or sociological notions that do not address the question of political or economic power.

60. Note that even the current emphases on matters of context and embodiment do not alleviate this problem significantly if they fail to address the question of power. In this sense, even so-called Christian Realism does not necessarily measure up to a deeper understanding of what is going on if it does not

engage in investigations of power in particular historical settings, which include the realities of class and views from the underside.

61. Victor Claar and Robin Kendrick Klay, *Economics in Christian Perspective: Theory, Policy and Life Choices* (Downers Grove, Ill.: InterVarsity Academic, 2007), 211.

62. This particular board was founded by my colleague at Perkins School of Theology, Isabel Docampo, and myself. For basic information on Workers' Rights Boards on the Jobs with Justice website, see http://www.jwj.org/projects/wrb.html (accessed 3/3/09).

63. This is exemplified by Sean McCloud, *Divine Hierarchies*, who studies working-class Christians without any notion of what this class is struggling against.

64. Some of these attacks become public only in hindsight, as the most blatant efforts are being reversed. A recent Associated Press report, for instance, notes that President Obama has signed a number of executive orders meant to "level the playing field." In this context, the following Bush administration policies were reversed, exposing only the tip of the iceberg of an increasingly slanted playing field. These orders will: "Require federal contractors to offer jobs to current workers when contracts change. Reverse a Bush administration order requiring federal contractors to post notice that workers can limit financial support of unions serving as their exclusive bargaining representatives. Prevent federal contractors from being reimbursed for expenses meant to influence workers deciding whether to form a union and engage in collective bargaining." "Obama Touts Middle-Class Task Force Led by Biden," AP Report (January 30, 2009), http://www.msnbc.msn.com/id/28933206/ (accessed 7/1/09).

65. Robert Brenner, *The Economics of Global Turbulence: The Advanced Capitalist Economies from Long Boom to Long Downturn, 1945–2005* (New York: Verso, 2006), 336.

66. In negotiations with unions, for instance, a company can argue that certain measures are not affordable, and the law requires them to open their books. There is no case where unions, after being shown the facts, have pushed unreasonable demands. See Michael Payne, "Unionization: A Private Sector Solution," 58.

67. Michael Zweig, "Economics and Liberation Theology," in *Religion and Economic Justice*, ed. Michael Zweig (Philadelphia: Temple University Press, 1991), 38.

68. Robert Dreyfuss, "Grover Norquist: 'Field Marshall' of the Bush Plan," *The Nation* (April 26, 2001), http://www.thenation.com/doc/20010514/dreyfuss (accessed 3/3/09).

69. John K. Williams, "Churchpeople, Socialism and Capitalism," in *Reader on Economics and Religion*, ed. John Sparks (Grove City, Pa.: Public Policy Education Fund, 1994), 34.

70. This insight is also part of the wider Christian tradition, although it is often overlooked in contemporary mainline Christianity. It is one of the key insights, for instance, of the medieval theologian Anselm of Canterbury.

71. Beverly Wildung Harrison, *Making the Connections: Essays in Feminist Social Ethics*, ed. Carol S. Robb (Boston: Beacon Press, 1985), 55.

72. Reinhold Niebuhr, *The Children of Light and the Children of Darkness* (New York: Scribner's, 1944), ix.

73. Karl Marx, "A Contribution to the Critique of Hegel's Philosophy of Right: Introduction," originally published in *Deutsch-Französische Jahrbücher* (February 1844; repr., Marxists Internet Archive, 2009), http://www.marxists.org/archive/marx/works/1843/critique-hpr/intro.htm#05 (accessed 3/3/09). Citations are to the Internet version. "The abolition of religion as the *illusory* happiness of the people is the demand for their *real happiness*." Emphasis in original.

74. Barbara Ehrenreich talks about the plight of white-collar workers in *Bait and Switch*; see, for example, 218.

75. Thomas Frank, *One Market Under God: Extreme Capitalism, Market Populism, and the End of Economic Democracy* (New York: Doubleday, 2000), 244.

76. See, for instance, the account of Herbert G. Gutman, "Protestantism and the American Labor Movement: The Christian Spirit in the Gilded Age," in *Protestantism and Social Christianity*, vol. 6, Modern American Protestantism and Its World, ed. Martin E. Marty (Munich: K.G. Saur, 1992); and Robert H. Craig, *Religion and Radical Politics: An Alternative Christian Tradition in the United States* (Philadelphia: Temple University Press, 1992). Craig mentions, for instance, a Christian socialist movement in Oklahoma and Texas, which in 1912 brought 20,000 people together for a meeting in Snyder, Oklahoma (109).

77. In the United States, I would like to highlight the work of Jobs with Justice (JwJ) and Interfaith Worker Justice (IWJ). The tradition of the Roman Catholic Worker Priests in France goes back to the middle of the twentieth century and initially inspired several Latin American liberation theologians.

78. Ehrenreich, *Bait and Switch*, 236.

3. God and the Free-Market Economy

1. Any Internet search on this topic provides a large number of hits. For example, http://www.ceofellowship.com/ (accessed 7/1/09); this organization was founded by Joe Greene, a former president of operations for Humana, who started his own company "based on biblical principles." The only example for the basis on biblical principles given on the website is that he used to pay his bills as early as they came in, not waiting thirty to sixty days in order to maximize interest. There is no mention, however, of whether he treated his workers differently than others in his position. See also http://www.ceoministries.org (accessed 7/1/09). The website advises: "The most important appointment in your day planner is your daily personal appointed prayer and study time. You must have an established daily appointment with the Chief Executive Officer of the Universe." It then asks whether the CEO has "established a time of corporate prayer with your business leaders and/or staff daily." See http://www.ceoministries.org/seminars.htm (accessed 7/1/09).

2. Bruce Wilkinson, *The Prayer of Jabez: Breaking Through to the Blessed Life* (Sisters, Ore.: Multnomah, 2000), 86–87, emphasis in original.

3. See: http://www.thejabezprayer.com/ (accessed 7/1/09). The link is to http://www.scripturalbusiness.com/ (accessed 7/1/09). This concept appears to be so natural that the Scriptural Business website does not even need to post a rationale or a mission statement. It simply states the following: "Welcome to the Scriptural Business website. Here you will find up-to-date articles on business, management, employee relations, hiring/firing, leadership, more than 18,000 downloads and a wealth of resources."

4. David Van Biema and Jeff Chu, "Does God Want You to Be Rich?" *Time* (September 18, 2006): 12, 48–56, http://www.time.com/time/magazine/article/0,9171,1533448,00.html (accessed 3/3/09).

5. Adam Smith, *An Inquiry into the Nature and Causes of the Wealth of Nations*, 5th ed., 1789 (London: Methuen and Co., Ltd., 1904), bk. IV, chapt. II, par. IV. The full quotation reads thus: "But the annual revenue of every society is always precisely equal to the exchangeable value of the whole annual produce of its industry, or rather is precisely the same thing with that exchangeable value. As every individual, therefore, endeavours as much as he can both to employ his capital in the support of domestic industry, and so to direct that industry that its produce may be of the greatest value; every individual necessarily labours to render the annual revenue of the society as great as he can. He generally, indeed, neither intends to promote the public interest, nor knows how much he is promoting it. By preferring the support of domestic to that of foreign industry, he intends only his own security; and by directing that industry in such a manner as its produce may be of the greatest value, he intends only his own gain, and he is in this, as in many other cases, led by an invisible hand to promote an end which was no part of his intention. Nor is it always the worse for the society that it was no part of it. By pursuing his own interest he frequently promotes that of the society more effectually than when he really intends to promote it."

6. Smith, *Wealth of Nations*, bk. IV, chapt. II, par. IV.

7. Adam Smith, *The Theory of Moral Sentiments* (New Rochelle, N.Y.: Arlington House, 1969), 264–65.

8. Smith, *Theory of Moral Sentiments*, 265.

9. Smith, *Theory of Moral Sentiments*, 265.

10. Claudius Luterbacher-Maineri, *Adam Smith—theologische Grundannahmen* (Freiburg: Herder, 2008), 331.

11. Smith prefers talking about the nature of things rather than about God, although the outcome is the same. In *Wealth of Nations*, bk. I, chapt. II, he argues that human nature is the reason for the division of labor. He finds "propensity in human nature . . . to truck, barter, and exchange one thing for another." In addition, he argues that, while animals are independent, human beings need each other. In Franz J. Hinkelammert, "Wirtschaft, Utopie und Theologie: die Gesetze des Marktes und der Glaube,"

in *Verändert der Glaube die Wirtschaft? Theologie und Ökonomie in Lateinamerika,* ed. Raúl Fornet-Betancourt (Freiburg: Herder, 1991), 68, the author identifies the early roots of this approach, which claim that the laws of the market have been established in nature by God, in historical developments between the sixteenth and the eighteenth century.

12. Johann Wolfgang von Goethe, in his famous play *Faust,* has Faust search for "that which keeps the world together at its core." ("*Das, was die Welt im innersten zusammenhält.*")

13. See also Luterbacher-Maineri, *Adam Smith,* 408.

14. Luterbacher-Maineri, *Adam Smith,* 409, reference to Alexander Rüstow, *Die Religion der Marktwirtschaft* (Münster: Lit Verlag, 2001), 27 and 31.

15. The Longview Institute, for instance, defines *market fundamentalism* in this way: "Market Fundamentalism is the exaggerated faith that when markets are left to operate on their own, they can solve all economic and social problems. Market Fundamentalism has dominated public policy debates in the United States since the 1980's, serving to justify huge Federal tax cuts, dramatic reductions in government regulatory activity, and continued efforts to downsize the government's civilian programs. While Republicans and conservatives have embraced Market Fundamentalist ideas, many Democrats and liberals have also accepted much of this mistaken belief system," http://www.longviewinstitute.org/projects/marketfundamentalism/marketfundamentalism (accessed 3/3/09).

16. Duncan K. Foley, *Adam's Fallacy: A Guide to Economic Theology* (Cambridge, Mass.: The Belknap Press of Harvard University Press, 2006), 3. "The most important feature of Adam Smith's work is not what it tells us concretely about how the economy works (although it tells us a great deal about that), but its discussion of how we should feel about capitalist economic life and what attitude it might be reasonable for us to take toward the complicated and contradictory experience it affords us. These are the discussions above all of faith and belief, not of fact, and hence theological" (xv).

17. Jung Mo Sung, *Economía, tema ausente en la teología de la liberación* (San José, Costa Rica: DEI, 1994), 207.

18. Hugo Assmann and Franz J. Hinkelammert, *Götze Markt,* trans. Horst Goldstein (Düsseldorf: Patmos Verlag, 1992), 27, referencing the book by George Gilder, *Wealth and Poverty* (New York: Basic Books, 1981).

19. Yale literature professor David Bromwich, "Our God That Failed," *The Huffington Post* (February 4, 2009), http://www.huffingtonpost.com/david-bromwich/our-god-that-failed_b_164112.html (accessed 3/3/09).

20. See the reference in Sheila C. Dow, "The Religious Content of Economics," in *Economics and Religion: Are They Distinct?* ed. Geoffrey Brennan and Anthony Michael Waterman (Boston: Kluwer Academic Publishers, 1994), 197.

21. Dow, "Religious Content of Economics," 199, 200. One of Dow's examples is the work of Chicago School economist Frank Knight.

22. This is a radically different way of interpreting transcendence, which in modern times has been established by the work of Karl Barth (see Joerg Rieger, *God and the Excluded: Visions and Blindspots in Contemporary Theology* [Minneapolis: Fortress Press, 2001], ch. 2), as well as by certain liberation theologians. A recent approach that also takes up such an alternative notion of transcendence is Mayra Rivera, *The Touch of Transcendence: A Transcendental Theology of God* (Louisville, Ky.: Westminster John Knox Press, 2007).

23. Warren J. Samuels, "The Methodology of Economics," in *Why Economists Disagree: An Introduction to the Alternative Schools of Thought,* ed. David Prychitko (Albany: State University of New York Press, 1998), 360.

24. Steve Keen, *Debunking Economics: The Naked Emperor of the Social Sciences* (New York: Zed Books, 2001), 3; emphasis in original.

25. In Paul Krugman, *The Return of Depression Economics and the Crisis of 2008* (New York: W.W. Norton & Company, 2009), 187, Krugman supports a "good old Keynesian fiscal stimulus."

26. The reforms that Krugman suggests have to do with tighter regulations on the financial sector that resemble regulations for banks and a stronger safety net for the financial sector. *Return of Depression Economics,* 189–90.

27. Krugman, *Return of Depression Economics,* 182, notes the attraction of supply-side economics in recent years. But he calls it a "crank doctrine that would have had little influence if it did not appeal to the prejudices of editors and wealthy men."

28. Thomas Friedman, *The Lexus and the Olive Tree* (New York: Farrar, Straus, Giroux, 1999), 435.

29. Friedman, *Lexus and the Olive Tree*, 464.

30. Friedman, *Lexus and the Olive Tree*, 464.

31. Friedman, *Lexus and the Olive Tree*, 465. Self-interest is nevertheless the guide even here: "The very reason we need to support the United Nations and the IMF, NATO, the World Bank and the various world development banks is that they leverage and magnify our power and our aid" (466).

32. In some ways, these reflections contradict the deeper beliefs in God's providential ordering of the world that will make all things come out all right. The explicit theological reflections of Friedman are on 468–70, *Lexus and the Olive Tree*.

33. See John Perkins, *Confessions of an Economic Hit Man* (San Francisco: Berrett-Koehler, 2004); see also Naomi Klein, *The Shock Doctrine: The Rise of Disaster Capitalism* (New York: Metropolitan Books, 2007), and our discussion of it in Néstor Míguez, Joerg Rieger, and Jung Mo Sung, *Beyond the Spirit of Empire: New Perspectives in Politics and Religion*, Reclaiming Liberation Theology Series (London: SCM, 2009), chaps. 2 and 4.

34. In William Wolman and Anne Colamosca, *The Great 401(k) Hoax: Why Your Family's Financial Security Is at Risk, and What You Can Do About It* (Cambridge, Mass.: Basic Books, 2003), the authors have chronicled the shift to 401(k) plans in relation to similar optimistic feelings about the market—an optimism that was never quite warranted.

35. Thomas Frank, *One Market Under God: Extreme Capitalism, Market Populism, and the End of Economic Democracy* (New York: Doubleday, 2000), 15.

36. Frank, *One Market Under God*, 16.

37. Summers's role is so important that he is giving briefings to the president every morning, just like the national security advisor.

38. Here is an example for a credit derivative: so-called credit default swaps (CDS) on U.S. government bonds, for instance, guarantee that if the U.S. Treasury defaults on its loans, other Wall Street companies will step in to secure the debt. The problem in this scenario, of course, is that it is not clear that private companies would be able to survive a crisis that would take out the U.S. Treasury. In other words, while a derivative carries a certain security, security is hard to achieve in a situation where the market as a whole is affected by downturn.

39. See the account by Peter S. Goodman, "The Reckoning: Taking Hard New Look at a Greenspan Legacy," *New York Times*, October 9, 2008, http://www.nytimes.com/2008/10/09/business/economy/09greenspan.html (accessed 3/3/09). For another account on the Web see also http://en.wikipedia.org/wiki/Robert_Rubin (accessed 3/3/09).

40. Goodman, "The Reckoning."

41. Perhaps Geithner's additional comment that "the current financial crisis has exposed a number of serious deficiencies in our federal regulatory system" gives us more reason to hope that systemic problems will be addressed, but Geithner, himself, is deeply involved in the history of these issues. Stephen Labaton, "Obama Plans Fast Action to Tighten Financial Rules," *New York Times*, January 24, 2009, http://www.nytimes.com/2009/01/25/us/politics/25regulate.html?th&emc=th (accessed 3/3/09).

42. "Geithner Apologizes for Not Paying Taxes," Associated Press report, January 22, 2009, http://www.nydailynews.com/money/2009/01/22/2009-01-22_geithner_apologizes_for_not_paying_taxes.html (accessed 7/1/09).

43. Mark Felsenthal and David Lawder, "Geithner Urges Bailout Reforms, Apologizes on Taxes," Reuters News Report, January 22, 2009, http://in.reuters.com/article/hotStocksNews/idINTRE50K19820090121 (accessed 7/1/09).

44. Goodman, "The Reckoning."

45. Sheryl Gay Stolberg and Stephen Labaton, "Obama Calls Wall Street Bonuses 'Shameful,'" *New York Times*, January 30, 2009, http://www.nytimes.com/2009/01/30/business/30obama.html?th&emc=th (accessed 3/3/09).

46. Alan Feuer and Karen Zraick, "It's Theirs and They're Not Apologizing," *New York Times*, January 30, 2009, http://www.nytimes.com/2009/01/31/nyregion/31bonuses.html?th&emc=th (accessed 3/3/09).

47. Paul Krugman, in *The Return of Depression Economics*, 186, has gone on record in this regard. He talks about "a full temporary nationalization of a significant part of the financial system." To clarify, he adds: "Just to be clear, this isn't a long-term goal, a matter of seizing the economy's commanding heights: finance should be reprivatized as soon as it's safe to do to."

48. David E. Sanger, "Nationalization Gets a New, Serious Look," *New York Times*, January 25, 2009, http://www.nytimes.com/2009/01/26/business/economy/26banks.html?th&emc=th (accessed 7/2/09).

49. Quoted in Sanger, "Nationalization Gets a New, Serious Look."

50. Quoted in Sanger, "Nationalization Gets a New, Serious Look."

51. Sanger, "Nationalization Gets a New, Serious Look."

52. See also Frank, *One Market Under God*, 21: "It's not that capitalists need us to believe in order to preserve their piles; it's that we must believe if we are to prosper."

53. Theologians related to the Radical Orthodoxy movement tend to build on this safety of pre-capitalist images of God. See, for instance, D. Steven Long, *Divine Economy: Theology and the Market* (New York: Routledge, 2000).

54. See also the comments of Christoph Deutschmann, "Die Verheißung absoluten Reichtums: Kapitalismus als Religion?" in *Kapitalismus als Religion*, ed. Dirk Baecker (Berlin: Kulturverlag Kadmos Berlin, 2003), 157.

55. See my introduction in *Opting for the Margins: Postmodernity and Liberation in Christian Theology*, American Academy of Religion, Reflection and Theory in the Study of Religion Series, ed. Joerg Rieger (Oxford: Oxford University Press, 2003), which was written at a time when such bubbles were chasing each other.

56. Walter Benjamin, "Kapitalismus als Religion," in *Kapitalismus als Religion*, ed. Dirk Baecker (Berlin: Kulturverlag Kadmos Berlin, 2003), 17.

57. See Joerg Rieger, *Christ and Empire: From Paul to Postcolonial Times* (Minneapolis: Fortress Press, 2007).

58. See Laurie Beth Jones, *Jesus CEO: Using Ancient Wisdom for Visionary Leadership* (New York: Hyperion, 1995). See also Laurie Beth Jones, *Jesus, Entrepreneur: Using Ancient Wisdom to Launch and Live Your Dreams* (New York: Three Rivers Press, 2002); and Bob Briner, *The Management Methods of Jesus: Ancient Wisdom for Modern Business* (Nashville: Thomas Nelson, 1996).

59. See http://walmartstores.com/AboutUs/289.aspx (accessed 3/5/09).

60. Note that the high priests who conducted Jesus' trials served at the pleasure of the Roman governor.

61. Assmann and Hinkelammert, *Götze Markt*, 16.

62. See David Prychitko, "Introduction: Why Economists Disagree: The Role of the Alternative Schools of Thought," in Prychitko, ed., *Why Economists Disagree*, 10.

63. William M. Dugger and Howard J. Sherman, "Comparison of Marxism and Institutionalism," in Prychitko, ed., *Why Economists Disagree*, 212–13, reference to the work of Thorstein Veblen.

64. Dugger and Sherman, "Comparison of Marxism and Institutionalism," 214.

65. Dugger and Sherman, "Comparison of Marxism and Institutionalism," 217.

66. Assmann and Hinkelammert (*Götze Markt*, 51), are right when they point out a tendency in economics to naturalize what is historical and to make that which is the product of human action—history—look as if it were natural.

67. See Ulrich Duchrow, *Alternatives to Global Capitalism: Drawn from Biblical History, Designed for Political Action* (Utrecht, Netherlands: International Books, 1995), 149–59.

68. Michael Zweig, "Economics and Liberation Theology," in *Religion and Economic Justice*, ed. Michael Zweig (Philadelphia: Temple University Press, 1991), 36.

69. See Dow, "Religious Content of Economics," 195.

70. Beverly W. Harrison, "The Fate of the Middle 'Class' in Late Capitalism," in *God and Capitalism: A Prophetic Critique of Market Economy*, ed. Norman Gottwald, Mark Thomas, and Vern Visick (Madison, Wis.: A-R Editions, 1991), 61.

71. Paul Samuelson and William D. Nordhaus, *Economics*, 13th ed. (New York: McGraw-Hill, 1989), 825; Samuelson and Nordhaus also note, however, that Smith did not always trust business owners.

72. Frances R. Woolley, "The Feminist Challenge to Neoclassical Economics," in *Why Economists Disagree*, 325.

73. The difference in income between men and women is well documented, as women earn, at best, two-thirds of what men earn. See Woolley, "Feminist Challenge," 311.

74. Woolley, "Feminist Challenge," 317.

75. Marianne Ferber and Julie Nelson, *Feminist Economics Today: Beyond Economic Man* (Chicago: University of Chicago Press, 2003), 7.

76. Ferber and Nelson, *Feminist Economics Today,* 8.

77. On this topic, see Joerg Rieger, "Reenvisioning Ecotheology and the Divine from the Margins," *Ecotheology* 9 (April 2004): 1.

78. The Worldwatch Institute, *State of the World 2009: Into a Warming World* (New York: W.W. Norton & Co., 2009).

79. Samuelson and Nordhaus, *Economics,* 41.

80. See Samuelson and Nordhaus, *Economics,* 47.

81. John Kenneth Galbraith, *The New Industrial State* (Boston: Houghton Mifflin, 1967), 49; for Galbraith's account on this issue, see pages 47–49. In his further assessment, however, Galbraith moves too quickly to assume that today it is no longer capital but "organized intelligence" which is the basis of power (57).

82. Herman E. Daly and John B. Cobb Jr., *For the Common Good: Redirecting the Economy Toward Community, the Environment, and a Sustainable Future* (Boston: Beacon Press, 1989), 19, 190, 203, 387.

83. See Assmann and Hinkelammert, *Götze Markt,* 10.

84. See the call for a *processus confessionis* that was passed at the twenty-third council meeting of the World Alliance of Reformed Churches in Debrecen, Hungary, in 1997: *The Call for a Church Process,* http://www.warc.ch/pc/debrecen/index.html (accessed 3/5/09).

85. For the background, see Michael Zweig, "Economics and Liberation Theology," 25. Zweig, writing in 1991, argues that "the Great Depression demolished this theoretic complacency in all but its most die-hard proponents."

86. The prayer can be found on the web at "The Deacon's Bench: Where a Roman Catholic Deacon Ponders the World," http://deacbench.blogspot.com/2009/01/rick-warrens-inaugural-prayer.html (accessed 3/5/09).

4. Consuming Desire vs. Resisting Desire

1. Ernst Bloch, *Das Prinzip Hoffnung,* vol. 1 (Frankfurt: Suhrkamp, 1959), 82 and the following, has shown how desire and hope are distinct as well as related.

2. In Marx's words: "The labor of the individual asserts itself as a part of the labour of society, only by means of the relations which the act of exchange establishes directly between the products, and indirectly, through them, between the producers." Karl Marx, *Capital: A Critical Analysis of Capitalist Production,* vol. 1, ed. Frederick Engels, trans. from 3rd German ed. Samuel Moore and Edward Aveling (New York: International Publishers, 1948), 44. See also Néstor Míguez, Joerg Rieger, and Jung Mo Sung, *Beyond the Spirit of Empire: New Perspectives in Politics and Religion,* Reclaiming Liberation Theology Series (London: SCM, 2009), chapt. 2.

3. Friedrich von Hayek, *The Constitution of Liberty* (Chicago: University of Chicago Press, 1960), 45.

4. The only theological treatment of desire and economics from a theological perspective is presented in the Brazilian theologian Jung Mo Sung's book, *Desire, Market and Religion,* Reclaiming Liberation Theology Series (London: SCM, 2007),

5. Martin Luther, "The Large Catechism," in *The Book of Concord,* trans. Theodore G. Tappert (Philadelphia: Fortress Press, 1959), 365. Luther reminds us, furthermore, that "money and possessions," "knowledge, intelligence, power, popularity, friendship, and honor" can also take the place of God.

6. Geoffrey M. Hodgson, "Institutional Economic Theory," in *Why Economists Disagree: An Introduction to the Alternative Schools of Thought,* ed. David Prychitko (Albany: State University of New York Press, 1998), 164.

7. Von Hayek, *Constitution of Liberty,* 45.

8. This issue is discussed in great detail by Robert Brenner, *The Economics of Global Turbulence: The Advanced Capitalist Economies from Long Boom to Long Downturn, 1945–2005* (New York: Verso, 2006).

9. This is one of the key points of my book, *Christ and Empire.* We cannot assume that any of our traditions have shaped up independently of empire. The good news is that empire is never able to control everything. In order to identify where true alternatives emerge, we need to dig deeper and find the "theological surplus." See Joerg Rieger, *Christ and Empire: From Paul to Postcolonial Times* (Minneapolis: Fortress Press, 2007).

10. Victor Claar and Robin Kendrick Klay, *Economics in Christian Perspective: Theory, Policy and Life Choices* (Downers Grove, Ill.: InterVarsity Academic, 2007), 240.

11. Paul Samuelson and William D. Nordhaus, *Economics*, 13th ed. (New York: McGraw-Hill, 1989), 41. In this context, profits "provide the rewards and penalties for business."

12. Walter Benjamin, "Kapitalismus als Religion," in *Kapitalismus als Religion*, ed. Dirk Baecker (Berlin: Kulturverlag Kadmos Berlin, 2003), 16, translation mine. "Das Verdrängte . . . ist aus tiefster, noch zu durchleuchtender Analogie das Kapital, welches die Hölle des Unbewußten verzinst." In my own work, I also have used psychoanalytical models in the analysis of the social and political rather than the individual unconscious. See, for instance, Joerg Rieger, *Remember the Poor: The Theological Challenge in the Twenty-First Century* (Harrisburg, Pa.: Trinity Press International, 1998).

13. John Kenneth Galbraith, *The Affluent Society*, 40th anniversary ed. (Boston: Houghton Mifflin, 1998), 115.

14. Galbraith, *Affluent Society*, 117.

15. Galbraith, *Affluent Society*, 120, 122.

16. Galbraith, *Affluent Society*, 121. "The notion that wants do not become less urgent the more amply the individual is supplied is broadly repugnant to common sense. It is something to be believed only by those who wish to believe" (124).

17. Galbraith, *Affluent Society*, 124, 125.

18. Galbraith, *Affluent Society*, 127.

19. William M. Dugger and Howard J. Sherman, "Comparison of Marxism and Institutionalism," in *Why Economists Disagree: An Introduction to the Alternative Schools of Thought*, ed. David Prychitko (Albany: State University of New York Press, 1998), 223.

20. "The businessman and the lay reader will be puzzled over the emphasis which I give to a seemingly obvious point. The point is indeed obvious. But it is one which, to a singular degree, economists have resisted." Galbraith, *Affluent Society*, 128.

21. Ralph Glasser, *The New High Priesthood: The Social, Ethical, and Political Implications of a Marketing-Oriented Society* (London: Macmillan, 1967), 12.

22. Glasser, *New High Priesthood*, 9. "Just as a little boy will imitate his grown-up brother's step and bearing in the fantasy hope that in doing so he will become infected by the real attributes of the man he wishes to become, so the imitative tendencies of adult consumers are one of the main planks in the platform of the new high priesthood in turning people's aspirations in directions favourable to certain marketing policies" (11).

23. John Hood, *Selling the Dream: Why Advertising Is Good Business* (Westport, Conn.: Praeger, 2005), 223.

24. Hood, *Selling the Dream*, 220.

25. Hood, *Selling the Dream*, 221.

26. Hood, *Selling the Dream*, 221.

27. Peter Stearns, *Consumerism in World History: The Global Transformation of Desire* (New York: Routledge, 2001), 44.

28. Stearns, *Consumerism in World History*, 55.

29. Stearns, *Consumerism in World History*, 56–57.

30. Stearns, *Consumerism in World History*, 141.

31. See, for instance, the account in Ulrich Duchrow, *Alternatives to Global Capitalism: Drawn from Biblical History, Designed for Political Action* (Utrecht, Netherlands: International Books, 1995), 35–43.

32. Michael Novak, *The Universal Hunger for Liberty: Why the Clash of Civilizations Is Not Inevitable* (New York: Basic Books, 2004), 70.

33. See Bobbie7-ga's answer to Brophy-ga's question about advertising statistics on http://answers.google.com/answers/threadview?id=56750 (accessed 3/3/09).

34. Paul King and David Woodyard, *Liberating Nature: Theology and Economics in a New Order* (Cleveland: Pilgrim Press, 1999), 67.

35. D. Stephen Long, *Divine Economy: Theology and the Market* (New York: Routledge, 2000), 270.

36. Max Stackhouse, "Introduction," in *God and Globalization: The Spirit and the Modern Authorities*, vol. 2, ed. Max L. Stackhouse and Don S. Browning, Theology for the Twenty-First Century Series (Harrisburg, Pa.: Trinity Press International, 2001), 30.

37. Long, *Divine Economy*, 78, 79.

38. Thomas Friedman, *The Lexus and the Olive Tree* (New York: Farrar, Straus, Giroux, 1999), 32–33.

39. Sung, *Desire, Market and Religion*, 32.

40. Dugger and Sherman, "Comparison of Marxism and Institutionalism," 214.

41. John Perkins, *Confessions of an Economic Hit Man* (San Francisco: Berrett-Koehler, 2004), xiv.

42. See Míguez, Rieger, and Sung, *Beyond the Spirit of Empire*, chaps. 2 and 4.

43. Robert Frank, *Falling Behind: How Rising Inequality Harms the Middle Class* (Berkeley: University of California Press, 2007), 48, 50.

44. Frank, *Falling Behind*, 118.

45. Frank, *Falling Behind*, xiii.

46. Frank, *Falling Behind*, 25.

47. Frank, *Falling Behind*, 78.

48. Frank, *Falling Behind*, 26.

49. Frank, *Falling Behind*, 94.

50. Frank, *Falling Behind*, 116.

51. Frank, *Falling Behind*, 125.

52. James Twitchell, quoted in Thomas Frank, *One Market Under God: Extreme Capitalism, Market Populism, and the End of Economic Democracy* (New York: Doubleday, 2000), 296–97.

53. Frank, *One Market Under God*, 29; emphasis in original.

54. Frank, *One Market Under God*, 50.

55. Frank, *One Market Under God*, 247.

56. According to a 2001 survey by the Barna Group. George Barna, *Researcher Predicts Mounting Challenges to Christian Church* (Ventura, Calif.: Barna Group, 2001), http://www.barna.org/barna-update/article/5-barna-update/43-researcher-predicts-mounting-challenges-to-christian-church (accessed 5/21/09).

57. See, for instance, M. Douglas Meeks, *God the Economist: The Doctrine of God and Political Economy* (Minneapolis: Fortress Press, 1989), 171. John Milbank has argued along similar lines.

58. Meeks, *God the Economist*, 171.

59. Meeks, *God the Economist*, 171–72.

60. Meeks, *God the Economist*, 179–80. See also Frederick Herzog, *God-Walk: Liberation Shaping Dogmatics* (Maryknoll, N.Y.: Orbis, 1988); and William T. Cavanaugh, *Being Consumed: Economics and Christian Desire* (Grand Rapids, Mich.: William B. Eerdmans, 2008).

61. Recently, the notion of gift-giving and its function in religion has been endorsed again by Philip Goodchild, *Capitalism and Religion: The Price of Piety* (London and New York: Routledge, 2002), 184. For a helpful critique of the limits of gift-giving see Kathryn Tanner, *Economy of Grace* (Minneapolis: Fortress Press, 2005), 49–61. "Gift exchange has some clear analogies with capitalist exchange," Tanner notes, since "at stake in gift exchange is one's social standing and social prestige" (52).

62. Meeks, *God the Economist*, 180; see also Meeks, *God the Economist*, 93: "The Gospels narrate the story of Jesus as the announcement and distribution of the righteousness of God's reign." Meeks understands the importance of work, but it does not feed into this conclusion: "The value of work has to do with increasing relationships among human beings and between human beings and God" (154); and "the future of democracy may be decided by the question of the democratization of the workplace" (155).

63. Stearns, *Consumerism in World History*, 62.

64. Stearns, *Consumerism in World History*, 68–69.

65. Stearns, *Consumerism in World History*, 70.

66. Stearns, *Consumerism in World History*, 128.

67. Sallie McFague's new awareness, expressed in her book, *Life Abundant*, differs from her earlier work at the point where she observes that "the market ideology has become our way of life, almost our religion, telling us who we are (consumers) and what is the goal of life (making money)." Sallie McFague, *Life Abundant: Rethinking Theology and Economy for a Planet in Peril* (Minneapolis: Fortress Press, 2001), xi. This is a crucial insight, but, in her account, the most dangerous problem is the consumerism of middle-class people in the first world, driven by the predominant values of individual desires and economic growth (81). As a result, the gap between rich and poor is growing, and natural resources are further diminished (14). North America has a leadership role in this process, for we oppress others "by being the world's major economic power and its chief exporter of consumerism" (33). The problem with this analysis is that we are left with the impression that things could be different if only those of us in the first

world would give up our love affair with consumerism, consume less, and focus less on the individual and more on the community and on nature. The thrust of McFague's economic analysis can, therefore, be put in therapeutic terms: we need to overcome our "addiction" to the consumer lifestyle (xii). What we need are "lifestyle limitations" and a "philosophy of enoughness" (33).

68. Stearns, *Consumerism in World History,* 139.

69. "As a society becomes increasingly affluent, wants are increasingly created by the process by which they are satisfied. . . . Wants thus come to depend on output. In technical terms, it can no longer be assumed that welfare is greater at an all-round higher level of production than at a lower one." Galbraith, *Affluent Society,* 129. Galbraith calls this the "dependence effect." "To furnish a barren room is one thing. To continue to crowd in furniture until the foundation buckles is quite another. To have failed to solve the problem of producing goods would have been to continue man in his oldest and most grievous misfortune. But to fail to see that we have solved it, and to fail to proceed thence to the next tasks, would be fully as tragic" (260). In an afterword written forty years later, he pleads to add the concerns of elimination of poverty and care for the environment—in order to save the "affluent society" (263).

70. Hugo Assmann and Franz J. Hinkelammert, *Götze Markt,* trans. Horst Goldstein (Düsseldorf: Patmos Verlag, 1992), 24, 39.

71. Anne Cronin, *Advertising Myths: The Strange Half-Lives of Images and Commodities* (London and New York: Routledge, 2004), 132.

72. Williams's fascinating story is told by Cedric Belfrage, *A Faith to Free the People* (New York: The Dryden Press, 1944).

73. See Bill Troy and Claude Williams, "People's Institute of Applied Religion," in *On Jordan's Stormy Banks: Religion in the South,* ed. Samuel S. Hill (Macon, Ga.: Mercer University Press, 1983), 56–57. Williams also lists the "oppressors of the people and enemies of justice," including "Ahab, Jezebel and other robber-murderers; Pharaoh with his taskmasters, magicians and soothsayers; the landlords with their winter and summer houses; church religion with its false prophets, high priests, priests of the second order; the Baals, Caesars, Herods and Pilates."

74. Richard A. Horsley, *Jesus and Empire: The Kingdom of God and the New World Disorder* (Minneapolis: Fortress Press, 2003), 13: "Trying to understand Jesus' speech and action without knowing how Roman imperialism determined the conditions of life in Galilee and Jerusalem would be like trying to understand Martin Luther King without knowing how slavery, reconstruction, and segregation determined the lives of African Americans in the United States."

75. The real, according to Lacan, is that which "is beyond the *automaton,* the return, the coming-back, the insistence of the signs." Jacques Lacan, *The Four Fundamental Concepts of Psycho-Analysis,* ed. Jacques-Alain Miller, trans. Alan Sheridan (New York: W.W. Norton, 1978), 53–54. The *automaton* here is the symbolic order, the master narratives that dominate a given context. In contrast with the postmodern fascination about metonymy—that is, the free flow of signification without referents of the dominant symbolic orders—Lacan maintains the importance of metaphor as well. *Metaphor* is defined as the replacement of one signifier by another in a process of repression. This process interrupts the free flow of signification and creates another level of reality underneath that which commonly counts as reality. Here is where the real is located. See Jacques Lacan, "The Agency of the Letter in the Unconscious or Reason Since Freud," in *Écrits: A Selection,* trans. Alan Sheridan (New York: W.W. Norton, 1977), 164.

76. One of the great advantages of Lacan's approach to psychoanalysis is that it is not limited to the analysis of the individual psyche but lends itself to the analysis of social processes, since it has been developed with broader social horizons in mind. See the use of Lacan in my books, *Remember the Poor,* and *God and the Excluded: Visions and Blindspots in Contemporary Theology* (Minneapolis: Fortress Press, 2001).

77. This notion of ambivalence is developed by Homi Bhabha, *The Location of Culture* (London: Routledge, 1994), 86. It is developed further in the context of theological discourse in Rieger, *Christ and Empire,* 11.

78. Michael Hardt and Antonio Negri, *Multitude: War and Democracy in the Age of Empire* (New York: Penguin, 2004).

79. Hardt and Negri (*Multitude,* 348, 356), point out that the "multitude" can be seen as a new human nature. Note also the rephrasing of Lacan's insight that the unconscious is structured like a language: "The multitude is organized something like a language" (339).

80. Troy and Williams, "People's Institute," 57.

81. McFague, *Life Abundant*, 48.

82. This is the approach taken in Rieger, *Remember the Poor*, and Rieger, *God and the Excluded*.

83. In Kevin Bales, *Disposable People: New Slavery in the Global Economy* (Berkeley: University of California Press, 1999), the author has shown that slavery is more widespread and more pernicious now than at any other point in human history.

84. The person "turned in on itself," *homo incurvatus in se*, was a classical way of expressing this.

85. This point is also made by an economist: see Karen I. Vaughn, "The Impossibility of a Theologically Sensitive Economics," in *Economics and Religion: Are They Distinct?* ed. Geoffrey Brennan and Anthony Michael Waterman (Boston: Kluwer, 1994), 245.

86. Jim Stanford, *Economics for Everyone: A Short Guide to the Economics of Capitalism* (London and Ann Arbor, Mich.: Pluto Press, 2008), 331.

87. See Frances R. Woolley, "The Feminist Challenge to Neoclassical Economics," in *Why Economists Disagree: An Introduction to the Alternative Schools of Thought*, ed. David Prychitko (Albany: State University of New York Press, 1998), 317–18.

88. Michèle Barrett and Mary McIntosh, *The Anti-Social Family* (London: NLB, 1982).

89. Rik Kirkland, "The Real CEO Pay Problem," *Fortune* (June 30, 2006), http://money.cnn.com/magazines/fortune/fortune_archive/2006/07/10/8380799/ (accessed 3/3/09).

90. Stanford, *Economics for Everyone*, 333.

91. Albert O. Hirschman, "Against Parsimony: Three Ways of Complicating Some Categories of Economic Discourse," in *Why Economists Disagree: An Introduction to the Alternative Schools of Thought*, ed. David Prychitko (Albany: State University of New York Press, 1998), 340, emphasis in original.

92. While Friedman later regretted the term, his Nobel Prize in 1976 was based in part on his study of the underlying phenomenon. "Unemployment below a structural level of balance thus leads, according to Friedman's theory, to a cumulative increase rate in prices and wages." This sentence is from a press release by the Royal Swedish Academy of Sciences, which awards the prize; see "This Year's Economics Prize to an American," http://nobelprize.org/nobel_prizes/economics/laureates/1976/press.html (accessed 3/3/09).

93. Hardt and Negri, *Multitude*, 311.

94. Hardt and Negri, *Multitude*, 336.

5. Rethinking God and the World

1. Antonio Gramsci, *Selection from the Prison Notebooks*, ed. and trans. Quintin Hoare and Geoffrey Nowell Smith (New York: International Publishers, 1971), 7.

2. A standard definition says that *theology* is "critical reflection on faith"; I have long argued for the importance of *self*-critical reflection, beginning with Joerg Rieger, *Remember the Poor: The Challenge to Theology in the Twenty-First Century* (Harrisburg, Pa.: Trinity Press International, 1998).

3. Both questions—where images of God come from and where they lead us—are important and must be no longer separated. In this regard, we can learn from each of the two opposing classical approaches: the approach of Max Weber, who has shown how theology influences economic developments, and the approach of Karl Marx, who has shown how theology is shaped by economic interests.

4. This is expressed in the following famous statement of Adam Smith, in *An Inquiry into the Nature and Causes of the Wealth of Nations*, 5th ed., 1789 (London: Methuen and Co., Ltd., 1904), bk. 1, chapt. II: "It is not from the benevolence of the butcher, the brewer, or the baker that we expect our dinner, but from their regard to their own interest. We address ourselves, not to their humanity but to their self-love, and never talk to them of our own necessities but of their advantages." Robert H. Nelson, *Economics as Religion: From Samuelson to Chicago and Beyond* (University Park, Pa.: Pennsylvania State University Press, 2001), 120, reports about different contemporary interpretations of self-interest and the tensions among economists between the followers of Samuelson and the Chicago School of Economics.

5. Nelson, *Economics as Religion*, 331: "The resistance of students is more moral than intellectual. If they must be exposed to many concrete examples that show how 'the market works,' it is because there is a strong initial ethical predisposition to reject the message."

6. Nelson, *Economics as Religion*, 9. Nelson notes the complexity: "Leading economists teach the acceptability of self interest in the market but the 'sins' of similarly opportunistic behavior in 'politics.'"

7. I show this for the case of Christology in my book, *Christ and Empire: From Paul to Postcolonial Times* (Minneapolis: Fortress Press, 2007).

8. Ulrich Duchrow and Franz Segbers, eds. *Frieden mit dem Kapital: Wider die Anpassung der evangelischen Kirche an die Macht der Wirtschaft* (Oberursel: Publik-Forum, 2008), 184, addressing a position paper of the German Evangelische Kirche (EKD), titled *Unternehmerisches Handeln in evangelischer Perspektive: Eine Denkschrift des Rates der Evangelischen Kirche in Deutschland* (Gütersloh: Gütersloher Verlagshaus, 2008), http://www.ekd.de/download/ekd_unternehmer.pdf (accessed 3/3/09).

9. In his preface to *Unternehmerisches Handeln*, 7, Bishop Wolfgang Huber supports profits as a necessity. The document even demands governmental protection (*"staatliche Sicherung"*) of competition.

10. See *Stuttgarter Nachrichten*, December 27, 2008, 1–2. This news report also notes that Pope Benedict XVI blamed self-interest as that which causes the fragmentation of the world in his 2008 Christmas message.

11. See also the discussion in Ulrich Duchrow and Franz J. Hinkelammert, *Property for People, Not for Profit: Alternatives to the Global Tyranny of Capital* (New York: Zed Books, 2004), 204 and the following.

12. *Message from the Tenth Assembly* (Winnipeg, Canada: Lutheran World Federation Tenth Assembly, July 2003), 17–18, http://www.lwf-assembly.org/PDFs/LWF_Assembly_Message-EN.pdf (accessed 3/3/09).

13. *Message from the Tenth Assembly*, 17–18.

14. *Message from the Tenth Assembly*, 19.

15. *Covenanting for Justice in the Economy and the Earth*, document GC 23-e (Accra, Ghana: World Alliance of Reformed Churches, 24th General Council, July 30–August 13, 2004), http://warc.jalb.de/warcajsp/news_file/doc-181-1.pdf (accessed 3/3/09).

16. "Economic Justice for All: A Pastoral Letter on Catholic Social Teaching and the U.S. Economy," the United States Conference of Roman Catholic Bishops, 1986, 1, 21, on the web: http://www.osjspm.org/economic_justice_for_all.aspx (accessed 5/7/09).

17. The Social Principles, par. 163, in *The Book of Discipline of the United Methodist Church 2008* (Nashville: United Methodist Publishing House, 2008), 118. See also *The Book of Resolutions of the United Methodist Church 2008* (Nashville: United Methodist Publishing House, 2008). It should be noted, however, that the United Methodist Church considers these resolutions as nonbinding for its churches, even though they have officially been endorsed by General Conference, the general assembly of the church.

18. Nelson, *Economics as Religion*, 289.

19. Dirk Baecker, "Einleitung," in *Kapitalismus als Religion*, ed. Dirk Baecker (Berlin: Kulturverlag Kadmos Berlin, 2003), 7, 9. "Whoever says money says spirit. And whoever says capitalism says religion" (translation mine). "*Wer Geld sagt, sagt Geist. Und wer Kapitalismus sagt, sagt Religion*" (12).

20. Christoph Deutschmann, "Die Verheißung absoluten Reichtums: Kapitalismus als Religion?" in *Kapitalismus als Religion*, 174; Deutschmann uses the German terms *Ernüchterung* and *Entwöhnung*.

21. John Wesley, journal entry of May 21, 1764; *The Works of John Wesley*, ed. Thomas Jackson, vol. 3 (Grand Rapids, Mich.: Zondervan, 1958), 178.

22. See, for instance, Ludwig Feuerbach, *The Essence of Christianity*, trans. George Eliot (New York: Harper Torchbooks, 1957).

23. This structure may not be visible during normal times, but it is much more in the open during extraordinary times, such as during capital campaigns.

24. This is how his biographer and friend Eberhard Bethge summarizes Bonhoeffer's position. Eberhard Bethge, *Dietrich Bonhoeffer: A Biography*, rev. ed., ed. Victoria Barnett, trans. Eric Moosbacher (Minneapolis: Fortress Press, 2000), 867. It was Bonhoeffer who, writing from a German prison cell, first discussed the value of seeing things from the underside. Dietrich Bonhoeffer, *Gesammelte Schriften*, vol. 2 (Munich: Kaiser Verlag, 1965), 441.

25. See Karl Barth, *Church Dogmatics*, vol. 2:1, ed. G. W. Bromiley and T. F. Torrance, trans. T. H. L. Parker and others (New York: Charles Scribner's Sons, 1957), 386–87.

26. See, for instance, the account in Joerg Rieger, *Remember the Poor: The Challenge to Theology in the Twenty-First Century* (Harrisburg, Pa.: Trinity Press International, 1998); and the contributions in Joerg Rieger, ed., *Opting for the Margins: Postmodernity and Liberation in Christian Theology*, American Academy of Religion, Reflection and Theory in the Study of Religion (Oxford: Oxford University Press, 2003).

27. *La Toma/The Take* is a film that not only chronicles the story but also the emotional involvement and struggle of the workers in this process. It is available on the web in full length: http://video.google.com/videoplay?docid=-6939956197822128063 (accessed 3/7/09).

28. Hugo Assmann and Franz J. Hinkelammert, *Götze Markt*, trans. Horst Goldstein (Düsseldorf: Patmos Verlag, 1992), 52.

29. Karl Barth, *Dogmatics in Outline*, trans. G. T. Thomson (New York: Harper & Row, 1959). For an account of how Barth's theology was shaped in relation to the struggles of workers and others, see Friedrich Wilhelm Marquardt, *Theology und Sozialismus: Das Beispiel Karl Barths* (Munich: Kaiser, 1972).

30. Michael Hardt and Antonio Negri, *Multitude: War and Democracy in the Age of Empire* (New York: Penguin, 2004), 157, emphasis in original.

31. This is the point made by M. Douglas Meeks, *God the Economist: The Doctrine of God and Political Economy* (Minneapolis: Fortress Press, 1989).

32. Friedrich A. von Hayek, *The Fatal Conceit: The Errors of Socialism*, ed. W.W. Bartley (Chicago: University of Chicago Press, 1988), 116–17.

33. See the North American Free Trade Agreement, "Chapter Eleven: Investments," http://www.sice.oas.org/trade/NAFTA/chap-111.asp (accessed 3/3/09).

34. Aristotle noted the problem in his own way: "It is when equals have or are assigned unequal shares, or people who are not equal, equal shares, that quarrels and complaints break out." Aristotle, *Nicomachean Ethics*, trans. J. A. K. Thomson (New York: Penguin, 1955), V:III, 178.

35. Most interpreters are now agreed on the centrality of the covenant and of relationship in the understanding of the biblical notions of justice. See, for example, Christopher D. Marshall, *Beyond Retribution: A New Testament Vision for Justice, Crime, and Punishment* (Grand Rapids, Mich.: William B. Eerdmans, 2001); and Walter Kerber, Claus Westermann, and Bernhard Spörlein, "Gerechtigkeit," in *Christlicher Glaube in moderner Gesellschaft*, Teilband 17 (Freiburg: Herder, 1981).

36. This is one of the basic arguments of my book, *God and the Excluded: Visions and Blindspots in Contemporary Theology* (Minneapolis: Fortress Press, 2001): inability to respect other human beings is related to the inability to respect God.

37. Karen Lebacqz, *Justice in an Unjust World: Foundations for a Christian Approach to Justice* (Minneapolis: Augsburg Publishing House, 1987), 11, proposes to begin with injustice not because it "offers better 'theoretical insights' but because it is the only honest place to begin, given the realities of our world."

38. "Between equal rights, force decides." Karl Marx, quoted in David Harvey, *Justice, Nature, and the Geography of Difference* (Oxford: Blackwell, 1996), 399.

39. I attempt a search for this energy without romanticizing it in my book, *Remember the Poor*. Of course, this is an ongoing process, as romanticization is a constant danger.

40. Elsa Tamez, *The Amnesty of Grace: Justification by Faith from a Latin American Perspective*, trans. Sharon Ringe (Nashville: Abingdon, 1993), 166.

41. In Islam, economic injustice is also seen as an important theological issue; see, for instance, the Qur'an, Sura LXX.

42. K. Koch, "sdq, gemeinschaftstreu/heilvoll sein," in *Theologisches Handwörterbuch zum Alten Testament*, vol. 2, ed. Ernst Jenni and Claus Westermann (Munich and Zurich: Christian Kaiser Verlag, Theologischer Verlag Zürich, 1984), 507–30.

43. Dieter Lührmann, "Gerechtigkeit III," in *Theologische Realenzyklopädie*, vol. 12, ed. Gerhard Krause and Gerhard Müller (Berlin: Walter de Gruyter, 1984), 419.

44. See Jewish theologian Moshe Weinfeld, "'Justice and Righteousness': The Expression and Its Meaning," in *Justice and Righteousness: Biblical Themes and Their Influence*, ed. Henning Graf Reventlow and Yair Hoffman (Sheffield: Sheffield Academic, 1992), 238. If space would permit, a narrative approach to biblical stories about God's justice would further demonstrate God's struggle to establish relationship in the face of broken relationships. Karen Lebacqz, *Justice in an Unjust World*, works out such a narrative approach.

45. See the examples in Weinfeld, "Justice and Righteousness," 242–43.

46. This is the point of Tamez, *Amnesty of Grace*. Marshall, *Beyond Retribution*, 93, describes what Paul and the writers of the Gospels share in common: God's justice is "a redemptive power that breaks into situations of oppression or need in order to put right what is wrong and restore relationships to their proper condition."

47. Gustavo Gutiérrez, *The Power of the Poor in History,* trans. Robert R. Barr (Maryknoll, N.Y.: Orbis, 1983), 8, 10.

48. John Perkins, *Confessions of an Economic Hit Man* (San Francisco: Berrett-Koehler, 2004).

49. Thomas Jefferson, "Letter to George Logan, November 12, 1816," in *The Writings of Thomas Jefferson,* vol. 10, ed. Paul Leicester Ford (New York: G.P. Putnam's Sons, 1892–1899), 69.

50. Karl Marx, *Capital,* vol. 1 (New York: International Publishers, 1967), 176.

51. Naomi Klein, *The Shock Doctrine: The Rise of Disaster Capitalism* (New York: Metropolitan, 2007), tells the story of the various means endorsed by Friedman and his supporters, including support of the military governments in Chile and elsewhere. Friedman explicitly endorsed the exploitation of situations of suffering, such as the aftermath of Hurricane Katrina in the New Orleans area (410).

52. Milton Friedman, *Capitalism and Freedom* (Chicago: University of Chicago Press, 1962), 14–15.

53. Friedman, *Capitalism and Freedom,* 15.

54. Friedman, *Capitalism and Freedom,* 16.

55. Duchrow and Hinkelammert, *Property for People,* 33–34.

56. Thomas Frank, *One Market Under God: Extreme Capitalism, Market Populism, and the End of Economic Democracy* (New York: Doubleday, 2000), 250.

57. Jeremy Rifkin, *The Age of Access: The New Culture of Hypercapitalism, Where All of Life is a Paid-For Experience* (New York: J.P. Tarcher/Putnam, 2000), for example, talks about *access* as that which matters more than ownership. One example is the leasing of cars, which is preferable for car companies, because it establishes an ongoing relationship of customer and company.

58. Friedman, *Capitalism and Freedom,* 26, 127–28. Emphasis added.

59. Friedman, *Capitalism and Freedom,* 120.

60. For a more developed argument of this matter see Rieger, *Christ and Empire,* chap. 7.

61. Friedrich August von Hayek, *The Constitution of Liberty* (Chicago: University of Chicago Press, 1960), 11.

62. See the account in Joerg Rieger, *Christ and Empire,* chap. 3.

63. Some exceptions are made for houses in walled cities, which do not have to be returned, but not for "houses in villages that have no walls around them," which are "classed as open country" (Lev 25:29-31). Fellow Israelites who are in positions of bonded labor must be released, but this rule does not apply to slaves who have been acquired from other nations (Lev 25:39-46). See also Duchrow and Hinkelammert, *Property for People,* 21–22, who point out how these traditions were already weakened by their own times.

64. John Wesley, "The Good Steward," Sermon 51, in *The Works of John Wesley,* sermons II, ed. Albert C. Outler, The Bicentennial Edition of the Works of John Wesley (Nashville: Abingdon, 1985), 283, emphasis in original.

65. In this sense, Wesley is more radical than John Locke, who is discussed in Kathryn Tanner, *Economy of Grace* (Minneapolis: Fortress Press, 2005), 40–46, and approaches the solution that Tanner suggests in the following sentence: "What if God does not even loan the world to us on conditions set by God's continued ownership of it, like some big landlord in the sky? What if God simply gives us what we need in an utterly gracious way?" (47–48). Wesley is, however, more interested in a mutual relationship of God and humanity than Tanner.

66. See Rieger, *Christ and Empire,* chap. 2.

67. See, for instance, Tanner, *Economy of Grace,* 85: "The whole point of God's dealings with us as creator, covenant partner, and redeemer in Christ is to bring the good of God's very life into our own." This is helpful because it opens new windows into the topic that are not commonly discussed, but the fact that God is taking a stand is missing here.

68. Grundgesetz für die Bundesrepublik Deutschland, I:14: "*Eigentum verpflichtet. Sein Gebrauch soll zugleich dem Wohle der Allgemeinheit dienen,*" http://www.bundestag.de/parlament/funktion/gesetze/Grundgesetz/gg_01.html.

69. Ronald Reagan, 1982 Economic Report of the President: "Political freedom and economic freedom are closely related." Reference in Paul Samuelson and William D. Nordhaus, *Economics,* 13th ed. (New York: McGraw-Hill, 1989), 829.

70. Michael Parenti, *Blackshirts and Reds: Rational Fascism and the Overthrow of Communism* (San Francisco: City Lights Books, 1997), 144.

71. See, for instance, the assessment of the former Soviet Union in Samuelson and Nordhaus, *Economics*, 838.

72. Victor Claar and Robin Kendrick Klay, *Economics in Christian Perspective: Theory, Policy and Life Choices* (Downers Grove, IL: InterVarsity Academic, 2007), 240–41.

73. Frank, *One Market Under God*, 276–306; Frank also shows how "cultural studies," an important development in the academy, often goes right along with these pro-market tendencies.

74. Johann Baptist Metz, *Faith in History and Society: Toward a Practical Fundamental Theology*, trans. David Smith (New York: Seabury Press, 1980), 89-90, argues that "the Church must understand and justify itself as the public witness and bearer of the tradition of a dangerous memory of freedom in the 'systems' of our emancipative society."

75. Nelson, *Economics as Religion*, 329.

76. Nelson, *Economics as Religion*, 330: "The market works."

77. By 1999, there were already one million homeless children in the United States; this number is the highest since the Great Depression in the 1930s. *The Dallas Morning News* (July 1, 1999). In 2009, this number has risen to 1.5 million children, according to the National Center on Family Homelessness. See http://familyhomelessness.org/?q–ode/1 (accessed 5/25/09).

78. Peter Senge and others, *Presence: Exploring Profound Change in People, Organizations, and Society* (New York: Currency Doubleday, 2005), 93.

79. For more information on Jesus' radical reversal and the concomitant practices see, for instance, Richard Horsley, *Jesus and Empire: The Kingdom of God and the New World Disorder* (Minneapolis: Fortress Press, 2003).

80. The Apostle Paul, in particular, has often been mistakenly identified with the interests of the powerful and the wealthy. Yet Paul constantly dealt with the question of how privilege distorts the emerging Christian traditions. See, for instance, his comments in 1 Cor 11:17-22. See also Neil Elliott, *Liberating Paul: The Justice of God and the Politics of the Apostle* (Maryknoll, N.Y.: Orbis, 1994).

81. Using the example of a patriarchal context, Lacan notes that women exist "only as excluded by the nature of things which is the nature of words." Jacques Lacan, "Seminar 20, Encore," (1972–73), in *Feminine Sexuality: Jacques Lacan and the École Freudienne*, ed. Juliet Mitchell and Jacqueline Rose (New York, London: W.W. Norton, 1985), 144. That is to say, unlike "man" and other signifiers of privilege, "woman" is not an ordinary part of the dominant order of things. In this order, women exist only as repressed. The limited advantage of women in this position is that as such they are involved in, but not restricted to, the functions of the dominant order like men. Women participate in what Lacan calls a certain "surplus-enjoyment," which escapes the authority and control of the powers of the dominant order to a certain degree and grants both a certain independence and a level of energy not available to the status quo (143–44). Slavoj Zizek, *The Sublime Object of Ideology* (London: Verso, 1989), 52, follows up on the notion of "surplus-enjoyment."

82. Hardt and Negri, *Multitude*, 212.

83. See also the argument in Hardt and Negri, *Multitude*, 350; Hardt and Negri, though, seem to discount the value of additional meetings too easily.

84. The significance of blind spots is one of the main themes of my book, *God and the Excluded*.

85. Unlike Stephen D. Long, *Divine Economy: Theology and the Market* (London: Routledge, 2000), who argues for the primacy of theology, I do not envision the relation of theology and economics in terms of a primacy.

86. See the prayer of Hannah, 1 Sam 2:1-10.

87. These numbers are quoted by UNICEF for the year 2007. See "Child Survival and Development," updated May 2009, http://www.unicef.org/media/media_45485.html (accessed 7/1/09).

Conclusion

1. This issue is frequently overlooked not only by Christian theologians but by others as well. Buddhist scholar David Loy is one of the non-Christian voices who has argued that the best way to address the religion of the market would be through "traditional religious teachings, which not only serve to ground us functionally but show us how our lives can be transformed." David Loy, "The Religion of

the Market," in *Visions of a New Earth: Religious Perspectives on Population, Consumption, and Ecology,* ed. Harold Coward and Daniel C. Maguire (Albany, N.Y.: State University of New York Press, 2000), 26.

2. For the latter see Heb 13:17; almost immediately following the previous passage referenced in the text above.

3. Joerg Rieger, *Remember the Poor: The Challenge to Theology in the Twenty-First Century* (Harrisburg, Pa.: Trinity Press International, 1998), chap. 3.

4. A welcome emphasis on the importance of ambiguity and ambivalence can also be found in the work of Marion Grau, *Of Divine Economy: Refinancing Redemption* (New York: T&T Clark International, 2004). Yet Grau does not give much consideration to the need of taking sides and establishing relationships of solidarity with and among those who are forced to endure the brunt of the pressures imposed by the free-market economy. Neither does Grau's God take sides, but becomes a "gambler and a courageous, hopeful investor in unpredictabilities, involved in subversive divine economic deals" (14).

5. John Maynard Keynes, "Economic Possibilities for Our Grandchildren" in *The Collected Writings, Essays in Persuasion,* vol. 9, 3rd. ed. (London: MacMillan Press, 1972), 330–31.

6. Ulrich Duchrow and Franz J. Hinkelammert, *Property for People, Not for Profit: Alternatives to the Global Tyranny of Capital* (New York: Zed Books, 2004), 157.

7. Point made by Steve Keen, *Debunking Economics: The Naked Emperor of the Social Sciences* (New York: Zed Books, 2001), 1.

8. According to Robert Lekachman and Borin Van Loon, *Capitalism for Beginners* (New York: Pantheon Books, 1981), 106, Keynes also endorsed a more egalitarian distribution of and control over investments, but this was never accomplished. David Prychitko, "Introduction: Why Economists Disagree: The Role of the Alternative Schools of Thought," in *Why Economists Disagree: An Introduction to the Alternative Schools of Thought,* ed. David Prychitko (Albany: State University of New York Press, 1998), 3, argues that the differences between Keynesians and Chicago School economists are not so great: "both groups held the same *basic* values of a dynamic, growing, efficient capitalist economy. . . . Keynes considered himself a realist in the classical liberal tradition." Emphasis in original.

9. On this interpretation of Barth see, for example, chapter 2 in Joerg Rieger, *God and the Excluded: Visions and Blindspots in Contemporary Theology* (Minneapolis: Fortress Press, 2001).

10. Jung Mo Sung, "Der Gott des Lebens und die wirtschaflichen Herausforderungen für Lateinamerika," in *Verändert der Glaube die Wirtschaft? Theologie und Ökonomie in Lateinamerika,* ed. Raúl Fornet-Betancourt (Freiburg: Herder, 1991), 92. See also Néstor Míguez, Joerg Rieger, and Jung Mo Sung, *Beyond the Spirit of Empire: New Perspectives in Politics and Religion,* Reclaiming Liberation Theology Series (London: SCM, 2009), chaps. 3 and 4.

11. Rom 8:21: "The creation itself will be set free from its bondage to decay and will obtain the freedom of the glory of the children of God."

12. The significance of the connection of our relation to God and our relations to other people—without identifying the two—is argued in my book, *God and the Excluded.*

13. Here is another place where the approaches of Max Weber and Karl Marx need to be connected. Images of God cannot be transformed in a vacuum but in relation to concrete material conditions, as Marx has rightly seen. Nevertheless, images of God that have been transformed in this way can also have important implications for social dynamics. Such implications were studied by Weber.

14. These numbers are quoted by UNICEF for the year 2007. See "Child Survival and Development," updated May 2009, http://www.unicef.org/media/media_45485.html (accessed 7/1/09).

15. On this topic see Joerg Rieger, ed., *Opting for the Margins: Postmodernity and Liberation in Christian Theology,* American Academy of Religion, Reflection and Theory in the Study of Religion (Oxford: Oxford University Press, 2003). The preferential option for the poor gains fresh importance in a postmodern world, where concern about the poor is either seen as special interest or gets lost in pluralistic perspectives.

Index